Studies in Women and Religion/
Études sur les femmes et la religion : 5

Studies in Women and Religion /
Études sur les femmes et la religion

Studies in Women and Religion is a series designed to serve the needs of established scholars in this new area, whose scholarship may not conform to the parameters of more traditional series with respect to content, perspective and/or methodology. The series will also endeavour to promote scholarship on women and religion by assisting new scholars in developing publishable manuscripts. Studies published in this series will reflect the wide range of disciplines in which the subject of women and religion is currently being studied, as well as the diversity of theoretical and methodological approaches that characterize contemporary women's studies. Books in English are published by Wilfrid Laurier University Press.

Inquiries should be directed to the series coordinator, Pamela Dickey Young, Queen's Theological College, Queen's University, Kingston, ON K7L 3N6.

STUDIES IN WOMEN AND RELIGION/
ÉTUDES SUR LES FEMMES ET LA RELIGION

Volume 5

Obedience, Suspicion and the Gospel of Mark

A Mennonite-Feminist Exploration of Biblical Authority

Lydia Neufeld Harder

Published for the Canadian Corporation for Studies in Religion /
Corporation Canadienne des Sciences Religieuses
by Wilfrid Laurier University Press

1998

This book has been published with the help of a grant from the Humanities and Social Sciences Federation of Canada, using funds provided by the Social Sciences and Humanities Research Council of Canada.

We acknowledge the financial support of the Government of Canada through the Book Publishing Industry Development Program for our publishing activities.

Canadian Cataloguing in Publication Data

Harder, Lydia Marlene, 1939-
    Obedience, suspicion and the gospel of Mark : a Mennonite-feminist exploration of biblical authority

(Studies in women and religion ; v. 5)
Includes bibliographical references and index.
ISBN 0-88920-305-9

1. Bible – Evidences, authority, etc.   2. Bible – Feminist criticism.
3. Bible. N.T. Mark – Criticism, interpretation, etc.   4. Mennonites –
Doctrines.   I. Canadian Corporation for Studies in Religion.   II. Title.
III. Series: Studies in women and religion (Waterloo, Ont.) ; v. 5.

BS480.H37 1998   220.13082   C98-930840-5

© 1998 Canadian Corporation for Studies in Religion /
      Corporation Canadienne des Sciences Religieuses

Cover design by Leslie Macredie, using an illustration reproduced from the 1975 *Froschauer Bibel*, with permission of Amos B. Hoover. Thanks to Dr. Margaret Loewen Reimer for her assistance.

Printed in Canada

Obedience, Suspicion and the Gospel of Mark: A Mennonite-Feminist Exploration of Biblical Authority has been produced from a manuscript supplied in camera-ready form by the author.

Order from:
WILFRID LAURIER UNIVERSITY PRESS
Waterloo, Ontario, Canada   N2L 3C5

Dedication

In memory of my mother and father
Margarete Koop Neufeld and Cornelius K. Neufeld
who embodied an openness to God's
revealing and saving presence

Acknowledgments

This book had its beginnings in a series of critical reflections by a circle of Mennonite women interpreting the Bible in the context of their daily tasks of housekeeping and homemaking. Thank you to the women of Waters Mennonite Church, Lively, Ontario, and First Mennonite Church, Edmonton, Alberta, who challenged me to keep my feet on the ground, even when exploring lofty visions. These early reflections were critically challenged in a circle of women gathered at St. Stephen's College in Edmonton. I remember with appreciation this ecumenical group of feminist women who encouraged me to seek further truth.

The convictions gained during those years of homemaking were challenged and acquired new forms of expression during the disciplined study that was required at the Toronto School of Theology. Thank you to Dr. George Schner who asked challenging questions, gave constant encouragement and read numerous versions of the same ideas during the writing of my doctoral thesis. Thank you also to Ellen Leonard, Marsha Hewitt and John Webster who offered critical and constructive comments. My appreciation also goes to Michele Rizoli, whose encouragement and technical help allowed this printed version of my ideas to materialize.

The final version of this book received its life during a time of vocational change when children had left home, formal studies had been completed and new vocational directions were being discerned. Special love and appreciation to my family and friends, who gave me reasons to pray, laugh and sing during a time of uncertainty and unrest. My husband, Gary, supported me with his love and caring as he freely took on additional homemaking tasks. Our children, Mark, Kendall and Kristen, provided welcome diversions with their many comings and goings. Many friends gave encouragement and counsel as they were drawn into countless theological discussions. Finally, a sincere expression of gratitude to the members of the Toronto United Mennonite Church, who continue to embody the love of God for me in their invitation to worship and in their practice of hospitality.

This book has been published with the help of a grant from the Humanities and Social Sciences Federation of Canada, using funds provided by the Social Sciences and Humanities Research Council of Canada. This support is appreciated and valued.

Table of Contents

Acknowledgments   vi

Introduction   ix

Chapter 1 — Methodological Strategies and Theological Focus   1
Hermeneutic Community: A Heuristic Tool   2
Discipleship: The Theological Focus   7
Methodological Strategy   13
A Critical and Constructive Model of Theology   20

**Chapter 2 — Discipleship and Authority: Mennonite
Hermeneutic Community**   25
Theological Convictions   28
Discourse Patterns   39
A Mennonite Ethos of Authority   55

**Chapter 3 — Discipleship and Authority: Feminist
Hermeneutic Community**   63
Theological Convictions   67
Discourse Patterns   78
A Feminist Ethos of Authority   94

Chapter 4 — Discipleship and Authority: The Gospel of Mark   99
Authority and Power: Definitions and Directions   101
The Creative Function of Kingdom Power   104
The Subversive Function of Kingdom Power   116
The Marcan Ethos of Authority and Power   133

Conclusion: An Invitation to Further Experimentation   145
A Hermeneutics of Discipleship   147
Biblical Authority   148

Selected Bibliography   151

Index of Authors and Subjects   162

Index of Biblical References   167

Introduction

> The pervasiveness of polarized thinking is so widespread as to make it appear essential to human comprehension. Yet, from a feminist viewpoint, to accept dualistic perception as an inevitable condition of human experience is to accept concurrently the inevitability of oppression.[1]

This book began as an experiment in feminist thought. It was designed to illuminate the creative and critical possibilities of relational reflection as envisioned by T. Drorah Setel in the context of the Mennonite theological tradition in which I stand. The issue that needed to be clarified was the authority of the Bible, a notion central to Mennonite theology, but one particularly susceptible to dualistic thinking and oppressive practice. The deliberate attempt to think relationally created new research questions. Could a discussion of biblical authority begin by respecting particular dialogue partners rather than subsuming their convictions under an abstract discussion of authority? What kind of a theological process would arise if a Mennonite hermeneutics of obedience was assumed to be distinct from a feminist hermeneutics of suspicion, but was not immediately seen as a polar opposite? How would clarifying relationships by describing significant connections and major disruptions assist me in constructing a new theological model of biblical authority? Could a definition of biblical authority be envisioned that allowed critical engagement with the text but that opened the reader to transformation and change? Could both obedience and suspicion be embraced as crucial moments in the hermeneutic process?

The experiment began by noting the manner in which the differences between a hermeneutics of obedience and a hermeneutics of suspicion were usually described in methodological discussions. In most writings, an unbridgeable gulf separated commitment to reading the Bible from a critical look at Scripture, a trust in the authority of the Bible from a trust in personal experience. The framework in which this separation made sense relied on a subject/object division, which produced other polarities in the theological enterprise. Thus spiritual and material, rational and emotional, good and bad, soul and body, divine and human, male and female were not only perceived as different, but were often described and evaluated as direct opposites. This dualism seemed to be inextricably linked to oppression because it devalued one pole of a continuum, thus justifying dominating practices based on the other pole.

Two aspects of theology were important to me in this experiment. First of all, both the methodology and the theological focus needed to allow for dialogue and relationship. Second, there needed to be a way to bring together theory and practice, an integration that is especially important in both Mennonite and feminist thought. The heuristic notion of *hermeneutic community* and the theological concept of *discipleship* provided the essential tools that allowed both of these aspects to be part of the process. These notions were readily available to me in my Mennonite tradition, but they have been further defined and clarified through my interaction with other theological and philosophical traditions.

The theoretical construct of hermeneutic community has been especially important to me in the way it includes the particular and the relational in its very definition. "Community" is a social category emphasizing participation in a common enterprise. "Hermeneutic" denotes a process that gives meaning and significance to experience with a text. Together, these terms emphasize communication and an interactive search for truth. They describe a conversation in which a variety of convictions about God and multiple individual interpretations continue to contribute to the community's identity. Thus the Bible and experience, past and present, social and personal, substance and function are linked in the language of a particular community, a language represented both by a tradition and by a discursive practice.

Discipleship is a theological notion rooted in particular history, yet one that is only relevant if that history testifies to the experience of the divine. It is a socially constructed term. However, its reality is dependent on the truth of a God who cannot be contained in the particular. It is a word associated with human identity and historical embodiment. However, it witnesses to God's revelatory and saving presence. The concept of discipleship therefore allows room for both the particular and the universal, the human and the divine to reveal themselves.

The methodology itself is a dynamic interweaving of theological convictions and interpretive practices, intended to invite the participation of others. The overall design of the analysis moves from a broad hermeneutical and theological discussion, to two particular communal discourses, to a number of individual voices within those discourses. It then turns to the hermeneutical conversation by the larger scholarly and church community around the meaning of particular biblical texts before it returns to the question of biblical authority.

Chapter 1 elaborates the methodological approach and places my particular methodological choices in the context of the hermeneutical discussion on biblical authority. Chapters 2 and 3 describe the experience with the biblical text as expressed by two hermeneutic communities—the first associated with the Anabaptist-Mennonite tradition and the second with feminist theological thought. Writings by John H. Yoder and Elisabeth Schüssler Fiorenza were chosen to illustrate the two approaches—a hermeneutics of obedience and a hermeneutics of suspicion. These descriptions of communal convictions and discourse patterns serve to illuminate the distinctive ethos of biblical authority in each community. It is these descriptions that give an external context to the internal sense of authority associated with my identity as a Mennonite feminist.

In chapter 4, the focus shifts to the biblical text. The interpretive approach attempts to be open to challenges from the text while retaining a critical edge rooted in Mennonite feminist experience. The ethos of authority expressed in the language of the Gospel of Mark is described by giving special attention to the relationship between parable and narrative, between the teaching of Jesus and the story that interprets that teaching.

Attention to experience and text was made easier because of my close connection with each community and my commitment to engagement with the text. This self-involvement, however, increased the danger of self-justification and of co-optation into an apologetic enterprise for either the Mennonite tradition or feminist theology. To lessen this danger, each community became a critical discourse partner for the other, as I searched for a non-oppressive, more relational model of authority. Because neither community was idealized, it was easier to be honest with the experiences of disillusionment and despair associated with my own experience of authority as exercised by each community. Thus the descriptions encouraged a process that illuminated the limitations of the tradition and discourse of each hermeneutic community as well as pointed to their strengths.

Rereading the Bible in this context opened new choices to me in relationship to both hermeneutic communities. A critical edge was created because of a new appreciation of the dynamic relationship between canon and community, Bible and church. The ethos of authority and power that I discovered in the Gospel of Mark suggested a new paradigm for envisioning biblical authority, a paradigm that does not separate the human practice of biblical interpretation from a response to God's revelation and salvation. This encouraged me to define more clearly both the convictions supporting the notion of biblical authority and the discourse practices that are congruent with these convictions.

This experiment in feminist thought was not designed to be a theoretical enterprise. It was to be both embodied thinking and reflective praxis. It was to be both self-involving and self-critical. The goals included both personal transformation and critical collaboration with others with the purpose of changing the broader authority structures of our many and diverse interpretive communities. Theology, in this model, is "a religious and ethical practice of critical inquiry and particular commitments" as called for by Elisabeth Schüssler Fiorenza and implied in the very notion of discipleship.[2]

I have identified my enterprise as Mennonite and as feminist in order to name the primary dialogue partners included in this study. This was not meant to exclude others. Instead, this book was envisioned as a way to invite other hermeneutic communities to reflect on their own particular convictions about biblical authority and to identify their own primary conversation partners. As we broaden the dialogue, we may discover that each of our distinctive construals of biblical authority is inadequate and needs to be transformed into a richer, more multifaceted understanding of God's authority as mediated through the Bible and the various communities that we name "church."

Endnotes

1   T. Drorah Setel, "Feminist Insights and the Question of Method," in *Feminist Perspectives in Biblical Scholarship* (Atlanta, GA: Scholars Press, 1985), p. 36.
2   Elisabeth Schüssler Fiorenza, "Commitment and Critical Inquiry," *Harvard Theological Review* 82, 1 (1989): 4.

Chapter 1

Methodological Strategies and Theological Focus

In my personal struggle to understand the nature of biblical authority, I read many feminist theological writings that began with assumptions foreign to me. These assumptions were considered foundational for Christian theology because they were accepted by a majority church tradition, whether Protestant or Catholic. As a member of a minority Christian denomination, I have often felt that these construals of biblical authority did not fully express my convictions born out of my Mennonite faith tradition. At times I have felt excluded from these conversations, silenced because my critical reflections were ignored and not understood. These feminist writings, however, introduced me to new ways of looking at biblical authority that challenged my static definitions and encouraged me to engage in a dynamic interactive search for deeper and richer meanings.

At the same time, I have often felt angered by a practice of biblical interpretation in Mennonite churches that was oppressive and stifling to many women in the congregations. Biblical interpretations by men condoned and encouraged a marginal role for women in Mennonite church institutions as well as in society. Despite strong affirmations of the church as a hermeneutic community, the pattern of communication and social interaction often did not encourage an active participation by women in the theological process of determining the meaning of biblical texts for the community. I therefore needed the encouragement of feminist theology to begin a critical reexamination of authority as construed by my own religious heritage.

Ambiguous experiences such as these suggested to me that a methodological approach to a study of biblical authority would need to include an examination of power relationships within interpretive communities, as well as an exploration of theological beliefs about divine and human authority. I would need to acknowledge the tension that results when persons were part of two communities, each with their own understandings and experiences. I did not want to begin with an abstract definition of power and authority which would neglect or subsume the distinctive ethos of authority that I had experienced in various contexts. Instead, I wanted the differing definitions and constructions to emerge from the study itself. My hope was that a deeper understanding of power would result as different conceptions of authority were brought into the conversation.

I began by assuming that power is essential to human reality in the sense that it describes a basic energy of life created by and expressed in the connection between relational beings.[1] In asking questions about authority and

1

legitimacy I wanted to consider the structured relationships that justified particular manifestations of power. I did not want to begin with a negative understanding, although I recognized that the terms power and authority evoke strong images and feelings for myself as well as for many other people. Instead, I accepted the fact that specific definitions and understandings of authority and power would need to be explored in particular contexts.

The heuristic use of *hermeneutic community* to designate the primary conversation partners proved to be helpful in identifying specific constructions of biblical authority. *Discipleship* was the common self-description that encouraged me to make a comparison between two socially constructed theologies, each with its own particular understanding of human and divine authority and power. The methodological strategies that were developed on the basis of these foci allowed both critique and commitment to be an aspect of my relationship with each of these communities.

A more detailed explanation of my methodological choices will demonstrate how my approach arose in response to the various claims to authority that I sensed not only in the external religious communities around me, but within my own psyche.

Hermeneutic Community: A Heuristic Tool

The Anabaptist-Mennonite tradition has insisted that biblical authority functions best in particular hermeneutic communities that interpret the Bible to structure their own communal life and practice.[2] With this basic conviction, Mennonites have broadened the discussion of biblical authority from a focus on the nature of the Bible, to explorations of the nature of the church and its reading habits. According to John H. Yoder, this notion of hermeneutic community was already a distinguishing characteristic of the Anabaptist tradition during the time of the Reformation. He speaks of the crucial difference between the Anabaptists and the other Reformers of the sixteenth century as "at the crucial point the Reformers abandoned their initial vision of the visible church, the hermeneutic community, and were obliged to shift the locus of infallibility to the inspired text and the technically qualified theological expert."[3]

For Yoder, the notion of hermeneutic community meant that the text could be understood best when disciples, committed to obedience, gathered to discern what the Bible had to say about their particular needs and concerns. Sometimes called *Gemeindetheologie* (community theology), this theology was not dependent for its authority on official leadership alone but rather on the active involvement of each member of the hermeneutic community in the interpretive process.[4]

In Mennonite tradition, the notion of hermeneutic community has surfaced repeatedly in order to emphasize the specific way in which Mennonites understood the ecclesial context of biblical interpretation. Biblical interpretation was to be oriented towards voluntary communities of worship and practice, rather than more universally to Christendom or society in general. The term implied that participants in the hermeneutic community were drawn into the argument precisely because "they agreed on the importance of the issue being debated."[5] Communities of discourse were defined not only structurally, by insisting on adult baptism as a mode of entry into the community, but also substantively, by the frame of reference in which discussions and disagreements took place. The hermeneutic community was that community of conversation in which goals, values and strategies were debated in order to establish community identity and practice. Mennonites named this community church.

In Mennonite history and tradition, the conversation often became limited to groups of people of the same ethnic identity and social class, living in close geographical proximity to each other. In fact, the term "Mennonite" is frequently understood to designate a group of people who live in communities physically separated from society by their alternative life styles. In reality, only a very small group of contemporary Mennonites can be identified by their distinctive dress, by their rejection of electricity and by their use of horses and buggies as a mode of transportation. Rather, Mennonites are a diverse group of people, speaking more than seventy languages, united not primarily by institutional structures but rather connected historically by the recognition of common faith origins and a number of common faith understandings.[6] This connection creates a common conversation about themes important to the Anabaptist movement, such as discipleship, adult baptism, the separation of church and state and peace-making.

The authority of the Bible in Mennonite tradition is rooted in the self-identity of the community as expressed in its discourse patterns as well as in the social/political shape of the church as a voluntary community of conversation. Hermeneutic community, as understood by Mennonites, refers to a specific group of people that claim a common hermeneutical stance arising out of a common self-identity leading to a common discourse. James McClendon, a Baptist theologian who has rediscovered his own Anabaptist roots, speaks of this as a "convictional community."[7] In his model the Bible and experience come together in particular communities that identify their own lived story—their tradition—with that of the disciples in the biblical story. For Mennonites, this identification determines the conversation that creates the shape of the church as a community of followers of Jesus.

A number of feminist biblical scholars and theologians are also focusing directly on particular convictional communities and the discourse patterns that give these communities their identity and influence their approach to biblical authority.[8] Letty Russell speaks about "the community of struggle which seeks to over-come the domination and dehumanization of half the human race." [9] Luise Schottroff focuses on the "Jesus movement of today," which reads the texts within the framework of liberation theologies.[10] Rosemary Ruether and Elisabeth Schüssler Fiorenza talk about "communities of critical consciousness" called women-church. These movements for change are often located on the boundaries of patriarchal church life but are connected by their common commitments to justice and freedom from patriarchal domination.[11]

Schüssler Fiorenza is the most clear in how these convictional communities of conversation relate to the church. She uses the term *ekklēsia* as a "political-oppositional" term to patriarchy, thus designating women-church as the particular social/political community that has captured the vision of the *basileia*, God's alternative world. She insists that Christian feminists cannot relinquish their biblical roots and heritage, but must find their sense of identity in the legacy and heritage of the disciples of the present and past. Christian feminist identity must be a communal-historical identity based on full participation of women in the hermeneutical process. She names this identity the discipleship of equals and makes it the locus of authoritative interpretation of the Bible.

Feminists who are calling for a more experience- and praxis-oriented approach to biblical interpretation may not designate these conversations as dialogues of a hermeneutic community. However, they assume that interpreters of the Bible choose to identify with particular communities of dialogue because they are committed to particular agendas. For Christian feminists, this agenda focuses on the full inclusion of women in the social and political interpretive process that yields authoritative interpretations for the church. These women are therefore forming particular communities of conversation that read the Bible in light of their own experience and vision. Though these feminists are not united by denominational commitments or geographical proximity, they are discovering their common roots in biblical religion, their common identity in women-church and their common hermeneutical stance in a non-oppressive process of interpretation.

The notion of hermeneutic community as a convictional community that reads the Bible in the context of its own experience is consistent with new consciousness in the larger hermeneutical discussion of the authority of particular communal traditions and patterns of discourse.[12] A shift from a focus on the individual interpreter in her/his subjectivity, to an emphasis on the interpretive community can be recognized in writings on hermeneutics ranging from philosophical discussions about language and interpretation, to theological discussions about the nature of church and its role in interpreting the Bible, to methodological discussions about reading practices in biblical scholarship.

Within philosophical hermeneutical theory several writers with diverse perspectives speak specifically about the community in which authoritative interpretation takes place. For example, Stanley Fish, a deconstructionist literary critic, comes to this conclusion:

> What I finally came to see was that the identification of what was real and normative occurred within interpretive communities and what was normative for the members of one community would be seen as strange (if it could be seen at all) by members of another. In other words there is no single way of reading that is correct or natural, only "ways of reading" that are extensions of community perspectives.[13]

Richard Bernstein, a philosopher who attempts to get beyond the dichotomy of objectivism and relativism in debates about the foundations of hermeneutical practice, recognizes the importance of what he calls dialogical communities for authoritative interpretation. He calls for dedication to "the practical task of furthering the type of solidarity, participation, and mutual recognition that is founded in dialogical communities."[14]

A number theologians are also calling for more clarification of the normative tradition and discourse patterns of the church—an institution particularly active in interpreting the Bible. Josè Mìguez Bonino, a Protestant liberation theologian, recognizes this when he ends his book on doing theology with a chapter on ecclesiology. He insists that a "Christian hermeneutics is unthinkable as a purely individual understanding. It necessarily presupposes a 'hermeneutical' community."[15] Paul Ricoeur, in applying his philosophical thought to a discussion of the ecclesial community, points out that "the confessing community is that place where the problem of the word is lived, thought, and announced as a struggle of religion and faith."[16] He realizes that "placed outside of a confessing community, the process of criticism and reinterpretation become what Kant called 'erudite exegesis' and, at its extreme, a mere exercise in logic."[17] And Lisa Sowle Cahill, a professor of Christian ethics, emphasizes the "crucial importance of community as the context of dialogue, as affording continuity to the interpretation of texts, and also as testing dialogue in action."[18]

Biblical scholars have added an additional dimension to this discussion of hermeneutic community by their social readings of the New Testament. James Sanders focuses on the process of the formation of scripture emphasizing that a pattern of interpretation and reinterpretation was already present in particular communities that formed the canon.[19] Wayne A. Meeks suggests that "the hermeneutical process has a social dimension at both ends" and proposes that "hermeneutics of social embodiment" would attend to both the social setting in which the text was first heard and the setting in which it is appropriated today.[20] Meeks thus raises the question of the hermeneutical relationship between these two contexts, a relationship that must be taken into account in any discussion of biblical authority.

Reader-response methodologies, in their promotion of self-conscious readings of the Bible, have also contributed to greater attention to the social/political context of interpretation.[21] These approaches to biblical studies focus on the readers of the text and on particular contexts that shape the way the text is read. These approaches have developed the notion of a "resisting reader" who does not automatically assent to the text but is open to looking at the text from new perspectives and with new assumptions, nurtured in particular contexts.[22] These methodologies urge readers to become more self-conscious about their Bible-reading practices, about the assent or resistance they give to particular biblical texts and about the community which authorizes specific interpretations.

These voices affirm that the term hermeneutic community can be a useful heuristic tool that encourages the naming of prior institutional and communal assumptions that govern an individual's approach to biblical authority. By concentrating on the particular context of biblical interpretation the term recognizes the rootedness of biblical authority in particular traditions and in particular patterns of discourse. Moreover, by moving the hermeneutical discussion into the area of reading practice the term helps to illuminate the relationship between communal convictions and communal discourse patterns.

Perhaps most important for the purposes of this project, however, is the way the notion of hermeneutic community encourages us to explore the dialectical relationship between the individual reader of a text and the specific social/political relationships that give authority to a particular interpretation. Hermeneutic community points to the interrelationship between the social environment in which we live and the internal acceptance or rejection of authority that we experience. This moves us away from thinking of ourselves as autonomous individuals able to stand on an external foundation from which we can judge the truth objectively. Instead, each of us participates in a number of distinct discourses, regulated by particular notions of authority and power. This awareness can illuminate the tensions we experience as we face hermeneutical choices in our various conversations. Opportunity is given for a conscious engagement of various aspects of authority that function internally, aspects which we may not easily admit. An analysis of the ethos of authority in a particular hermeneutic community can therefore encourage self-analysis and self-critique.

The following two aspects of the hermeneutic relationship are assumed when the term hermeneutic community is used to describe a social/political community that is involved in reading and interpreting the Bible:[23]

The community is hermeneutically constructed. This suggests that the community that reads the Bible will be affected by the symbolic universe inscribed in or projected by the biblical writings. Social embodiment or the community-shaping function of a canonical text must be understood if one wishes to examine the construal of biblical authority in a community. While Mennonites have largely emphasized the positive aspects of this relationship, feminists have pointed out that biblical interpretation has also led to the oppression and domination of women. This difference points to the need to analyze more closely the particular way in which each of these communities understands the community-shaping power of the text and the embodiment of that authority in community tradition and discourse.

The process of biblical interpretation is a social/political process. This moves beyond individual interpretation to acknowledge communal involvement in the process of determining the meaning of texts. What is needed is a description and clarification of the social/political context that influences how members of the community participate in this process. This would mean exploring the patterns of discourse within a community and examining the theological assumptions which legitimate or support these patterns. While Mennonites have emphasized the right of marginal Christian communities to interpret the Bible in light of their own needs and concerns, feminists have stressed the freedom of women to interpret the text for themselves. Further clarification is needed about the way each community understands the embodiment of communal authority in its patterns of social discourse.

In any hermeneutic community, both of these dimensions play a role in bringing about the intrinsic relationship between Bible and personal experience. By using the term hermeneutic community as a heuristic tool, attention can be paid to the unique ways in which these two aspects are understood in each community. The authority of the Bible, therefore, arises out of the distinctive ways in which the power of the text to form community tradition and the authority of the discourse partners in the interpretive process come together in hermeneutic communities that continue to read and interpret the Bible.

Discipleship: The Theological Focus

Letty Russell has highlighted the importance of a process of revisioning of the church by Christian feminists. In her book, *Church in the Round: Feminist Interpretation of the Church*, she uses the metaphor of "God's new household" to identify the gathering of the followers of Christ around the table of hospitality.[24] This table is characterized by a new view of authority, an authority that invites the marginal to join in the "round table talk" of the community. Elisabeth Schüssler Fiorenza explicitly identifies the *ekklēsia* as the discipleship of equals and makes it the locus of authoritative biblical interpretation for women-church. She uses the traditional term *ekklēsia* for her radical democratic concept of the church as the locus of feminist interpretation. For these Christian feminists, discipleship is connected with a particular approach to biblical authority as well as with a particular notion of church.

Traditionally, Mennonites have also associated discipleship with a distinctive understanding of the church and its approach to biblical authority. For Harold Bender, the Anabaptist-Mennonite movement began with personal appropriation of the biblical Word of God but included a new vision of the church and its mission of discipleship.[25] With others in the "Believer's church" tradition, Mennonites such as Bender and John H. Yoder insisted that an obedient response by the community of disciples to the Bible defined the church and its mission.[26]

This convergence suggests that the conversation between Mennonite and feminist hermeneutic communities can be furthered by using the notion of the church as a community of disciples to specify the conversation partners. Communities of interpretation that agree on the importance of the relationship between discipleship and the process of biblical interpretation can then become critical discourse partners. Individual interpretations of discipleship by representatives of these communities (Schüssler Fiorenza and Yoder, for example) can then be fruitfully compared. Thus the network of theological terms, concepts and practices connected with discipleship in each community becomes the focus of the exploration and discussion.

It is striking that both Mennonites and Christian feminists have used an identity as disciples to question traditional ecclesial definitions of authority.[27] Both began as protest movements rooted in a new sense of self-involvement in the interpretative process. Both have understood the need for just relationships between conversation partners within the church community. Both have been marginal movements often seen as outside of the established authority of mainstream churches. A brief overview of the historical beginnings of these hermeneutic communities will point to similarities and differences.

Mennonites have a four-hundred-year history that can be traced to what is variously called the Radical Reformation, the Left Wing of the Reformation or the Anabaptist movement. This movement has stressed "Believer's church" or "Free church," as a form of church rooted in a faithful community. Crucial to Anabaptism was the call for freedom to interpret the Bible in the interests of those gathered to hear God's word. These believers identified themselves with the disciples in the biblical record and insisted that God was their primary authority. The social-political implications of this identification were evident in the time of the Reformation when the autonomy of the local congregation from the religious and secular establishment was at stake. Persecution and banishment followed the creation of these counter-culture communities who insisted on following their own convictions constructed through intense dialogue within the communities themselves.

Anabaptist Mennonites have thus insisted on defining the church as primarily congregations of committed disciples and have resisted placing authority in an institutional hierarchy or in scholarly expertise. This congregational authority was one in which the individual participated but in which there was to be community accountability.[28] The term discipleship thus described both the participatory hermeneutical process and the particular self-identity of the community as church.

The fact that it has never become clear whether Anabaptists fit any better into the Protestant camp than they did into the Roman Catholic Church testifies to an identity that was often relegated to the margins of the Christian faith.[29] Anabaptists were outcasts from both major traditions and at the time of their beginnings were severely persecuted by all the established churches. Added to this was the fact that, as a protest movement, Anabaptism did not develop homogeneously and become unified by adopting a centralized institutional structure or theological framework. Anabaptism could not even be identified by the name of one or two theological leaders who articulated its central doctrines. The status of the Anabaptist-Mennonite community as a church has been suspect and therefore it has often been designated as a sect.

Feminism is a growing movement within society and church that names the injustice and oppression felt by women in not being perceived and valued as "fully human and fully equal."[30] During the last two centuries various movements associated with women's liberation or feminism have arisen to work for change in social/political structures and institutions, including the church. In search for a self-identity that is not dependent on men's naming of women's experience, a number of Christian feminists have begun to question their relationship to church institutions. As they began to notice that their voice had been missing in intellectual and theological work, as well as in the institutional structures of the church, women began to assert their own identity and to name their own spiritual home in terms such as women-church or discipleship. For Rosemary Radforth Ruether and Miriam Therese Winter, this includes stressing the discovery of women's own spirituality and empowerment through genuine community and inspiring liturgy in women-church.[31] For Schüssler Fiorenza, women-church means specifying more clearly that discipleship implies a discipleship of equals or an equality from below. For others, such as Russell, new relationships within the community are signalled by terms that link authority with partnership.

There are definite implications for the nature of the church in this way of identifying Christian identity. A primary implication is that the church is now made up of women and men liberated from patriarchal assumptions that marginalize and oppress women. This identity presents a challenge to many of the more common sociological/theological understandings of church. Since denominational boundaries, as well as the boundaries between church and society are crossed, many people do not know how to speak of these convictional communities of conversation formed not only around the Bible but around common vision, commitments and practices of inclusion.

This overview suggests that for both Mennonites and feminists, terms such as discipleship function to define not only a basic communal self-identity but also the social/political discourse patterns of the hermeneutic community. This focus on the political shape of the discourse has meant a radical questioning of the institutional definitions of church and a challenge to established forms of communication and authority. These challenges to authority have meant that feminist hermeneutic communities are often located on the edge of established church life.

Though the term discipleship seems to serve a similar function in both conversational contexts, Mennonites and Christian feminists have usually not belonged to the same hermeneutic community. The ambivalence that Mennonite women have felt about the feminist movement is often paralleled by the disinterest in and ignorance of Mennonites by many feminists. This barrier between the communities signals some crucial differences in the definition of discipleship embraced by each community of discourse. It also suggests some significant differences in the hermeneutical process that provides the crucial link between the Bible and experience in each community.

It is therefore not surprising that some Mennonite women who identify themselves as feminists feel caught between the authority exercised by the Mennonite community and the authority exercised in the feminist community. Two aspects of the experience of these Mennonite women need further exploration because each of them claim some authority in terms of discipleship:

The Authority of Tradition

The history of the Anabaptist-Mennonite hermeneutic communities testifies to a suspicion of theological/ecclesial traditions. John H. Yoder has suggested that for the early Anabaptists one of the implications of discipleship was that, though the congregation would recognize the assistance of a teaching tradition, it was not to be bound by that tradition or its creeds, but only by the truth of the texts as discerned by the present hermeneutic community.[32] This was based on the conviction that tradition too could be sinful. The concern for faithful restoration and moving forward in the history of salvation implied that the practicing congregation of disciples needed to discern the present movement of the Spirit. Anabaptists thus radically questioned the consensus of the past in established churches that claimed to be universal and therefore true. This suspicion of tradition implied a concrete identification of apostasy and sin within the history of the church.

Yet Mennonites have not only been critical of tradition, they have also created a tradition. For Mennonite women, this tradition, particularly the tradition of discipleship as obedience, service and self-denial, has sometimes not been life-giving.[33] The theology of peace, justice and non-violence that has characterized the Mennonite community has generally not examined the power relationship between women and men.[34] Some Mennonite women therefore find commonality with other feminists who are looking for alternatives to the authority of theological/ecclesial traditions. For some religious feminists, these traditions must be left behind in order to recover the insights and wisdom of goddess traditions and extra-biblical writings. For others, the traditions that have meaning are the counter-voices, the minority reports of women in the tradition. But for all feminists, to identify with the tradition, as it is now proclaimed and taught by the institutional church, is not enough. Feminists assert that "not only have women been excluded from shaping and interpreting the tradition from their own experience, but the tradition has been shaped and interpreted against them."[35] The universality of the claims of patriarchal tradition is therefore being questioned and a new authority is given to women's history and experience.

This means that for many Christian feminists, including some Mennonite women, their own experience "is painfully split within itself."[36] A fear of being co-opted into patriarchal religion alternates with a fear of not being accepted by the faith tradition of which they are a part. Yet an identity as a disciple demands a relationship to the tradition in which discipleship was first modelled and proclaimed. Any exploration of the authority of the biblical text needs to come to terms with the authority and function of the tradition of discipleship in each hermeneutic community.

The Authority of Discourse Patterns

In Mennonite tradition, the notion of discipleship has implied that theology discussed in theoretical terms was not sufficient. Instead, strong and specific statements had to be made about actual congregational involvement in the process of discernment.[37] For the early Anabaptists, this meant removing authority from specialized theologians and hierarchical authorities and placing it instead into the hands of the ordinary believer. The process was to be a "binding and loosing" process in which the congregation as a whole was responsible for church discipline, as well as church teaching. No specialist separated from concrete life situations could take away the prerogative of all of God's people to discern the truth.

Mennonite women, however, have not been fully included in this process of congregational discernment.[38] The common identity of men and women as disciples has not challenged the societal division between the personal-domestic and the communal-public sphere that separated men's and women's responsibilities.[39] Many Mennonite women have accepted a silent or passive role in the congregational discernment process, not very different from the role women have had in other churches.

Mennonite feminists thus join with other women in looking more closely at the relationship between the language of faith and the social/political institutions which structure the theological dialogue. They question the discourse patterns that have been established in the church institutions and in the scholarly domain and challenge power relationships and their effect on the communal discourse. They wonder how inclusive the term discipleship really is if women are excluded from the discernment process.

There is a certain discomfort for feminist theologians, including Mennonite theologians, in this critical discussion. As scholars, these women are beginning to recognize the contradictory existential and ideological condition in which they find themselves in belonging to both a marginalized and oppressed group, as well as to an academic elite. For Christian feminists, this raises the issue of how an identity of discipleship influences the choice of conversation partners in the feminist hermeneutical discussion.[40] Women wrestle with the issues of power and status and with questions of setting boundaries in their own hermeneutic community. Therefore, a discussion of the authority of biblical interpretation will need to give greater attention to the political patterns of discourse in each of these hermeneutic communities.

Discipleship in the Biblical Text

In order to test whether Mennonites and feminists belong to the same discipleship tradition and discourse, it is helpful to go back to the origins of this term in Christian tradition. As Lisa Sowle Cahill has pointed out, a communal orientation to the authority and use of the Bible probably works best "for a community whose form as well as commitments are analogous to those of the New Testament, that is, the enthusiastic discipleship 'household'."[41] This suggests that both Mennonite and feminist communities identify themselves as disciples because they perceive a strong analogy between themselves and the first disciples of Jesus. Analogy, however, is not to be understood as denying all differences between communities. Rather, analogy implies that there are enough similarities between communities so that discipleship continues to be appropriate in describing the identity and practices of the community.

An analysis of discipleship as used in present communities must therefore also wrestle with the use of the term in the New Testament gospels.[42] The Gospel of Mark has been chosen to test the analogy of discipleship because it presents the "earliest sustained portrait of disciples" and is thus a primary paradigm for later pictures of discipleship, including those in the other gospels.[43] At the same time, this historical, canonical text represents discontinuity and distance as well as continuity and connection. Because it is accepted as Scripture within Christian communities, it has traditionally had the function of challenging and confronting present understandings. This implies that there may be a critical edge to a study of the gospel which can add depth to an examination of the distinctive tradition and discourse patterns of the Mennonite and feminist hermeneutic communities.

Methodological Strategy

> Hermeneutics seems to me to be animated by this double motivation: willingness to suspect, willingness to listen: vow of rigor, vow of obedience. In our time we have not finished doing away with idols and we have barely begun to listen to symbols.[44]

The starting point of theology in a theoretical model that stresses hermeneutic community is not a discussion of a philosophical foundation expressed as a transcendental a priori or a phenomenological analysis of abstract structures of possibility.[45] Rather, theology begins by recognizing a specific discourse as the linguistic manifestation of the life and practice of a particular community. It begins by exploring this discourse as it is rooted in traditional speech and practice as well as in its development through ongoing conversations around the meaning of particular texts. John H. Yoder emphasizes this when he insists: "What must replace the prolegomenal search for 'scratch' is the confession of rootedness in historical community."[46]

The notion of hermeneutic community can therefore prevent a false dichotomy between personal experience and the Bible by shifting the attention to the specific communities which form the social/political pre-suppositions of the readers. The confession of rootedness in historical community forces interpreters to pay attention to the network of beliefs and practices which express the traditional interpretations of individual biblical texts. It encourages them to name the theological convictions which have influenced their own practice of Bible reading. A new awareness of their own personal involvement in the discourse of their community and its issues of authority and power can result from this kind of analysis.

James William McClendon's definition of theology can be helpful here. He speaks about theology as "the discovery, understanding, and transformation of the convictions of a convictional community, including the discovery and critical revision of their relation to one another and to whatever else there is."[47] In this definition theology is both a descriptive discipline that tries to discover the actual convictions by which a community lives, and a constructive discipline that becomes involved in the critical revision of these convictions. The focus on particular community convictions implies the pluralistic nature of theology, but also includes the challenge of critical dialogue between individuals and communities. Theology is thus interested in both the concrete historical manifestations of community beliefs and the rational theoretical discussion of their interrelationship.

Convictions, for McClendon, are beliefs that are so self-involving that a community would become significantly different if they were to be relinquished. Convictions can be articulated in many forms including confessions of faith such as doctrines and creeds, ethical principles, foundational narratives or even hymns and liturgies. By their very nature, however, convictions are not disembodied ideals but rather are part of the community ethos, that mixture of discourse and action, tradition and behaviour that characterizes and identifies a community. Theology, therefore, cannot do its task unless it has first of all heard community proclamation and seen or experienced community life.

In a model of theology that stresses convictional community, both the text and the community will be named and described in specific ways.[48] It will not suffice to speak in universal terms of the "church" or the "Bible." Though a general pattern of discourse may emerge, this pattern is based on specific experience with particular texts and particular communities. Each convictional community has unique ways in which individual texts connect or are discontinuous with its vision and practice because each text is construed in unique ways by the normative community interpretation.

Theology deals with the question of truth but admits that this truth is only found in the convictions of particular communities. This implies that theology is a human activity that is limited in wisdom, vision and faithfulness. Yet theology deals with the search for truth in a systematic manner, as implied by the emphasis on the "relation" of convictions to one another and to whatever else there is. Theology is therefore not narrowly confined to the description of the interrelationship of the community's convictions. Theology also enters into dialogue with "whatever else there is," that is, with the convictions held by other communities. This can lead to mutual affirmation, challenge and a critique which does not accept the cynicism of relativism.

The term "transformation" points to the creative aspect of the theologian's task. It involves not only clearly articulating the identity and vision of a community as expressed in its convictions but includes a critical and constructive exploration of further dimensions and new domains that can be changed by this vision. Transformation thus implies a "redescription" of reality in terms of the framework of convictions that the analysis has uncovered.[49]

Theologians and biblical interpreters whose discussions of authority are rooted in hermeneutic community self-consciously participate in the ongoing transformation of the community's vision and practice. Their interpretations become part of the dynamic process of identifying authoritative convictions. They are involved in the interactive politics of the community's interpretive practice.

In order to prevent self-justification, theologians must remain open to the possible disruptions that the experience of others or the rereading of the biblical text can bring to their own normative language.[50] They cannot uncritically or naively place authority in any one writing, whether contemporary or canonical. However, they also cannot become skeptical, assuming that normative statements or truth claims cannot be made. Rather, in this model of analysis, the theological process itself reveals the authoritative relationships that are present between individuals and within the community. A double strategy of listening and suspicion, commitment and critique, allows the political patterns of relationships to be revealed, critiqued and transformed. This strategy becomes clearer through a closer examination of the notions of *tradition* and *discourse.*

Communal Tradition: Self-involving and Political

Hans-Georg Gadamer, speaking from the sphere of philosophical hermeneutics, has redefined the role that tradition plays in the hermeneutical process.[51] His analysis of the phenomenon of understanding focuses on the crucial way that tradition mediates between the text and the individual reader in the production of authoritative readings of a text. Gadamer asserts the *continuity of meaning* in historical tradition, thus connecting past and present in an authoritative relationship. This challenges a discrediting of the authority of tradition in the name of reason commonly accepted since the Enlightenment. At the same time Gadamer does not wish to restore the authority of a mythical past as in romanticism. In his model, authority is linked to the *Mitzugehoerigkeit,* or "belongingness," to the text that is experienced by members of a language community. The authority of tradition is based on a model of understanding in which the community assumes that the reader is related to the world of the text and the text is related to the world of the reader.[52]

The notion of hermeneutic community implies this sense of belonging or relationship to the text prior to the actual practice of reading a particular text. To understand how the authority of the text is construed in a particular community requires that this belongingness be made explicit. Because this connection is hidden in the "pre-understandings" or prejudices with which interpreters come to the text, they may be unaware of the power of tradition. They may not realize that a particular tradition is the framework within which things are first perceived and defined and that a dynamic hermeneutic process depends on a critical engagement with this tradition. Gadamer explains the process this way:

> In fact the horizon of the present is being continually formed, in that we have continually to test all our prejudices. An important part of this testing is the encounter with the past and the understanding of the tradition from which we come. Hence the horizon of the present cannot be formed without the past. . . . The hermeneutic task consists in not covering up this tension by attempting a naive assimilation but consciously bringing it out.[53]

In this model, understanding or interpretation is not to be thought of so much "as an action of one's subjectivity, but as the placing of oneself within a process of tradition in which the past and present are constantly fused."[54]

This means that hermeneutics is closely related to practice. Application is not appended to the interpretive process but is integral to it. In fact, tradition can only exist through appropriation. This does not imply, however, that authority means blind obedience to the tradition. Gadamer is again helpful when he substitutes "recognition" of tradition for obedience to it. He contends that acknowledgement, cultivation or affirmation of tradition is just as much a matter of choice and reason as revolution and renewal of tradition. The essence of authority for Gadamer has to do with knowledge and personal involvement in the process of tradition formation. Thus "the authority of persons [texts] is based ultimately, not on the subjection and abdication of reason, but on recognition and knowledge—knowledge, namely that the other is superior to oneself in judgment and insight and for this reason his [her] judgment takes precedence."[55]

Gadamer's discussion is helpful for an analysis of authority in hermeneutic communities, because it allows us to see tradition as a self-involving process. Authority choices are made in the process of wrestling with the tradition. This means that communal tradition cannot be understood as a static entity but must always be understood as changing and evolving as interpreters judge between rival claims to truth. This implies that in the dialogical process between text and interpreter there is both a questioning of the text by the present interpreter and a partial negation of one's own horizon (that is, the tradition in which one stands). This encourages an openness to being questioned by the text. In studying the relationship between experience and text within the Mennonite or feminist hermeneutic community, the dynamic self-involving nature of each tradition must be taken into account.

Both Mennonites and feminists have criticized the way in which an emphasis on objectivity and scholarly detachment has allowed scholars to deny their self-involvement in the theological process. Mennonites have concentrated on the relationship of knowing and doing. For them, self-involvement shows itself in the practice of the interpreter. Feminists have stressed the biases which are part of the reading of every text. They have emphasized the hidden bias of patriarchal hermeneutical practice. As Mary Ann Tolbert points out:

> The fiction of an objective reading of a text asserts itself when the biases guiding the interpreter match closely the biases undergirding the evaluating group. . . . No value-neutral position exists nor ever has. Feminist hermeneutics stands over against patriarchal hermeneutics, an advocacy position for the male-oriented, hierarchically established present cultural power system.[56]

These remarks by Tolbert point to a hidden danger in Gadamer's theory of language that is of particular concern to feminists.[57] Tolbert has suggested that his theory tends to stress surrender and fidelity to the biblical text more than critical consciousness and discriminating judgments. Because Gadamer's theory gives the false impression that all persons enter the conversation on equal terms, he cannot deal adequately with interpretation as a process embedded in relationships of power structured by institutions. Jürgen Habermas, in the philosophical tradition of Marx and the Frankfurt school, has spelled out how the hermeneutical process can be hindered not only by misunderstanding but also by systemic distortions caused by work and power.[58] He insists that language too can be a "medium of domination and social power; it serves to legitimate relations of organized force."[59] Thus the aim of interpretation must be not only new understandings but also emancipative action.

Liberation theologians, including feminists, insist that biblical interpretation is by definition engaged in furthering the interests of a particular community with its institutions and structured patterns of relationships. Interpretation is always "interpretation for" and is best described as both an engaged and a political process. Theologians in this critical stream of thought therefore insist that ideological suspicion must always be part of the theological process. They point toward a liberation approach that seeks to include those previously marginalized and excluded from communal institutions and patterns of discourse that embody tradition.

The notion of *hermeneutic community* used in this study includes an emphasis on the dynamic process of tradition formation, as well as a focus on tradition as pre-understanding. The process of tradition formation is acknowledged as being both rhetorical and political. In this model of the community-text relationship, belongingness to a tradition bridges the distance between text and experience. This belongingness, however, also points to the need for a critical examination of the self-interested nature of claims to truth and the resulting power relationships. By bringing tradition as pre-understanding and tradition as political discourse together in the notion of hermeneutic community, a strategy is encouraged that includes the possibility of both commitment and critique.

Communal Discourse: Authoritative and Innovative

George Lindbeck, in his book *The Nature of Doctrine,* suggests that comparing religions to languages and to cultures will give us a new way to speak about the constancy and change, diversity and unity, which characterize the beliefs and practices of religions. His theory places the emphasis on the comprehensive interpretive scheme of each community, which uniquely structures individual human experience and understanding of the self and of the world. His theory can be helpful in understanding the role of a particular theological concept such as *discipleship* in identity formation and in determining the discursive practices of individuals rooted in particular hermeneutic communities.

A primary assumption of Lindbeck's model is that human experience is shaped, moulded and constituted by the external word. Experiences cannot be expressed and understood unless there is a language that gives the vocabulary and grammar for communication. Lindbeck suggests that this overall religious scheme can be understood as an idiom that makes possible the description of realities, the formulation of beliefs, and the experiencing of inner attitudes, feelings, and sentiments. . . . it comprises a vocabulary of discursive and nondiscursive symbols together with a distinctive logic or grammar in terms of which this vocabulary can be meaningfully deployed. . . . its doctrines, cosmic stories or myths, and ethical directives are integrally related to the rituals it practices and the institutional forms it develops. This undercuts any appeal to unmediated experience whether from a transcendental or existential standpoint.[60]

In this model, religious communities, including Mennonite and feminist communities, have distinctive languages or idioms that characterize the discourse. The use of the term discourse shifts the focus to the use of language in communication. Similarities between languages can be ascertained by comparing the distinctive patterns of story, belief, ritual and behaviour used in communal conversation as much as by comparing the common vocabulary. In Lindbeck's theory, doctrines and theological concepts are not primarily claims to truth or expressive symbols of God but "communally authoritative rules of discourse, attitude and action."[61] These rules allow for diverse expressions of truth claims and of religious experience in changing conditions.

Change or innovation in the community's language is not understood primarily as the result of individuals gaining new inner experiences which begin to change the external cultural-linguistic framework. Instead, change occurs because of the interaction of the interpretive scheme with changing situations. This means that the interpretive scheme "develops anomalies in its application in new contexts."[62] These anomalies produce negative effects and experiences, even according to the religion's own norms, and therefore lead to discoveries of concepts that remove the anomalies. Thus change and dynamic movement are always part of the way community and text interact as texts are performed in community discourse and practice.

An emphasis on discourse in a cultural-linguistic model does not necessarily mean that a hermeneutic community is isolated in its own sectarian community. Instead, broad contact with the wider culture can result in innovative, creative redescriptions of the community's own theological language as well as creative conversations between hermeneutic communities. Every conversation will begin, however, by assuming distinctive ideas and practices based on each community's unique relationship to the Bible and to contemporary experience. Only through a dialogical process will the similarities come to light that would encourage two communities to form an enlarged hermeneutic community based on similar convictions. Thus the integrity of each community is respected in the dialogue.

Lindbeck's understanding of religious discourse is important in establishing a way to describe the distinctive and unique understanding of discipleship in each of the hermeneutic communities. His approach suggests that a theological term such as discipleship needs to be explored in terms of its function in the larger network of beliefs and practices in a particular community discourse. An examination of the use of a term within its own hermeneutic community constitutes the first step in a theological discussion, even before establishing its more general propositional or experiential meaning.

Theologians must learn to attend to the particularities of communal discourse, whether biblical or contemporary, before assuming continuity and commonality based on the common use of a term such as discipleship. Therefore they must begin with intratextual study and reflection in order to see which normative narratives or histories are treated as the paradigmatic instantiation of a discipleship ethos and ethic in the community or in the Bible. Innovation as well as authoritative grammar can more easily be described if the rules that accompany the use of the term in each case could be ascertained.

Though Lindbeck's cultural-linguistic model is helpful in understanding discourse patterns, its emphasis on intratextuality must be approached with caution. When Lindbeck discusses theological method, he construes the biblical text in a formal way, as a self-contained intratextual world that has the capacity to "absorb the universe." [63] Both Mennonites and feminists have noted a conservative tendency in this more literal use of the notion of intratextuality. Feminists have noted that his theory assumes that the Bible is the paradigmatic instantiation of the semiotic code for a community. [64] His theory, therefore, hides his commitment to a particular view of the authority of the text by focusing on grammatical rules.

Yoder has also warned that cultural-linguistic categories such as story or narrative may hide implicit philosophical assumptions about authority. A particular biblical narrative can become a sub-set of the general notion of narrativity, thus assuming a kind of authority associated with narrative forms. He suggests that vigilance is needed to defend "the particularity of Abraham and Samuel, Jeremiah and Jesus from reduction to mere specimens of a new kind of universals, namely narrative forms, lying deeper than the ordinary events and sufficient to explain them." [65]

The claims to truth that are hidden by a focus on the grammar or the narrative unity of the text need to be exposed and highlighted in order that their claim to universality can be critically evaluated. This includes a more adequate analysis of the construal of the text by the community, a construal that does not hide implicit claims to truth about authority or history. Lindbeck's theory needs to be modified in order to include the wide variety of ways in which the text and the community can interact in the hermeneutical process.

A cultural-linguistic approach to discourse accepts the notion that experience is mediated by the language of a particular community. The critical task of theology can be part of the intratextual task if theology begins by noting the faithfulness or unfaithfulness of the community to its own norms and paradigmatic narratives, whether these are embodied in text or experience. [66] This description of the theological language acts as a constructive process that includes critique. It also provides the basis for a dialogue with other communities about their norms, thus introducing a second moment of critical reflection. A creative moment may follow, as the language of each community shifts to explain the anomalies that have come about because the context has changed to include the other in the conversation. A double strategy can therefore occur within a theological discourse that is both authoritative and innovative because it attends to the particularity of discipleship in the hermeneutic community and in the biblical text.

A Critical and Constructive Model of Theology

These understandings of tradition and of discourse leads us to a model of theology in which two interpretive strategies must occur simultaneously. The first arises out of the sense of belonging that comes when a particular biblical interpretation has become part of the tradition. This leads to an intratextual reading that examines how certain convictions, experiences and texts have shaped the identity and practice of a community. This strategy is constructive in that it attempts to redescribe or elaborate the pattern or network of beliefs and practices of a community in order that the experiences of authority that are described in that writing can be better understood. It attempts to listen carefully to community language and then to creatively and constructively render this language intelligible to others.

The second strategy recognizes the historical character of theological and biblical writings and emphasizes the distance between the perspectives of the various discourse partners. It is suspicious of transcendental statements and is critical of any appeals to universality (whether in the name of experience or of the biblical text) that do not take into account the particular historical nature of the writing or the social-political process of communication. This strategy is primarily critical and suggests that radical change and innovation may be needed in the community's theological formulations. It enters the discourse of a community as a disruption and seeks to transform the language of tradition in order to resolve the contradictions and anomalies that have developed in community experience.

Both description and critique will characterize the first part of this study of biblical authority. The primary task will be to describe the network of convictions and practices that characterize an identity of discipleship in the tradition and the pattern of discourse in two distinct hermeneutic communities: the Mennonite community and the Christian feminist community. Reflections arising out of the differences between them will begin the critical process. This exposes the struggle to work out an authoritative process of biblical interpretation in each community and allows it to be evaluated in the context of an enlarged conversation. This first task is thus focused on illuminating the ethos of biblical authority in each community as experienced in the new context created by the dialogue between communities.

The second task shifts to the biblical text. Again, commitment and critique intertwine as the text is reread by someone standing self-consciously in both communities. The understanding of discipleship that emerges from this rereading uncovers both continuities and discontinuities in Mennonite and feminist definitions and identifications. A critical dialogue with these past understandings can begin, a dialogue which opens new choices to the interpreter. It is these choices that can bring new possibilities to each community, as the interpreter adds her voice to the larger community discourse.

The theological method, as well as the theological focus, contributes to a study that refuses to accept the polarity commonly assumed by many scholars—a polarity that places commitment and suspicion at opposite ends of objective scholarship.This study asserts the relationship between subject and object, in particular historical communities. It therefore assumes that self-involvement, as well as self-criticism, are part of responsible theological scholarship.

Endnotes

1   Rita Nakashima Brock, *Journeys by Heart: A Christology of Erotic Power* (New York: Crossroad, 1992), p. 25.
2   Perry Yoder, "The Role of the Bible in Mennonite Self-Understanding," in Calvin W. Redekopp and Samuel J. Steiner, eds., *Mennonite Identity* (New York: University Press of America, 1988), p. 76. The focus on hermeneutic community is especially important among those groups influenced by the "Anabaptist Vision" as outlined by Harold S. Bender, *The Anabaptist Vision* (Scottdale: Herald Press, 1944). My analysis will concentrate on this hermeneutic community of Mennonites. For an overview of the diverse approaches to systematic theology among Mennonites, see A. James Reimer, "Anabaptist-Mennonite Systematic Theology," *The Ecumenist* 21, 4 (May/June 1983: 68-72.
3   John H. Yoder, "The Hermeneutics of the Anabaptists," in Willard Swartley, ed., *Essays on Biblical Interpretation* (Elkhart, IN: Institute of Mennonite Studies, 1984), p. 308. Both the term "hermeneutic community" and "hermeneutical community" have been used in the Mennonite tradition. I will be using the former term in this work in order to put equal emphasis on "hermeneutic" and on "community."
4   Walter Klaassen, *Anabaptism: Neither Catholic nor Protestant* (Waterloo: Conrad Press, 1973), p. 47.
5   John D. Roth, "Community as Conversation," in H. Wayne Pipkin, ed., *Essays in Anabaptist Theology* (Elkhart, IN: Institute of Mennonite Studies, 1994), pp. 35-50.
6   For statistical information about Mennonites worldwide and for a description of Mennonite groups in Canada, see Margaret Loewen Reimer, *One Quilt, Many Pieces*, 3rd ed. (Waterloo, ON: Mennonite Publishing Services, 1990).
7   James Wm. McClendon, *Ethics* (Nashville: Abingdon, 1986), p. 23.
8   In this work the dialogue is particularly with those Christian and Jewish feminists who continue to read and struggle with the Bible as an authoritative book. A good example of writings on the issue of biblical authority by these feminists is the collection of essays in Letty Russell, ed., *Feminist Interpretation of the Bible* (Philadelphia: Westminster

Press, 1985). I will be using the term "feminist" to refer to this larger community of dialogue. However, when I speak about communities of dialogue concerning an identity of discipleship, I am referring more directly to Christian feminists who identify with the faith of the disciples of Jesus.

9   Letty Russell, "Liberating the Word," in ibid., p. 17.

10   Luise Schottroff, "Working for Liberation: A Change in Perspective in New Testament Scholarship," in Fernando F. Segovia and Mary Ann Tolbert, eds., *Reading from This Place, Vol. 2* (Minneapolis: Fortress Press, 1995), p. 188.

11   Rosemary Ruether, "Feminist Interpretation: A Method of Correlation," in *Feminist Interpretation of the Bible*, p. 122, and Elisabeth Schüssler Fiorenza, "The Will to Choose or to Reject: Continuing our Critical Work," in ibid., p. 127.

12   I have explored the relationship between the Mennonite notion of hermeneutic community and these directions in hermeneutical theory in my unpublished ThM thesis entitled "Hermeneutic Community: The Contemporary Relevance of an Anabaptist-Mennonite Approach to Biblical Interpretation" (Edmonton, AB: Newman College, 1984).

13   Stanley Fish, *Is There a Text in This Class? The Authority of Interpretive Communities* (Cambridge: Harvard University Press, 1980), p. 15.

14   Richard J. Bernstein, *Beyond Objectivism and Relativism: Science, Hermeneutics, and Praxis* (Philadelphia: University of Pennsylvania Press, 1983), p. 231.

15   José Miguez Bonino, *Doing Theology in a Revolutionary Situation* (Philadelphia: Fortress Press, 1975), p. 132.

16   Paul Ricoeur, "Tasks of the Ecclesial Community in the Modern World," in *Theology of Renewal*, ed. L.K. Shook (Montreal: Palm Publishers, 1968), p. 246.

17   Ibid., p. 232.

18   Lisa Sowle Cahill, "The New Testament and Ethics: Communities of Social Change," *Interpretation* 44, 4 (October 1990): 384.

19   James Sanders, *Canon and Community* (Philadelphia: Fortress, 1987).

20   Wayne A. Meeks, "A Hermeneutics of Social Embodiment," *Harvard Theological Review* 79 (1986): 184.

21   Janice Capel Anderson and Stephen D. Moore, *Mark and Method: New Approaches in Biblical Studies* (Minneapolis: Fortress Press, 1992), pp. 50-83.

22   Judith Fetterley, *The Resisting Reader: A Feminist Approach to American Fiction* (Bloomington and London: Indiana University Press, 1978).

23   These two aspects are mentioned in a lecture by George Lindbeck, "Deconstructing Modernity," *J. J. Thiessen Lectures* (Winnipeg: Canadian Mennonite Bible College, October 20-21, 1992), audiotape # 1. Lindbeck begins the lecture by recalling how his suggestion of the theme of hermeneutical community was greeted with pleasure by the conference planners. He had been unaware of this term in the Mennonite tradition when he proposed the theme. His emphasis is largely on the first aspect while in Mennonite tradition the term was usually used to emphasize the second aspect.

24   Letty Russell, *Church in the Round: Feminist Interpretation of the Church* (Louisville, KY: Westminster/John Knox Press, 1993).

25   *Biblical Revelation and Inspiration* (Scottdale, PA: Mennonite Publishing House, 1959).

26   Donald F. Durnbaugh, *The Believers' Church: The History and Character of Radical Protestantism* (London: Macmillan Company, 1968), pp. 209-220.

27   A focus on the theological notion of discipleship does not negate the sociological, psychological and material motives involved in a protest movement. It also does not negate the various other theological themes involved in justifying a protest movement. It is, however, important to note that in both the Mennonite and feminist movement,

discipleship has been used to assert the relationship between Christian identity and a political process that questioned institutional structures.

28 John H. Yoder, "The Hermeneutics of Peoplehood: A Protestant Perspective on Practical Moral Reasoning," *Journal of Religious Ethics* 10, 1 (1982): 291-308.

29 Walter Klaassen, *Anabaptism: Neither Catholic nor Protestant.*

30 Russell, "Liberating the Word," p. 14.

31 Rosemary Radforth Ruether, *Women-Church* (New York: Harper and Row, 1989); Miriam Therese Winter, "The Women-Church Movement," *Christian Century* 106 (March 8): 258-260.

32 Yoder, "The Hermeneutics of the Anabaptists," p. 21.

33 Nadine Pence Frantz, ed., "Women: Bearing the Cross of Discipleship," *Women's Concerns Report* 89 (March/April 1990): 1-14, and Lydia Harder, "Discipleship Reexamined: Women in the Hermeneutical Community," in Harry Huebner, ed., *The Church as Theological Community* (Winnipeg, MB: CMBC Publications, 1990), pp. 202-206.

34 Gayle Gerber Koontz, "Freedom, Discipleship and Theological Reflection," in Daniel Schipani, ed., *Freedom and Discipleship* (Maryknoll, NY: Orbis Books, 1989), p. 173.

35 Rosemary Ruether, "Feminist Interpretation: A Method of Correlation," *Feminist Interpretation of the Bible*, p. 112.

36 Mary Ann Tolbert, "Protestant Feminists and the Bible: On the Horns of a Dilemma," *Union Seminary Quarterly Review* 43, 1-4 (1989): 1.

37 Yoder, "The Hermeneutics of the Anabaptists," p. 23.

38 In some Mennonite traditions this supportive and submissive role was symbolized by the wearing of the prayer veil by the women. See the theological justification for this custom in the booklet by Paul M. Miller, *The Prayer Veiling* (Scottdale: Herald Press, 1956).

39 Elisabeth Schüssler Fiorenza has discussed this division in her book *In Memory of Her*, p. 86.

40 Koontz, "Freedom, Discipleship and Theological Reflection," pp. 174-175.

41 "The New Testament and Ethics," p. 394.

42 For a more comprehensive study of discipleship and authority, other biblical texts and other hermeneutic communities would be drawn into the conversation. However, in a model of theology based on hermeneutic community, all generalizations would begin with particular interpretations.

43 John R. Donahue, *The Theology and Setting of Discipleship in the Gospel of Mark* (Milwaukee, WI: Marquette University Press, 1983), p. 11.

44 Paul Ricoeur, *Freud and Philosophy* (New Haven: Yale University Press, 1970), p. 27.

45 For a discussion of the search for foundations in theology see Francis Fiorenza, *Foundational Theology* (New York: Crossroad, 1984).

46 *The Priestly Kingdom* (Notre Dame, IN: University of Notre Dame Press, 1984), p. 7.

47 James Wm. McClendon, Jr., *Ethics* (Nashville: Abingdon, 1985), p. 23.

48 David H. Kelsey discusses biblical authority by examining particular works of various theologians and their "imaginative construal of scripture." He hints that this construal is related to the construal of "church," but does not focus on the social/political dimension of the interpretive process. See *The Uses of Scripture in Recent Theology* (Philadelphia: Fortress Press, 1975).

49 Lindbeck, *The Nature of Doctrine* (Philadelphia: Westminster Press, 1984), p. 118.

50 In describing the various ways in which theologians can appeal to the notion of experience, George Schner suggests that experience can enter a theological argument not as foundational but as interruptive, bringing a moment of discontinuity into a larger, already established context. I assume that the Bible can also function this way. See

George Schner, "The Appeal to Experience," *Theological Studies* 53, 1 (1992): 54.

51   Hans-Georg Gadamer, *Truth and Method* (London: Sheed and Ward, 1975).

52   *Wahrheit und Methode* (Tübingen: J.C.B. Mohr, 1960), p. 274; (*Truth and Method*, p. 258).

53   *Truth and Method*, p. 273

54   Ibid., p. 258.

55   Ibid., p. 248

56   "Defining the Problem: The Bible and Feminist Hermeneutics," *Semeia* 28: 118.

57   Elisabeth Schüssler Fiorenza, *Bread Not Stone: The Challenge of Feminist Biblical Interpretation* (Boston: Beacon Press, 1985), p. 133.

58   *Theory and Practice* (Boston: Beacon Press, 1973), pp. 1-40, and *Knowledge and Human Interest* (Boston: Beacon Press, 1968).

59   "A Review of Gadamer's *Truth and Method*," in *The Hermeneutic Tradition* (Albany: State University of New York Press, 1990), p. 239.

60   Lindbeck, *The Nature of Doctrine*, p. 33.

61   Ibid., p. 18.

62   Ibid., p. 39.

63   Ibid., pp. 116-117.

64   Mary Ann Tolbert suggests that the work of Lindbeck is one example of an attempt to preserve the traditional authority of Scripture by not declaring openly the fictional nature of biblical writings. See *Sowing the Gospel* (Minneapolis: Fortress Press, 1989), p. 25.

65   Yoder, *The Priestly Kingdom*, p. 36.

66   Ibid., pp. 113-124

Chapter 2

Discipleship and Authority: Mennonite
Hermeneutic Community

When the historian Harold S. Bender identified discipleship as the heart of the
Anabaptist/Mennonite tradition in his classic 1944 synthesis of the Anabaptist
vision, he spoke to the needs of a community struggling with its identity as a
minority church within the larger North American culture.[1] His way of
construing the essence of the Christian faith around an historical ideal found
broad resonance in many Mennonite churches concerned with remaining
faithful to the Christian faith. Vigorous research into the historical roots of
Mennonites thus provided the stimulus for a new articulation of the self-
identity of a community. The fact that this identity was expressed as
discipleship, a concept clearly rooted in the Bible, allowed it to become a
central notion in Mennonite theology within a short period of time.

The recovery of the Anabaptist vision began with an apologetic concern
to correct a picture of sixteenth century Anabaptism as "sectarian fanaticism
or as a renewed kind of works religion."[2] The identification of Anabaptism
with the Peasants' War of 1525 and the Münster incident of 1534-35 was
rejected, along with the charge of heresy that had made Anabaptism irrelevant
or even dangerous to the broader church. Instead, the confessional writings of
Anabaptists were studied by men like Harold Bender, John Horsch and J.C.
Wenger in order to gain a new picture of the nature and goals of this minority
movement within the church.[3] Through this process the bias in church history
which favoured the major denominations was identified. Increasingly the
origins and heritage of the Mennonite church were presented positively,
creating a more respectable image of Anabaptism's role in the Reformation.

Bender's presidential address to the American Society of Church History was symbolic of this effort to convince other Christians that Anabaptism
was a valid part of the Reformation. In fact, in Bender's eyes, Anabaptism had
taken the Reformation to its proper conclusion by emphasizing the practice-
oriented nature of the Christian faith. Discipleship, the church as a brotherhood
and the ethic of love and nonresistance were identified as the core of commonly
held beliefs characteristic of "evangelical and constructive Anabaptism."
Bender summarized the essence of Anabaptism in this way:

> The whole life was to be brought literally under the lordship of Christ in a
> covenant of discipleship, a covenant which the Anabaptist writers delighted to
> emphasize. The focus of the Christian life was to be not so much the inward
> experience of grace of God, as it was for Luther, but the outward application
> of that grace to all human conduct and the consequent Christianization of all
> human relationships. The true test of the Christian, they held, is discipleship.

The great word of the Anabaptists was not "faith" as it was with the reformers, but "following" (*Nachfolge Christi*).[4]

The apologetic concern was matched by an equal concern for a renewal of authentic life in the institutional Mennonite church. The study of Ana-baptism became the search for an ideal, an identification of those elements in history that could provide new vitality and vision for a church that was seen to be increasingly influenced by the norms of the larger society. Thus the Anabaptist vision served to challenge the church with a "call to radical dis-cipleship" at a time of crisis in its life.[5] *Mennonite Quarterly Review*, a scholarly periodical, as well as the more informal pamphlet series, *Concern*, were established by Mennonite scholars to ask questions of Christian renewal and to encourage the Mennonite church to become again a radical Christian movement. Historical studies thus served to ask critical questions of the current theology and life of the Mennonite church.[6]

The significance of this time of reaffirmation of a tradition must be understood within the larger social setting of Mennonites in North America during the first half of the twentieth century. After a period of isolation in rural communities, Mennonite young people were beginning to enter the academic and intellectual world around them, including the world of scholarly theology and biblical studies. It was a time of identity confusion in which Mennonites felt drawn into the battle lines already firmly established by the theological discussions between liberalism, with its optimistic expectations of American society, and traditional Protestantism, with its insistence on loyalty to the Bible. Leaders, absorbed with working out the process of change and accommodation to cultural patterns, were not equipped with the educational tools necessary to articulate their own theological understanding of biblical authority. An alliance with Fundamentalism by a significant number of Mennonite leaders was inevitable.[7] This focused the issue of biblical authority on the literal inter-pretation of the Bible and on a particular theory of inspiration not congruent with the pre-theological biblicism of most Mennonites.[8]

At the same time Mennonite biblical scholars were embracing historical-critical methods of biblical interpretation. An articulation of biblical authority was needed that would allow Mennonites to affirm the Bible as the "trustworthy guide of faith and life" in a way that was congruent with their self-understanding and their practice of biblical studies.[9] The Anabaptist vision, with its way of connecting church and Bible within history, became a model for asserting biblical authority in the present life of the church. Historical study thus stimulated the articulation of an explicit, scholarly Mennonite theology that attempted to be true to a tradition that was neither Protestant nor Catholic, but rather presented a third option.[10]

The influence of the recovery of the Anabaptist vision began to be seen in the educational efforts and in the more explicitly theological writings of

Mennonites. This is evident in the *Foundation Series* curriculum for children, youth and adults, which was widely used in Mennonite churches across North America during the 1970s and 1980s. Discipleship was a central learning goal.[11] The influence of Anabaptist studies can also be recognized in the intensive study process on the nature of theological education initiated by Associated Mennonite Biblical Seminaries during the 1960s. The publication of *The People of God: A Mennonite Interpretation of the Free Church Tradition* provided theological undergirding for the work of the seminaries. The purpose of Associated Mennonite Biblical Seminaries was to be a "Christian community of scholarship and discipleship in the Free Church tradition."[12] C. Norman Kraus' book, *Jesus Christ our Lord: Christology from a Disciple's Perspective,* illustrates the centrality of the Anabaptist understanding of discipleship in systematic theology.[13]

Recent contextual studies of Reformation history have given a less idealistic picture of Anabaptism. They have emphasized Anabaptist plurality and the polygenetic nature of Anabaptism. The presence of core beliefs that established an ideal community is being questioned.[14] An occasion for conferences and essays devoted to an analysis of the educational, theological and sociological ethos that emerged in Mennonite circles under the banner of the "Anabaptist vision" was provided by the fiftieth anniversary of the publication of Harold S. Bender's essay. Arnold Snyder, commenting on these analyses, suggests that what was so convincing about Bender's vision was that it combined two seemingly disparate currents: "The 'Discipleship' called for by true Anabaptist followers of Christ involved both a visible 'separation from the world' as well as an active engagement in the world."[15]

Discipleship has gained centrality in Mennonite articulations of theology and continues to be a strong focus for unity among the various Mennonite branches. For many Mennonites, it continues to express the "imaginative construal" of what "the Christian thing is all about." [16] Studies of Anabaptist theology continue to serve as normative for Mennonites. Discipleship remains a vital framework for biblical studies. As Yoder points out, Anabaptism has come to designate not "a century but a hermeneutic," not merely a historical period but also a particular theological emphasis.[17]

The theological approach named Anabaptism may therefore be represented by some Anabaptist figures but is often considered valid apart from that period of history. For example, a periodical entitled *Anabaptism Today*, published by the Anabaptist Network in London, England, involves Christians from many different denominations. In its definition of Anabaptism as "Christian discipleship in the radical tradition," it illustrates a movement that assumes a distinctive theology that goes beyond the institutional Mennonite church.[18]

In a recent sociological study entitled *The Mennonite Mosaic: Identity and Modernization*, the authors suggest that the tensions among Mennonites in the last decades have largely been related to tensions between theology influenced by the Anabaptist heritage, and theology influenced by Fundamentalism.[19] Frequently, these tensions have focused on an understanding of biblical authority and biblical interpretation, especially interpretation related to women's roles. Though Fundamentalism was characterized in this study by a belief in biblical inerrancy, it contrasted with Anabaptism by being correlated with less knowledge about the Bible. At the same time, it was distinguished from Anabaptism in that it held more strongly to traditional female roles.[20] A study of the theology and practice of discipleship as articulated in Anabaptist-Mennonite tradition is therefore crucial for understanding an approach to biblical authority that contrasts with Fundamentalism, while insisting on the critical place of the Bible in the life of the church.

My analysis will begin by describing the particular theological convictions about God that have informed the construction of discipleship communicated through my Anabaptist-Mennonite heritage. The sources for this "redescription" are taken from a broad variety of Mennonite writings in order to demonstrate the consensus on a hermeneutics of obedience as the appropriate approach to biblical authority. Secondly, the discourse patterns of the community will be illuminated by looking at several writings of John H. Yoder as paradigmatic instances of the language of discipleship. He has been chosen because of the central place that discipleship has in his writings and because he is often thought of as the representative theologian of the Mennonite tradition. His articulation of a hermeneutics of obedience will be discussed as it relates to the social/political practice of biblical interpretation in the Mennonite hermeneutic community. This will result in a description of the ethos of authority as it is expressed and practised in a specific hermeneutic community.

Theological Convictions

The centrality of discipleship in Mennonite tradition is rooted in several key theological convictions about the divine/human relationship. These are not often expressed in systematic theological formulations because Mennonite theology is oriented to the practical application of beliefs. Instead, the key convictions about God's presence in the world are implicitly assumed or only partially articulated in the many essays or sermons that speak to the current issues of the congregations.[21] Though unsystematic, these various threads of theology do form a network of beliefs, which together point to a hermeneutic of obedience as the appropriate response to God.

In this redescription, these convictions are organized in a trinitarian framework in order to allow for easier comparison with other Christian hermeneutic communities. This is not a completely foreign imposition because in their written confessions of faith Mennonites continue to accept the classic

Christian understanding of God as triune.[22] However, the work of the triune God is understood in a specific way by Mennonites, who have interpreted the Bible within their own historical context These more general doctrinal statements are thus filled with their own substantive content. A redescription in a trinitarian pattern can make this unique emphasis and focus explicit.

Jesus—The Incarnation of Revelation

> The authority of Scripture cannot be separated from the authority of Jesus Christ who reveals God most fully, completely and clearly. In Jesus also, the riddle of how the divine and human live together is resolved through demonstration.[23]

Anabaptist-Mennonite theology is probably most often described by its focus on Jesus as the ultimate authority for faith and life. The verse from 1 Corinthians 3:11, "For no other foundation can any one lay than that which is laid, which is Jesus Christ," has served as a kind of motto for Mennonites from the time it first appeared in all the writings of Menno Simons, the sixteenth century priest from whom the Mennonites received their name.[24] This motto was based on the conviction that Jesus was the final, most complete revelation of God's will for all humanity (Heb.1:1-2).

For Mennonites, it followed that Jesus defined most clearly what life in obedience to God looked like.[25] This meant that not only the death and resurrection of Jesus, but his teaching and daily life, his character and actions, were revelational and therefore normative for the moral life of the disciples of Christ.[26] The incarnation of God in Jesus, someone who lived a human life, made it possible to understand the intention of God for all people. Christ's humanity revealed what it meant to be created in God's image and allowed persons and communities to follow in the way of Jesus. In Mennonite theology, the invitation to discipleship was an invitation for all of humanity to again live according to God's intention. Thus John H. Yoder insisted that "the way of discipleship is the way for which we are made; there is no other 'nature' to which grace is a *superadditum*."[27] The affirmation of the Lordship of Jesus was the central conviction that allowed Mennonites to see the possibility of human and divine in relationship to each other. This "compatibility" of the human and divine in Jesus was an essential conviction because it encouraged Mennonites to see a new relationship between God and humanity, between Spirit and flesh. This new relationship was modelled by Jesus, who though he was Lord, became servant. As Swartley points out, "Precisely when Jesus suffers and dies, testifying to his complete humanity, the Gospel of Mark declares that then, in that context, he is truly Son of God, divine (Mark 15:37-39)."[28] God chose to exercise Lordship by becoming servant, thus modelling a way for humanity to relate to God (Phil. 2: 6-11). Revelation, therefore, has a dual impact on our knowledge of the divine-human relationship. In his identification with humanity, Jesus reveals the self-giving quality of God's love and thus God's initiative in relating to persons. In his choice to become servant, Jesus reveals an obedient response to divine love. Thus he shows what a human response to God should look like.

The conviction that God chose to be revealed through the words and works of a particular person and a particular story has encouraged Mennonites to see God continuing to work in the particularity of ongoing history, including their own communal interpretation of the biblical text.[29] As Yoder pointed out, the historicity of the documents of the canon means that we are:

> left in the continuing uncertainty of life within history, the arbitrariness and the particularity of all historical existence, and the arbitrariness and particularity of hermeneutics within history, which is precisely where we ought to be, since that is where God chose to be revealed in all the arbitrariness and particularity of Abraham and Sarah, Moses and Miriam, Jeremiah, Jesus and Pentecost, Luke and Paul, Peter and John.[30]

The relationship between Testaments was not seen as "flat" but historical, related through a story of promise and fulfilment.[31] For example, Mennonites pointed to authoritative critique by Jesus of those perspectives in the Old Testament that were seen as only preparing for the coming of the kingdom of God through Jesus.[32] The Bible was therefore to be read "directionally" or historically, rather than understood as a collection of timeless "parabolic anecdotes for allegorical application or propositional communications ready for deductive exposition."[33] For some Mennonites, this implied that the New Testament superceded the Old Testament in authority, creating an uneasy relationship, not only with the Old Testament but with the Jewish community and its Scriptures.[34]

This reduction of the Old Testament's authority is parallelled by a strong emphasis on Jesus as the primary authority. In Mennonite understanding, Jesus brought about a new kind of historical reality. His life, death and resurrection were seen to be a "historical hinge or watershed," in that he fulfilled in himself the promises of the Old Covenant, thus initiating the New Covenant.[35] The covenant church continues this movement in history by embodying the Jesus story.[36]

For Mennonites, it is Jesus' life and teachings that form "the base line," against which all people must evaluate their own commitment and activity.[37] As pointed out by Ben Ollenburger: "For the Anabaptists Jesus Christ ceased to be, as he was for Luther, a forensic act of justification. The Anabaptists viewed Christ as one to be imitated as a judge of ethics, and as standing in judgment over the ethics of the old eon. Christ is a person to be obeyed."[38]

The importance given to Jesus' earthly life in providing ethical guidance for the church today is illustrated by the importance of the notion of modelling in the *Foundation Series* curriculum for children. "God provided a model for Jesus. Jesus provided a model for his followers. The apostles provided models for the believers that followed them. Today, parents, teachers and other adults provide models of discipleship."[39]

To identify with the Jesus story, to take Jesus as model, meant that the specific content of the biblical narrative was important. The distinction between the historical Jesus and the canonical Jesus was not considered crucial because it was assumed that the early church lived in faithful discipleship. The text provided a true witness to Jesus in the particular context of the writer. Therefore, Anabaptist-Mennonite communities have attempted to model their life after the life of Christ and the life of the early Christian communities as recorded in the Bible. The interpretation of the biblical narrative in a typological manner became the primary theoretical justification for any moral action by individuals or community.

The specific instructions given by Jesus in the Sermon on the Mount (Matt. 5-7), the example of Jesus in his rejection of the use of power to dominate people, and his obedient suffering and death on the cross have inspired Mennonites to envision the church as a servant church. They have interpreted the way of Jesus in the Gospels to be one of love and non-violence and have emphasized those strands in the Epistles and in the Old Testament, which agreed with these themes. The mission of the church has therefore been understood as one of communal witness to the reconciliation and servanthood that Jesus himself brought. The term "incarnation" has been used not only to describe the Word becoming flesh through Christ but also to describe the message of God becoming flesh through God's people. As stated by Harry Huebner, the disciples were to "carry on the incarnation of Immanuel by themselves being the presence of God among the people in a manner like Jesus."[40]

Regeneration or conversion to the way of Christ, and suffering and cross-bearing as evidence of obedience, were considered essential for anyone claiming to have revelational knowledge of God. "Knowledge of Christ comes in walking *with* him, and only then can one understand what is written *about* him."[41] Salvation was thus defined as identifying with Christ and achieving an intimacy with God that led to a true knowledge of the divine will. As summarized by C.J. Dyck:

> the way of the cross, discipleship, leads to that kind of intimacy with the living Christ by which his will becomes that of the disciple, not simply cognitively, but totally and increasingly, and in the process, transforming him [her] into the image of Christ. When this happens discipleship becomes not only a hermeneutical principle to uncover biblical meanings but opens up the very meaning of life itself.[42]

Central to the notion of discipleship in Mennonite tradition is the doctrinal conviction that Jesus was the unique incarnation of God in history as a *Servant/Lord*. His life and death modelled a relationship with God that demonstrated both the self-giving love of God and the obedient response of humanity. This *revelation has historically been embodied in the New Testament text,* which gives identity and ethical guidance to disciples who choose to live a life of obedience and servanthood modelled after that of Jesus.

God—The Creator/Saviour

> The manner in which God's creative power is manifest in Christ, then, is the clue to understanding the creation process. Or, to put it slightly differently, incarnation as it was realized in Jesus is the recreative process by which the original intention of God in creation is being achieved. . . . When the incarnate Word is identified with the word of creation, we learn that creation is also an act of grace.[43]

For Mennonites, understanding creation as an act of grace means it is understood through the lens of God's redemptive action in creating a new humanity. Both creation and salvation happen at God's initiative and are God's gift to humanity. However, because God's original intention in creation is obscured through sin, a new creative action is necessary in order for humanity to really acknowledge God as Creator. For Mennonites, the theological discussion of creation becomes a sub-set of the soteriological and ecclesial aspects of God's activity.

Jesus is understood as the last Adam, the prototype of the image of God. In this way, he defines in his own being what is meant by the new creation. So too the church, as body of Christ, is understood to be God's new creation. Salvation is the creation of a new people of God whose identity and character reflect the creative initiative of God (1 Cor. 5:17). God is the loving Creator who continues the work that was begun in creation as narrated in Genesis and will finally bring it to completion in the eschaton depicted in Revelation. This Creator/Saviour was usually named Father in Mennonite theological writings.[44]

The creation of a people obedient to the intention of God in creation is understood by Mennonites to be central to God's original purposes and therefore central to the gospel.

> The work of God is the calling of a people, whether in the Old Covenant or the New. The church is then not simply the *bearer* of the message of reconciliation, in the way a newspaper or a telephone company can bear any message with which it is entrusted. Nor is the church simply the *result* of the message. . . . That men [and women] are called together to a new social wholeness is itself the work of God which gives meaning to history.[45]

The creation of the one humanity, as stated in Ephesians 2:14-15, 3:3-6, is itself the mystery that is now to be proclaimed, the first fruits of a kingdom already here. God's grace brings about reconciliation to God and reconciliation between individuals and thus fulfils the intention of creation. The close connection between the purpose of God in creation and the purpose of God in salvation is made visible by the linkage of creation and salvation in the church. Mennonites can speak of God's creation of a people as an "interpretive thread," which runs through the entire Bible from the "call of Abraham through the assembly of the messianic community around the resurrected Jesus to the future culmination of all reality in the kingdom of God."[46]

Anabaptist-Mennonites have insisted that God's new creation has a particular political shape that embodies the gospel message of reconciliation. The people of God are living epistles, known and read by all (2 Cor. 3:2). Mennonites have rejected the normativity of Christendom and have insisted that the "Constantinian shift" which made the church the state religion and therefore part of established society also distanced the church from the biblical understanding of the people of God.[47] Instead, Mennonite theology has emphasized the pilgrim and alien quality of the church's political reality as a minority community, which lives in nonconformity to the values of the larger culture.

In Mennonite tradition, the importance of nonconformity (Rom. 12:1) or separation arises out of this understanding of the faithful church as a new social reality. The distinctiveness of the church has been expressed in various ways, including language, culture, clothing styles or refusal to participate in various political processes. Primarily, nonconformity has been symbolized by an alternative ethic, which emphasized the way of peace and reconciliation including service, nonresistance and the rejection of violence.

This commitment to nonconformity is based on an eschatological view of history in which the church has an important role in the creative purposes of God. The term "kingdom of God" describes this larger creative purpose.

> the kingdom of God has come through the death and resurrection of Christ and is historically visible in the church which is the realm where Christ's lordship is acknowledged. . . . The suffering and martyrdom of the faithful is the result of the conflict between two kingdoms, two worlds, two ages which are the locus of a cosmic struggle between God, the Creator and Redeemer and all the powers of evil which oppose him [sic].[48]

The church, in its radical obedience, becomes the sign of the coming kingdom, of the creative purpose of God, as it lives out its calling to be an alternative presence in the world, a moral community embodying the values of the kingdom of God. The church must therefore disengage itself from the contemporary culture in which it is immersed in order to clearly discern the discrepancies between that culture and the way of Christ. It cannot be invisible but instead must become a visible instrument of grace in the world. This visibility must be social in order to embody reconciliation and peace in its very being.

The mission of the church arises out of this identity as a servant church, created by God to proclaim and embody God's good news of the kingdom. The political shape of the church as an alternative society is crucial because only then can it fulfil its mission, not only to proclaim but also to embody God's creative purpose in the midst of a society that has failed to give ultimate allegiance to God. To be able to respond to God in radical obedience, the community must be made up of those who voluntarily commit themselves to obey God. It must be made up of disciples willing to follow Jesus' example in his commitment to the kingdom of God. Therefore, Mennonites have insisted on adult baptism as a sign that the community is entered by mature choice, marked by conviction and commitment.[49] Commitment is also recognized by the submission of the individual to the counsel and admonition of fellow members. There is a covenantal quality to the discipline of the community, which includes both freedom and accountability. Yoder has emphasized that this kind of community is called forth by God and presents a real alternative to the "coercive givenness of establishment" or the "atomistic isolation of individualism."[50]

The shape of this community is to be derived from the Bible, the primary witness to God's creative activity in history. The Bible testifies to God's initiative within history through the calling forth of a community of disciples from the larger society of Jews and Gentiles to live in faithful obedience. The Bible records both God's creative, saving action and the response of the people as they are embodied in community life. A statement on biblical interpretation adopted by the Mennonite General Assembly in 1977, recognized that biblical authority rests in this conviction that the Bible and the obedient community of disciples are intrinsically connected by the creative work of God.

> The Bible is the *Book of the people of God*. It is the testimony of God's people to the prophetic Word and historic events. Through this Word and these events God created a special people with a peculiar political shape among the nations. . . . The Bible is truly at home within the believing community which gave the Bible its shape. The Bible in turn has shaped the people of God. . . . The unique authority and rule of God in Christ which is set forth in the Bible can become apparent only in the voluntary faith and obedience of the responding community.[51]

In Mennonite theology, God as *Creator/Saviour* invites human participation in the *new creation, historically embodied in a new community of reconciliation.* This participation is marked by commitment and obedience and is named discipleship. This new creation, the moral community, is already described in the Bible as a sign of the coming kingdom of God. The new community must therefore be characterized by its obedience in following Jesus and its nonconformity to the values of the larger society.

The Spirit—The Enabler of Discernment

One way that Mennonites speak of the Holy Spirit is as the "guarantor of our salvation now in process (2 Cor. 5:5, Gal. 5:5)."[52] The Spirit who raised Jesus from the dead also continues to bring new life to those who are called the first fruits or down-payment of God's redemptive activity (Rom. 8:11). It is through the Spirit of God that "the world was created, prophets and writers of Scripture were inspired, [and] the people were enabled to follow God's law."[53] It is through the Spirit that the particular historical event and word of Jesus became God's incarnational presence in the world. It is the Spirit who enables disciple-ship and thus enables obedience to the revelatory knowledge of Christ. It is the Spirit who enables the experience of salvation and who invites participation in the new creation of a reconciled community.

By relating the work of the Spirit to creation, salvation, and revelation, Mennonites have stressed the continuity of God's presence throughout history. This provided a basis for saying that the Spirit would continue to make "the written Word active in our lives and in the world."[54] Historically, the struggle to define the Spirit's work often focused on the process of biblical inter-pretation. Some Anabaptists expressed this struggle by stressing the need to bring the "inner" and "outer" word together in the interpretive process. They were thereby insisting that "a biblical text without the penetration and testing of personal appropriation is a dead letter."[55] Hence Anabaptists stressed the reciprocal relationship between obedience and understanding, suggesting that although it was obedience that opened the mind to the revelatory Word of God, it was the Spirit that made the Word powerful and alive, kindling the kind of obedient response that makes knowing possible.[56]

The conviction that the Holy Spirit would illuminate the mind of those who came to the Bible with love and obedience also meant regarding knowledge without obedience as blind, distorted and idolatrous (1 John 2:3-11; 1 John 4:6-21; John 14:15-24; 1 Cor. 10:5).[57] Therefore, faithful discernment of truth and of God's will are considered central tasks of the community of disciples. This task was not placed in the hands of the individual alone, nor in the hands of particular leaders. Instead, this discernment was placed in the context of a community gathered for worship and decision-making. The "rule of Paul" (a term already used by Zwingli for 1 Corinthians 14:26-29) was used by the Anabaptists to stress that each person should express his/her convictions and then the congregation should decide who spoke more nearly according to the Bible. As Yoder points out, this means that "the tools of literary analyses do not suffice; that the Spirit is an interpreter of what a text is about only when Christians are gathered in readiness to hear it speak to their current needs and concerns."[58]

The authority of the community to discern God's will for its life and work came from the basic guiding principle—the "rule of Christ" (Matt. 18). In this text, Jesus gives his disciples the responsibility to "bind and loose."

David Schroeder points out that this is part of the larger biblical pattern of how God relates to humanity.[59] God as a loosing and binding God was already demonstrated in the Exodus, with its focus on freedom and salvation (loosing) and on Mt. Sinai, with its revelation of the covenant responsibilities (binding). This pattern can also be seen in Jesus' life when he freed people from bondage in order to bind them to do the will of God. So too disciples are "loosed" from communities of unbelief and sin to be created anew, as "a chosen race, a royal priesthood, a holy nation, God's own people" (1 Pet. 2:9). The confidence found in a community identity of discipleship is related to the confidence found in a community process guided by the Spirit. As Schroeder goes on to say:

> If we are desirous to know the will of God, earnest in our deliberation, willing to commit our lives to a clear word from God, and rely on the leading of the Spirit there will come in the midst of our deliberation the moment when "it seemed good to the Holy Spirit and to us" (Acts 15:28) that we should do thus or so. There will be a moment when we will know what is of God.[60]

Marlin Jeschke's book, *Discipling in the Church*, is based on an interpretation of Matthew 18 that makes a strong point that a discipleship church cannot be developed without an understanding of mutual discipline and accountability in the community.[61] The use of the ban (exclusion from the community) in Mennonite church history was an attempt to recognize the abandonment of the way of Christ by certain people and a way to bring about repentance, forgiveness and reconciliation. This meant that the community created boundaries through a process of discernment assumed to be guided by the Spirit. According to Marlin Jeschke, the rule of Christ meant "to do some-thing about sin in the church but to do it Christ's way." [62] This was based on the conviction that "Only that Spirit which conforms to Jesus Christ, as we know him through the Scriptures, can reliably guide our faith and life." [63] For Anabaptist-Mennonites, this ruled out the use of physical violence to bring about change in the church or in society.

Mennonites believed that since the Resurrection of Jesus, we are living in a new period of God's action in the world, the age of the Spirit. The process of discernment created by the work of the Spirit among a group of people was understood as crucial in defining the church, for it was only with this function that the church could become a "tool for changing both societies and personalities."[64] Thus a hermeneutics of obedience meant obedience to the guidance of the Spirit in the context of a community of disciples.

In summary, in Mennonite theology God, as *Holy Spirit,* enables human involvement in a process that brings revelation and salvation together in the new creation of God in history. This *involvement is embodied in a process of binding and loosing,* which frees people to live in discipleship, but also enables the discernment of good and evil. This discernment comes about when the

Spirit enlivens the process of biblical interpretation within a community willing to hear and obey the Word of God.

God's Authority in History

In the theological language of Mennonites, biblical authority rests with the triune God and God's continuing presence *in history.*[65] The revelational knowledge of God is based first of all on Jesus in all his historical particularity and is then expanded to God's work in creation and God's continuing activity through the Holy Spirit. Though in Mennonite understanding God's presence has been incarnated most clearly in Jesus, the obedient Servant/Lord, it continues to be embodied in the work of God the Creator/Saviour in the creation of a new community of reconciliation, and in the work of the Holy Spirit who enables participation in a discernment process of binding and loosing.

The theology of discipleship depends upon a notion of divine *incarnation* or *embodiment* in history that continues beyond the historical event of Jesus. The present authority of God is *mediated* by the embodiment of God's activity in a *human text*, a *human community* and a *human discernment process.* Discipleship is defined as the response of obedience to this authority of God. The response is shaped by the model of Jesus in the biblical text, expressed through a commitment to the new community and discerned in a binding and loosing process within that community. Therefore, a hermeneutics of obedience clearly describes the openness of a community to God's authority, as mediated through these human intermediaries. This openness is evident in a hermeneutic community that identifies itself with discipleship in the Bible, participates in the creation of a community of reconciliation and is involved in the discernment of God's will on earth. The church as hermeneutic community is therefore constituted by God's gracious presence and action in the world and is made up of disciples who recognize their dependence on God's grace. Such an identity moves the church toward becoming a dynamic community, open to living out the truth as discerned through a participatory process of interpretation.

Hidden in Mennonite theology, however, is a primary assumption that can move the church in an entirely different direction. The network of beliefs surrounding discipleship and authority assumes that a hermeneutic community will be shaped by biblical interpretation and will live in accordance with God's will. It emphasizes the continuity between Jesus as described in the text and discipleship as lived in the New Testament account and in the twentieth century. Revelational insight and knowledge are assumed to move from the Old Testament to the New Testament and from the Bible to the present church community. This suggests that divine authority can be claimed by these intermediaries to authorize their interpretation of God's will.[66] It creates an understanding of the Bible and the church as pure, "without spot or wrinkle," able to truly incarnate God's presence in history.

This authoritative claim by a particular hermeneutic community can lead to interpretive practices that close the community to the embodiment of God's will in other people and other communities. It can make the Mennonite community exclusive and lead to the disregard of other hermeneutic communities who also read the Bible. One example comes from the Mennonite approach to the Old Testament. Waldemar Janzen, a Mennonite professor of Old Testament, has pointed out a certain neutralization of the Old Testament as authoritative canon and an ignoring of the text as a full-fledged conversation partner in the search to know God.[67] This demotion of the Old Testament has promoted a supersessionist approach to the Jewish people, thus taking away their dignity as a unique people of God with their own particular relationship to their Hebrew Scriptures. Janzen has also pointed out a certain "disdain for the mainline churches which are seen to have somehow stayed back in the lesser fullness of the Old Testament in the areas of laws, politics and war."[68] A context is created which allows interpreters of the Bible to promote their own interests, in the guise of divine authority, while downplaying the integrity of others.

In Mennonite theology not enough attention has been placed on the human practice of biblical interpretation and its difference from divine revelation. Discipleship has been defined "from above," with a focus on Jesus as divine and the Bible and church as participating in this divine authority. Therefore, the Mennonite definition of discipleship does not wrestle with the realism of the New Testament description of the disciples, who were often tempted to justify their own setting of boundaries by an appeal to divine authority.

A hermeneutics of obedience may allow a misuse of human authority within a community. It can describe a commitment to the Bible, the community and the interpretive process that does not take into account the limitations embodied in a human-authored book, a human built-institution and a human-organized political practice. It can hide the fact that some interpreters within the community may be using biblical interpretation to seek their own interests. A hermeneutics of obedience can encourage an uncritical, naive acceptance of a human authority rather than promoting an openness to God. This stance could move the church away from dynamic change to a more static acceptance of the status quo. This means that in Anabaptist-Mennonite theology an ambiguity surrounds the use of the term obedience. This ambiguity needs further examination through the exploration of the actual discursive practices in the Mennonite hermeneutic community.

Discourse Patterns

An examination of the ethos of authority that characterizes the discourse patterns within the Mennonite hermeneutic community will illuminate the relationship of discipleship and obedience from a somewhat different angle. Ethos emphasizes the customary, habitual ways of thinking and acting, the pattern of values that is revealed in the institutional shape of the community, as well as in the actual practices of the community.[69] Examining the ethos of a community is important because Mennonites have insisted that biblical interpretation not only shapes theological truth but also shapes and informs the practices of a community of disciples. The social/political shape of the church, as well as its rituals and ethical practices, must therefore be in continuity with the ethos of authority in the early communities of disciples. According to Nicholas Nash, the very way the community is constituted can be seen as a "performance" of scripture.[70]

The writings of Yoder articulate a vision for the shape of the church and for patterns of discourse within the community on the basis of a definition of discipleship that he argues is gleaned from interpretation of biblical texts. His vision for the church, articulated in the *Politics of Jesus*, has become persuasive for many Mennonites because it integrates key convictions of the community.[71] His book thus provides an example of the normative language of discipleship. Yoder has also written specifically about how this applies to a number of practices of the community. A summary of the ethos of authority which arises from his approach will be followed by an analysis of this ethos, both from personal experience in the Mennonite church and as gleaned from conversations and writings of a broader group of Mennonites, including other women. This exploration will give a more concrete example of the direction that a hermeneutics of obedience has taken in the practice of Mennonite congregations.

Discipleship as Revolutionary Subordination

Yoder is clear that his study of the New Testament texts is an attempt to relate the Jesus of the canonical Gospels to the discipline of social ethics, especially in its concern with the issues of power and revolution.[72] In order to do so he reads the gospel narratives with one persistent question in mind: Is there in the ministry and claims of Jesus a particular "social-political-ethical option" that can guide the social life of people today?[73] He insists that hearing the answer given in the Bible depends on setting aside the usual negative assumptions about biblical relevance that are common in ethical discussions today.

Yoder begins by concentrating on the canonical Luke to show that:

Jesus was, in his divinely mandated (i.e. promised, anointed, messianic) prophethood, priesthood and kingship, the bearer of a new possibility of

human, social, and therefore political relationships. His baptism is the inauguration and his cross is the culmination of that new regime in which his
disciples are called to share.[74]

Thus Yoder insists that Luke pictures Jesus as the creator of a new
social and political reality, a community of disciples committed to alternative
patterns of life that challenge the powers of the world around them. Luke 4: 18-
19 is a summary of Jesus' platform for the inauguration of the kingdom of God,
a kingdom that fulfilled the prophesy of the Jubilee vision as articulated in
Leviticus 25. It is clear that this vision included "a visible socio-political
economic restructuring of relations among the people of God, achieved by his
[God's] intervention in the person of Jesus as the one Anointed and endued
with the Spirit."[75]

Yoder points out that certain sociological traits were most
characteristic of the community of disciples, characteristics which also describe
any group that sets about to change society. These include a visibly structured
fellowship, voluntary commitment to the fellowship, and a lifestyle distinct
from that of the crowd.[76] This distinctness is the nonconformed quality of
involvement in the life of the world, an involvement that challenges the powers
that be and leads to the cross—the price of social nonconformity. This
nonconformity is characterized by a trust in God's power and a rejection of the
use of violence and controlling power to bring about change in human history.

Yoder traces the pattern that he finds in the accounts of Jesus in the
Gospels through to the Epistles and the rest of the New Testament. He focuses
particularly on the "in Christ" language of the Epistles, which challenges
believers to live in such a way that their behaviours or attitudes correspond to
or participate in the nature of their Lord. These traditions of discipleship or
imitation are found throughout the Epistles. Yoder's conclusion is that there is
but one realm in which participation with Christ is demanded, the realm of
political and social relationships. He concludes: "Servanthood replaces dominion, forgiveness absorbs hostility. Thus—and only thus—are we bound by
New Testament thought to be like Jesus."[77]

Yoder then turns to an examination of Christ and the language of
"principalities and powers" as found in the Pauline literature. He finds that
language particularly helpful in understanding the structured power relationships of our society. He points out that in Pauline thinking the powers and
structures were created good but now participate in the fallenness of all
creation by becoming the masters and guardians rather than the servants of
humanity. This leads Yoder to insist that the primary task of the church is to be
in itself "the proclamation of the Lordship of Christ to the powers from whose
dominion the church has begun to be liberated."[78]   The church must
demonstrate through its existence, Christ overcoming the powers. Therefore,

the church must concentrate on not being seduced by the powers that tend to dominate society.

The task of communal discernment is therefore placed in the centre of church life. This discernment concentrates on recognizing when the confession of Christ as Lord requires that the church challenge the powers that are embodied in social and political structures. He illustrates what is meant by this discernment by examining the "revolutionary subordination," which he sees in the ethical codes of the New Testament. Throughout this discussion he insists that the model of Jesus was the central factor in the social ethics of the New Testament writers who were writing for a community of disciples..

Yoder emphasizes several aspects of the *Haustafeln*, or household codes, that he sees as revolutionary. The first of these focuses on the subordinate person who is challenged to take personal moral responsibility to make of his/her status or position a meaningful witness and ministry. This means that the wife cannot rely on her husband, nor a slave on the religious unity of the household, to determine their faith. They are "freed for obedience" by the resurrection of the crucified One.[79] Second, this call includes the dominant person, because the call to subordination is reciprocal. The existing order is thus relativized and undermined. Yoder recognizes that the practical, concrete and sweeping impact of these imperatives comes in this call to the superordinate person.[80]

When Yoder goes on to speak of the presence of similar patterns of ethical thought in the rest of the Epistles, he points to what he sees as a uniform pattern of "creative transformation," arising out of the stance of servanthood, derived from the example and teaching of Jesus. A new world regime, which violently replaces the old is not the mandate of Christians who follow in the steps of Jesus. Instead, "the old and new exist concurrently on different levels."[81] Yoder summarizes this as a stance of revolutionary subordination, of willing servanthood in the place of domination that "enables the person in a subordinate position in society to accept and live within that status without resentment, at the same time that it calls upon the person in the superordinate position to forsake or renounce all domineering use of his status."[82]

The church can live out the newness of the kingdom within whatever structures the society has because it knows that these structures are crumbling and passing away, and that "moral or personal value" is not determined by these structures. Yoder thus insists that the ethic of Jesus "was transmitted and transmuted into the stance of the servant church within society, as indicated precisely in the *Haustafeln*."[83]

A stress to not conform to society's norms begins as Yoder speaks about the kind of subjection and respect that the disciple has for the authority of government. He stresses that function exercised by government is not the function to be exercised by Christians. However able an infinite God may be to work at the same time through the sufferings of his believing disciples who return good for evil and through the wrathful violence of the authorities who punish evil with evil, such behaviour is for men [women] not complementary but in disjunction.[84]

While God orders government, God does not morally approve of all that government does. Christians, though accepting their subjection to government, retain their moral independence and judgment and may at times suffer because of their obedience to Christ.

The willingness to suffer is then not merely a test of patience or a dead space of waiting for God to act; it is a participation in the character of God's victorious patience with the rebellious powers of his creation. In Yoder's view, Christians subject themselves to government because it was in so doing that Jesus, as our prime example, revealed and achieved God's victory.[85]

In the final chapters of the book, Yoder places these discussions of the ethical and social stance of the church into the context of God's righteousness and grace, which reconciles people to each other. For Yoder the essence of the gospel proclamation is

the triumph of God's love in his [God's] own sustaining of his [God's] creation in that he [God] blesses equally insider and outsider, friend and enemy, in such a manner that the genuineness (Jesus said, "perfection") of our love is also made real at the point of its application to the enemy, the Gentile, the sinner. There is a sense in which the ethics of marriage and the prohibition of adultery, or the ethics of work and the regulation of attitudes toward slavery, or the opening up of communication and the prohibition of falsehood are all part of the promise of a new humanity enabled and created by God and already being received by men [women] of faith.[86]

The key to being God's people is not effectiveness, but patience, obedience and faithfulness in the midst of the rebellious powers. It is not the primary duty of disciples to make history move in the right direction or to manage society. Rather, it is Christ's resurrection that assures Christians of the ultimate triumph of God's purpose. This is a reminder that the way of the cross, the way of love, will finally triumph. This way is only meaningful if Christ is who he said he is, the Master.[87]

To summarize, Yoder's biblical interpretation results in a theological vision of discipleship that determines the political shape of the discipleship community. This political shape has two dimensions:

First of all, discipleship implies a commitment to a particular Christian behaviour, to an ethical lifestyle as a follower of Jesus. According to Yoder, discipleship is a substantial, binding, costly social stance that gives direction to decision-making in the social and political realm of life. Servanthood, subordination and non-violence are central to this new order, made visible in an alternative community, the faithful church that embodies and mediates the reconciling love of God through its lifestyle. Therefore, the community will live in non-conformity to the larger society.

Second, a confession of discipleship also makes an important truth claim. By rejecting any human power that attempts to dominate or manipulate history according to its own definitions of good, Yoder undermines human agency as the controlling factor in history. This revolutionary thinking is characteristic of disciples who insist that the power of God will finally triumph. They trust in God to direct history while seeing themselves as continuing to embody God's love in the world. This confession suggests that the community of disciples will be a minority community that is not concerned with directing history by using political power.

Yoder's primary concern is therefore the shape of the church as an alternative social and political entity in the midst of a society that is not ordered according to the ethic and truth of Jesus. A hermeneutic of obedience is expressed in Yoder's emphasis on the continuity between the ethic and truth claims of the obedient community of disciples today and the ethic and truth claims already asserted in the New Testament, especially as embodied in Jesus. He assumes that this ethic and this truth claim result in a new normative order in which the usual societal distinctions that determine power and authority are considered "relatively unimportant."[88] This raises the question of how this new order is actually experienced by members of the community. Can the church, a social and political institution, actually practice this new order when the old order still strongly influences the sense of personal autonomy and freedom that men and women of the community experience?[89] Does the costly stance of non-conformity also encourage women to challenge the patriarchal social hierarchy in the community?

Authority and Power in Discipleship Practice

In an article entitled "Sacrament as Social Process: Christ the Transformer of Culture," Yoder has named five practices that he sees "described and mandated" in the New Testament.[90] These practices concern both the internal activities of the Christian congregation and the ways the church interfaces with the world. According to Yoder, these practices are rooted in the normative events of the revelation of Christ and as such are a crucial part of living in the community as disciples. These practices are "incarnational processes" that "pioneer a paradigmatic demonstration of both the power and the practices that define the shape of restored humanity."[91] They therefore show how the *revolutionary subordination* described in Yoder's interpretation can be put into practice in the hermeneutic community.

This shift to practice implies a shift from the language of vision to the language of performance. Performance language only becomes true for a community when a congruence occurs between vision and reality. This shift requires that attention be paid to how various members of the community evaluate the performance of these practices. The analysis will consider the writings of both women and men in order to point out how these particular practices have functioned in the Anabaptist-Mennonite community. The distinctive ethos of authority that emerges from this analysis demonstrates how *revolutionary subordination* has worked itself out in the practice of biblical interpretation within the Mennonite community.

Fraternal admonition. This practice, called the "rule of Christ" by early Protestants, is interpreted by Yoder to be a "process of human interchange combining the mode of reconciling dialogue, the substance of moral discernment, and the authority of divine empowerment."[92] This practice of binding and loosing is based on the passage in Matthew 18 in which Jesus gives his disciples instructions dealing with sin and offense. These terms had a meaning in rabbinic thought referring to making something obligatory or not obligatory. Binding and loosing, or mutual admonition, was the way in which a community regulated its life together. According to Yoder, the goal of mutual admonition was reconciliation, forgiveness and the experience of again being fully included in the community.

A number of the reformers in the sixteenth century recognized that this function was to be assigned to the Christian community. However, Yoder suggests that it was the radical reformers who continued to insist on congregational conversation and decision making rather than giving the authority to make decisions for the church to the civil powers. It is in the congregation, the *ekklēsia*, that there is this close relationship between the confession of Christ as Messiah (Matt.16) and the assignment to bind and loose—the assignment to speak to one another *in God's name*. The confession of discipleship and the practice of mutual admonition are thus closely tied to ethical living in the Spirit of Christ.

Central to the process described in Matthew 18 is the movement from concrete situations involving a few members, to the broader discussion involving many members. According to Yoder, distortions of this process tend to emphasize discipline as a punishment designed to impose right standards on a whole society. In Yoder's view, this process is intended to encourage a person to "grow freely in the integrity with which he [she] lives out the meaning of his [her] freely-made commitment to Christ."[93]

The notion of fraternal admonition has functioned in Anabaptist-Mennonite history to *claim the authority* of the minority church over against the political authority of government or hierarchical structures of the established church.[94] The authority of the community was not to be taken over by the state, the school, or any secular organization, such as social work, psychiatry or legal organizations. The issues of war and peace, which have created tensions between Mennonites and the state, have frequently challenged the community to insist on its right to make decisions on its own behalf. Authority in this model comes through mutual conversation and decision-making in the community of disciples. The emphasis has therefore been on "authority in which the individual participates and to which he or she consents."[95] It was an authority based on God's presence within the community of God's disciples.

In the history of the Mennonite church, however, the practice of fraternal admonition has served another purpose. It was understood as the primary way to establish and maintain order and unity within the community. The ban is the topic of the second article of the Schleitheim Confession of 1527, where it shall be practised in order that "we may all in one spirit and in one love break and eat from one bread and drink from one cup."[96] Admonition was carried out primarily by the leaders and if that proved unsuccessful was expressed through a congregational decision to ban or excommunicate an errant member. This has led to great variations in opinion among the churches as to when discipline is necessary. It has also led to disputes over strictness, over details of the rules or over enforcement within the congregation. At times it has led to schisms within the church and sometimes new congregations were started as a result of a dispute over matters of discipline.[97]

Mennonite women have experienced the power of "brotherly" admonition, as it was usually called, used against them. As Melanie A. May points out, this interpretation of Matthew 18 privileged community decision over the well-being of individual members of the community, thereby privileging those with power in the community.[98] It led to denial of the abuse of power and authority within the community because it privileged privacy over public accountability. In a community in which public decision-making is usually placed in the hands of the male members of the community, this means that male authority is privileged over female authority. For female members of the community, subordination to community decisions meant subordination to community decision making in which women often had no part.

The experience of women testifies to a "tyranny of disciplined community" and to the "coercive dynamics" that some leaders used to deny their power while emphasizing God's authority.[99] Though very little systematic analyses has been done on authority structures, personal accounts by women are beginning to challenge the institutionalized inequities operative in interpersonal relationships within the communities.[100] Dorothy Yoder Nyce notes that the writing and preaching of Mennonite male leaders between 1920 and 1950 reinforced women's nonconformity to the world, a nonconformity expressed in the wearing of a prayer veil, "a constant reminder" of women's limited role and their necessary submission to men.[101] Though no comparison has been made between the public confession required of women disciplined for sexual activity resulting in pregnancy and the silence surrounding sexual abuse by male members of the community, it is clear that Mennonites have only recently applied peace teachings to the issue of violence against women.[102] When only men hold the "office" of minister, mutual admonition is slanted in the direction of male dominance.

The rule of Christ can therefore be understood as having at least two primary functions in the Mennonite community. It has been used to counter the authority and power of alternative community structures. It has also been used to enforce conformity to community norms that encouraged women's inferior status. In both cases, the claim to authority lay in the insistence that God's will could be known in the community as it read the text while guided by the Holy Spirit.

Universality of charisma. The mode of group relationships in which every member of the body has a distinct role is based on passages in Ephesians 4, 1 Corinthians 12 and 1 Peter 4:10. Yoder describes this as a "universalization of giftedness, with every member having his or her charismatic role, whose exercise the community helps define, celebrates, and monitors."[103] This means that every member is gifted by the Holy Spirit according to the grace of God to contribute to the "fullness of Christ" (Eph. 4:13), the full embodiment of Christ in the world.[104]

Leadership within the group was recognized as one of the gifts of the Holy Spirit. Diversity of gifts was considered natural and honour was to be ascribed to what are often considered the lesser gifts. Yoder describes this process as an "empowerment for the humble."[105] This emphasis on the gifts of the Spirit was to contribute to a sense of equality, without minimizing the need for leadership. Love and service were considered the highest gifts and thus no one could be denied the possibility of exercising that gift (1 Cor. 13).

In the history of Anabaptist-Mennonites, this theology functioned in several ways. First of all it was used to reject the authority of a sacerdotal class and an educated elite. It served to make all leadership roles functional. The phrase "the priesthood of all believers" was often used to emphasize the equality among the members, thereby freeing lay members to critically evaluate their leaders. Power was also given in this way to charismatic leaders in the community who were often not part of the institutional structure. These leaders were to be servants of the community.

During the early years of Anabaptism, the leadership authority of persons such as Conrad Grebel, Felix Mantz and Balthaser Hubmaier emerged through the power of their convictions, and was recognized by persons who gathered around them. Lois Barrett, in an article on Anabaptist women, suggests that it was the emphasis on the gifts of the Spirit which gave courage to Mennonite women who assumed authority in a patriarchal church and society. For example, Elizabeth Dirks, who was said to be a colleague of Menno Simons, became a teacher of many people. Her subsequent arrest testifies to the courage and strength given through the conviction that it is God who gives leadership gifts.[106]

As leadership became more routinized however, the prophetic gifts were submerged and the leadership office became more important.[107] A theology of gifts soon began to differentiate between the gifts of men and the gifts of women. J.C. Wenger, one of the early leaders in articulating the Anabaptist vision, suggested the following division in his booklet, *Separated Unto God*: "Women need the strength and leadership of men, and men need the grace and virtue of women."[108] In his biblical interpretation he tries to show that Paul believed in a divine order of "God—Christ—man—woman." He goes on to say what this means for him: "Just as Christ in the divine economy is subordinate to the Father so woman is to be subordinate to man in function and administration. This of course is a matter of rank, not of quality or importance."[109]

This division between male and female roles allowed the men, in their function as leaders, to name "service" in the home as the special gift of women, while naming their own dominant roles in the church as "servant-leadership." Biblical passages such as 1 Timothy 2:8-15, which based male superordination on an order established already in creation contributed to this view. Not only did the Holy Spirit not give women leadership gifts but it was already described in Genesis that women should not have authority over men. Elmer Martens concludes his recent study of these passages with these words:

> the above exposition would mean a broad exercise of gifts for all—men and women. Clearly women, to whom dignity is to be accorded, have broad avenues for public ministry. At the same time it seems necessary that a respect for role differentiation be maintained. One might envision, for example, that women would preach, serve on boards, perhaps be ordained (given an understanding of ordination as affirmation, rather than entitlement to authority). But officially designated leadership roles, such as senior pastor, would be reserved for men.[110]

This has meant that the public sphere of decision-making was largely reserved for men, while the domestic sphere was open to women. It is clear that the authority structures in the Mennonite church were not very different from those which prevailed in all of society.[111]

The universality of charisma functioned to empower those who wished to reject the authority of designated leaders by virtue of education or clergy status. However, it also gave power to persons who wished to keep leadership in the hands of the male members of the community, by suggesting that the different roles were already established in creation. In both cases, the authority to name gifts was rooted in the community who assumed that this authority was given by the Holy Spirit and was mandated by the Bible.

The Spirit's freedom in the meeting. The vision of the social process of decision-making was given even more guidance by the instructions in 1 Corinthians 14:21-29 about how to hold a meeting in the power of the Spirit.

This process has often been called the "rule of Paul" in Anabaptist-Mennonite circles. It emphasizes the right of all who have something to say to have the floor, while others "weigh" what has been said. It gives priority to prophecy but limits that authority by stressing the need for interpretation by others of what is said. Acts 15 tells the story of this process in action.

The rule of Paul, as Yoder describes it, recognizes the need for order in a community. However, the authority to keep order is one in which each member has the right to participate and speak. At the same time everyone is accountable to the other members and is to be open to challenge and admonition. The context of this process is worship and the goal is helping the congregation to discern and live according to the gospel. Authority is based on simple that God as Spirit is at work to "motivate and monitor his own in, with, and under this distinctive, recognizable, and specifically disciplined human discourse."[112]

During the Reformation, this stress on the right process of congregational decision making placed the discussion on a different level than it had been at first. Not only were the principles that were to be applied in detecting heresy important but the procedure of the meeting was also used as a mark to check out the validity of the claims. Were all persons free to speak? Was every speech heard and weighed so that all could enter the conversation? According to Yoder, in Anabaptist history the "rule of Paul" was used to insist on open congregational process over against the order that institutional structures could maintain. It was used by the Radical Reformation to insist on "the elbow room to keep on calling for change as new items arose on the agenda of reform."[113]

Anabaptist-Mennonite churches, however, have also insisted that this freedom of the Spirit was to be set in a context of created order. 1 Corinthians 14:29 is followed by verse 34 in which women are told to be silent. These verses were interpreted to mean that an active role for men and a passive role for women was basic to the process of the Spirit in the congregation. Women were therefore not ordained as leaders who could be part of the active process of communal change. Women were not heard in the public meetings of the congregation as they accepted the implicit understanding that the Spirit did not speak through women. As Di Brandt points out, the roles deemed suitable for women were roles that demanded their silence in the decision-making arena of the community:

> Women figure in Mennonite writing, as in public life, almost without exception as a terrible absence. The boards of our church conferences continue to be male-dominated despite active participation in church life by women members. Is it surprising therefore that the agenda of our theological and organizational discussions continue to reflect a male bias at the expense of other groups in the Mennonite community?[114]

The rule of Paul was used in the churches both to insist on the authority of a process of dialogue as well as to insist that this process meant different things for men than for women. Listening was understood to be more suitable for women, while the active involvement in the process was deemed more suitable for men.

Historically, Mennonite women have made a place for themselves in auxiliary organizations, which have existed alongside the main body of the church. Here they have been active, nurturing an alternative identity based on service and love. Yet women today are beginning to recognize that what is needed "is not so much a recovery of the Anabaptist vision, as a perpetual re-vision of it."[115] What is needed is a dynamic process that does not allow a static definition of roles. This revisioning will not be done if passive participation is expected from half of the congregation.

The authority of the dynamic work of the Holy Spirit in the community has functioned in Mennonite history to claim a dynamic process over against the static ordering of institutions. This dynamic process, however, was set within assumptions that accepted active roles for only some members of the community. Thus it also functioned to marginalize women from the active work of community transformation.

Breaking bread. The Eucharist is an "act of economic ethics" for Yoder.[116] This understanding is based on the "words of institution" in the gospels but also on the communal meals narrated in Acts of the Apostles. The emphasis is on the sharing of material substance in the community of disciples. The economic solidarity that is naturally part of the family has now been made broader. Eating bread together *is* being part of the family, and is not only symbol of this fact. Yoder thus calls the Eucharist "sacramental," to distin-guish it from a more "sacramentalist" definition in which a particular action is pulled out of daily life and given a distinctive meaning.

For Yoder, the Lord's Supper is a decentralized, particular and personal practice in continuity with Jesus' sharing of bread and fish in the post-Passion world. It includes the common purse of the "wandering disciple band who leave their prior economic bases to join the movement."[117] Eating together is a crucial activity of belonging to a new community in which Christ's presence creates the unity and reconciliation that holds people together.

For Mennonites, sharing through activities of relief and development has been of central importance. Service "in the name of Christ" has been the motto of the Mennonite Central Committee, the service branch of the church. This has meant that the sharing of bread with others has come to be a primary way of inviting others to join in the community of those who live by love and service. In Yoder's description of the Lord's Supper, a worship ritual is tied to both mission and ethics.

One distinctive emphasis of the Anabaptists in the sixteenth century was the close relationship of communion and ethical living. They refused to participate in Catholic or Protestant Mass because of a perceived lack of authenticity and love in the worship and life of the leaders and churches. They rejected the claim to holiness of certain observances and ceremonies of the church, insisting instead that holiness came only with ethical living in a community "united with God in his will and purpose in and through Jesus Christ."[118] The meal of fellowship was seen as an incorporation into the body of Christ. The focus was on the commitment to live and suffer for the sake of Christ and the community. Self-sacrifice in the name of Christ was at the centre of this commitment. Celebrating the Lord's Supper in small intimate communities was a way of saying that communion with God and each other did not have to be tied to certain sacred things, places, times or people. Rather, the sharing of food in love was itself an expression of the holiness that God gives to God's people.

The close tie between communion and ethical living contributed to giving another function of communion more prominence. Communion came to symbolize unity, love and peace in the community. This meant that when members of the community did not live up to the standards of the group they could be excluded from the communion table. A practice of "closed" communion discouraged an "open" discussion of conflict. Strife and dissension were denied or covered up in order to give the appearance of peace and unity.

The Supper also reflected the differences in role, evident in other areas of community life. These role differences became most clear around the table, the symbol of unity in the Mennonite home and church. Until recently, only men served in this community ritual. Public decision making and public service in worship were connected through their designation as male tasks. This meant that the observance of the Supper served not only to invite others into the community but also functioned as a primary way to signal the status differences between men and women in the church. Women continued to serve in the church kitchens, an extension of the kitchens in the home, while men served in the public worship. As Magdalene Redekop describes it:

> It was my father who made the decision to offer hospitality to the Indians, but it was my mother, my sisters and I who served the food and made the beds. While the *Bruderschaft* [brotherhood] was making the important decisions in the main body of the church, the *Frauenverein* [women's fellowship] was in the basement getting the food ready.[119]

The celebration of the Lord's Supper empowered Anabaptist-Mennonites to include themselves as full members of Christ's body, without relying on the ceremonies and rituals of the established churches. In its broader understanding of sharing bread, it motivated the extension of the community to others through acts of service and hospitality. However, it also served to exclude from the community those who were considered sinful or those who raised conflict issues. Differences in status were not overcome in the meal of unity and fellowship.

Induction into the new humanity. For Mennonites, baptism is the worship ritual that inducts persons into a new community in which "all prior given or chosen definitions of identity are transcended."[120] Social classifications based on class or category are no longer basic to ones identity. (Gal. 3:28, Eph. 2, 2 Cor. 5:16-17). This "egalitarianism or interethnic reconciliation" is enabled by the new creation which is signed and sealed by baptism. The New Testament is witness to the fundamental breakthrough of the Jew-Gentile barrier in the new humanity created by God. It therefore relativizes prior stratifications and classifications, giving them lesser importance than one's identity as a member of the church.

Anabaptists were nicknamed re-baptizers because they insisted on the voluntary nature of this act. Adult baptism signified that each person had the freedom to voluntarily join the community. Even those born into the community were to be given the opportunity, at the age of "accountability," to decide whether to join the church.[121] Thus adult baptism was a way to insist on religious freedom and to reject the use of violence and force to bring people into the church.

At the same time, the focus on the priority of spiritual identity allowed the community to minimize particular ethnic, gender or racial identities. When the majority or the powerful in a community were of a particular "race," an ethnic group or the male gender, it meant that the community identity was largely determined by that group. Thus Swiss-German Mennonites or Russian-German Mennonites were considered to be part of the community in a different way than French, black or aboriginal Mennonites.[122]

The practice of baptism could therefore implicitly be used to obscure differences between people and to emphasize conformity. The failure to recognize the identity of women as female disciples with their own particular experiences was part of this tendency. As Mary Schertz points out: "In our effort to disassociate ourselves from the abuses of western individualism, we [Mennonites] have introduced ideas and practices that come very close to sacrificing the sanctity of the individual for the good of the community."[123] Schertz goes on to point out how this notion of community has helped condone violence against women.

While the focus on adult baptism in Mennonite theology freed persons to choose their identity in Christ and to choose to belong to a community, it also forced some members to deny essential aspects of their identity in order to conform to norms established by the dominant members of the community.

To summarize, each of these practices, based on the interpretation of particular texts and assumed to be empowered by the presence of the Spirit in the community, has been used in at least two ways in community discourse:

(1) First of all, these interpretations have been used to assert communal authority over any other power from the outside that threatened the community. Each practice could be used by a community to assert itself over against the dominant religious and secular traditions that would threaten its unique identity. These practices have thus empowered the community to live in nonconformity to the culture surrounding it and to live according to what the community learned in its own experience of discipleship. The interpretations by Yoder have therefore encouraged freedom of choice over against forces outside the community that would limit that choice. They have encouraged a dynamic process of discernment in the community—a process that empowered a minority church threatened from the outside. (2) At the same time, each of these practices has also been used to assert community power over minority positions in the community and to insist on conformity by all members to a static community norm. The community discourse has thus encouraged a rigid interpretation of roles within the community and stifled diverse opinions and ideas. Unique identities and experiences were discouraged in the name of normative biblical interpretation in the community. The victims of this use of power were often women or minority groups who were not encouraged to be active members of the hermeneutic community. Obedience came to mean obedience to community norms established by the more powerful in the community.

These oppressive practices were possible because of the way the community ethos of servanthood was experienced in differing ways by the various members of the community. The ethic of servanthood could easily be internalized to imply passivity and submissiveness by those who were used to being dominated and feeling powerless in their role in the larger society. Thus they were encouraged to accept their status and low position in the community in silence and to express this in servanthood and compliance in community relationships. These women and men felt that they were obeying God's divine authority embodied in the church. Since political structures were considered unimportant in the larger scheme of God's direction of history, the pain and anger created by unjust political relationships within the community was also trivialized. Interpretations of particular biblical passages by the powerful in the community affirmed this internalization.

This same ethical directive of servanthood could be internalized by the powerful in the community to deny the reality and importance that status and authority based on economics, education, race, class or gender gave to them. Social differences could be denied and power could be disguised in terms like "servant leadership." Focusing only on the ideals and visions in the Bible allowed the dominant to ignore the many references within the biblical narratives to social differences and the way these played into the choices demanded by discipleship.

The differing ways in which the community discourse is experienced by members of the community again raises the issue of authority in biblical interpretation. How can there be true discernment of the authority of God if mediation of that authority is via a human text and a human community?

Authority in the Interpretive Process

This analysis of the distinctive discipleship discourse in the Mennonite community suggests that at times a closed "hermeneutical circle" has been created. *Experience* and the biblical *text* interact in such a way in the interpretive process that transformation of the community is cut off and the status quo is maintained.[124] Particular interpretations came to be authorized by the community and as practices became routinized their existence came to be justified by further biblical interpretation. Thus the community was not only influenced by its reading of the texts but the community practices also in turn began to influence the interpretations of the texts. The critical edge of this interpretive process emerged only when more active participation by individuals and minority groups forced the dynamic process to continue.

The biblical interpretation by Yoder in *The Politics of Jesus,* and the "performance" of these texts in community practice illustrate this hermeneutical circle. Yoder's interpretations are consistent in the way his theology of discipleship, defined as revolutionary subordination, correlates with the pattern of authority described by the five practices. Yoder's primary concern is to challenge the power of the church institution, derived from a church-state alliance that came with the dominance of Christianity in the Western world. In that sense, his views are revolutionary, rooted in the authority of the Lordship of Jesus and concretely expressed in the community of disciples over against the authority of other institutions. *Subordination* in this context does not mean unquestioning obedience but the willingness to suffer at those points where the stance of the community collides with other powers and authorities. The way of the cross is then understood to be a stance of strength arising out of the empowerment that comes from trust in God. This stance is *revolutionary* in the way it refuses to control or use violent means to bring about change. It thus suggests an alternative to other models of being church in the world. It challenges the Mennonite church to continue to question the use of the institutional power of the church to exercise control in the larger society. Rather than trying to become a dominant force in society, the church is witness to God's love by its stance of servanthood and reconciling love. This interpretation spells out some of the implications of an Anabaptist heritage during the middle of the twentieth century when Yoder conceived his book.

At the same time Yoder's interpretation does not critically examine the way obedience and subordination can be used by the powerful within church institutions to encourage submission and acceptance to their rule. The critique comes from women who have only recently broken their silence and begun to

speak about their experience. These women suggest that a focus on the way of
the cross and suffering has often been used to enforce obedience by those who
were most dominant and powerful in the community. The notion of the cross
and self-sacrifice has indirectly supported male control, as women followed the
teachings of the church. This kind of obedience arises out of lack of strength
and power and a loss of any sense of personal autonomy. Community practices
have often corresponded to unarticulated cultural patterns, which have been
fused with the community's understanding of discipleship. There is nothing
revolutionary about these practices because they *conform* to larger cultural
patterns of dominance and control.

Yoder's reading of the New Testament reflected his own primary
interest in church/state relationships as a theologian and ethicist. He did not
seem to be aware of how his position as professor at a university and his
predominantly male conversation partners influenced his interpretation of the
household codes. When he began to dialogue more directly with women, there
were small changes that testify to the importance of diverse conversation
partners.[125]

Yoder's biblical interpretations can easily be used to justify an existing
order because the ethical stance that he assumes tends to give the power to
change structures of the community to those who are given the leading position
in the community—the husband, the master and the father.[126] This conforms to
power as defined by the larger society, rather than power as defined by Jesus.
In Yoder's view, women, slaves and children are to change their attitudes so
that they can more willingly serve and in that way they may change the
dominant partner who may then make changes in the system. His interpretation
does not show evidence of understanding the different ways in which the
dominant and the marginal tend to hear these words.

What makes these interpretations particularly powerful is that they are
represented as being legitimated by God. Together with the Mennonite community, Yoder asserts that the authority with which the community acts is based
on a confidence that God is acting through the community's interpretation of
the Bible. Human agency is seen as unimportant and therefore is not explicitly
examined. This allows leaders in the community to use Yoder's interpretation
in oppressive ways and encourages those who are marginal to accept their
subordinate place in the hermeneutical process of the community.

A Mennonite Ethos Of Authority

The critical redescription of biblical authority in the Mennonite church has
focused on both tradition (as articulated in theological convictions) and
community discourse patterns (as embodied in biblical interpretation and
community practice). It has affirmed discipleship as a primary theological

construction that has brought Bible and experience, text and community and God and humanity into a relationship with each other within history.

The ethos of authority that has emerged in this analysis depends on understanding the church as both a community of disciples and a hermeneutic community that interprets the Bible in order to hear and obey God's voice. Convictions about God's relationship to humankind, as well as human patterns of response to God, form the basis for authoritative interpretation within the church community.

Within this ethos of authority, the Bible is understood as canon, as that literature "in which we are prepared to find criteria for truth."[127] One crucial implication for a community in accepting the canonical authority of the Bible is that this book will be read and interpreted again and again in the community. This brings about a simple statement of authority for a community of disciples. In order to be a disciple, one must read, interpret and live according to the truth as discovered through this process. This implies that the church as a community of disciples, and the Bible as a communicator of God's revelation and salvation, become the locus of authority. They are the true home of the Christian, held "passionately and uncompromisingly against all our homelessness."[128] This brings church and Bible into a dialectical relationship in which the power of the text will be life-giving and energizing for the community.

However, the analysis has also shown that two alternative directions can result based on these convictions. Some communities seek certainty by equating the Mennonite institutional church with the faithful community of disciples. The institution is then seen as a contemporary embodiment of divine authority. This would lead to interpretations that would justify and legitimate present structures and practices of the church. The hermeneutical process would become static, serving the interests of the leadership of the community. Biblical interpretation could then be used to dominate and control those on the margins of the community. In this model, convictions about truth would be treated as conclusions rather than invitations to deeper readings of the text. The assumed continuity between text and community would justify this approach. Obedience would be interpreted as obedience to revelation, embodied in the community's interpretation of the text.

A second direction is also possible. This direction would move the community to ongoing interpretation of truth in dialogue with the Bible. Other voices from the many communities of disciples outside of the Mennonite church would be invited into a conversation about revelation, salvation and discipleship. Particular attention would be paid to the minority voices on the margins of the communities. This second direction would allow room for the disruptive power of God as mediated through a broadening of the community's experience and through new readings of the text. The dialectical relationship between community and text would remain open as the conversation shifts and changes in response to new conversation partners. Biblical interpretations would focus on the discontinuity between text and community, creating tension that would require repentance and change. Obedience would be seen as obedience to the movement of God's Spirit, and would result in salvation and transformation of the community.

Where does this leave me in terms of my own approach to biblical authority? Do I recognize these two directions within myself? Which direction do I take? This redescription of my context within the Mennonite church has given me new eyes with which to see the alternative routes possible within my tradition. I can now see that a hermeneutics of obedience, which draws rigid lines around human embodiments of revelation and salvation, fails to include the dynamic, freeing movement of the Spirit of God. I know that this interpretation cannot adequately deal with human relationships and the temptations to use power to dominate others. I will therefore move beyond a search for certain truth to an analysis of power and domination. Feminist theology, with its promise of non-oppressive interpretation, will be invited to become a crucial partner in this conversation.

However, the Mennonite claim that the church is a hermeneutic community because it returns again and again to the biblical texts for its identity and its criteria for truth, is important to me. To be a disciple as understood in the Mennonite church, implies an acceptance of the canonical status of the biblical books. No theological discussion of authority and power has integrity for me without including the biblical text as a serious conversation partner. Therefore, I will include the study of a particular text in the ongoing discussion of authority. I will continue hoping that I may discover God's voice through human mediation of the text. This hope acknowledges the risk of hearing a disruptive voice, a voice that would remind me that accepting God's authority implies an openness to being transformed and changed.

Endnotes

1   Harold S. Bender, "The Anabaptist Vision," in Guy F. Herschberger, ed.,*The Recovery of the Anabaptist Vision* (Scottdale, PA: Herald Press, 1967), pp. 29-54. This essay has been widely quoted and its popularity can be seen by the number of times it has been reprinted in various anthologies. It was originally given as the presidential address to the American Society of Church History, December 1943, and appeared in print in *Church History* 13 (March 1944): 3-24 and with slight revisions in *Mennonite Quarterly Review* 18 (April 1944): 67-88. In 1994 a number of scholarly conferences commemorated this event and its importance for the Mennonite church. See *The Conrad Grebel Review* 12, 3 and 4 (Fall 1994,Winter 1995) for articles and reflections on this event.
2   John Howard Yoder, "The Recovery of the Anabaptist Vision," *Concern* 18 (July 1971): 6.
3   Guy F. Hershberger, *The Recovery of the Anabaptist Vision*, pp. 1-10.
4   Bender, "The Anabaptist Vision," p. 42.

5   Paul Peachey, "The Modern Recovery of the Anabaptist Vision," in *The Recovery of the Anabaptist Vision*, p. 336.

6   A good example of this call to renewal is the article by John H. Yoder, "Anabaptist Vision and Mennonite Reality," in A.J. Klassen, ed., *Consultation on Anabaptist-Mennonite Theology* (Fresno: Council of Mennonite Seminaries, 1970), pp. 1-46.

7   Norman Kraus, "American Mennonites and the Bible," in Willard Swartley, ed., *Essays on Biblical Interpretation* (Elkhart, IN: Institute of Mennonite Studies, 1984), p. 131.

8   Ibid., p. 139.

9   "The Common Confession 1896" (Printed in the 1959/1968/1984 Constitutions of the General Conference of Mennonites in North America); Howard John Loewen, *One Lord, One Church, One Hope and One God: Mennonite Confessions of Faith* (Elkhart, IN: Institute of Mennonite Studies, 1985), p. 106.

10 Walter Klaassen, *Anabaptism: Neither Catholic nor Protestant* (Waterloo, ON: Conrad Press, 1975).

11 Virginia A. Hostetler and Lawrence Martin, *The Foundation Series Handbook: A Guide to the Children, Youth and Adult Curricula* (Nappanee, IN: Evangel Press; Scottdale, PA: Mennonite Publishing House; Newton, KS: Faith and Life Press; Elgin, IL: Brethren Press, 1986), pp. 5-6.

12 Ross Thomas Bender, *The People of God: A Mennonite Interpretation of a Free Church Perspective* (Scottdale, PA: Herald Press, 1971), p. 182.

13 (Scottdale, PA and Kitchener, ON: Herald Press, 1987).

14 Werner Packull, "From Monogenesis to Polygenesis: The Historical Discussion of Anabaptist Origins," *Mennonite Quarterly Review* 49 (1975): 83-121.

15 "The Anabaptist Vision: Historical Perspectives," *The Conrad Grebel Review* 12, 3 (Fall 1994): 231.

16 David H. Kelsey uses this expression to speak about the diverse construals that theologians have of the biblical text, *The Uses of Scripture in Recent Theology* (Philadelphia: Fortress Press, 1975), pp. 205-207.

17 "Anabaptist Vision and Mennonite Reality," p. 5.

18 See, for example, the front and back page of *Anabaptism Today* 11 (February 1996) which explains some of the goals of this network. Theologians and ethicists such as Stanley Hauerwas and James Wm. McClendon have also been influenced by Anabaptism, particularly in their understanding of the church in its social/political function in society. See Charles Scriven, "The Reformation Radicals Ride Again," *Christianity Today* 34, 4: 13-15.

19 J. Howard Kauffman and Leo Driedger, *The Mennonite Mosaic: Identity and Modernization* (Scottdale, PA and Waterloo, ON: Herald Press, 1991), p. 253.

20 Ibid., pp. 254-255.

21 Until recently Mennonites have been known for their objection to "abstract" theology. They have therefore not had a systematic theology—at least not one similar to the kind that Catholics, Lutherans or Calvinists have developed. A consultation in 1983 representing the three largest Mennonite groups in North America was not able to come to a consensus of the kind of systematic theology that could be done from a Mennonite perspective. The papers given at this consultation are printed in Willard Swartley, ed., *Explorations of Systematic Theology* (Elkhart, IN: Institute of Mennonite Studies, 1984). However, Mennonites have done theology more informally, usually in the mode of biblical interpretation or ethical reflection on particular practices. A. James Reimer raised the issue of the nature of theology in *The Conrad Grebel Review* and the debate was carried on in the following issues of the periodical. See "The Nature and Possibility of a Mennonite Theology," *The Conrad Grebel Review* 1, 1 (1983): 33-55.

22   Howard John Loewen, *One Lord, One Church, One Hope, and One God: Mennonite Confessions of Faith*, pp. 38-39. See also the strong statement on the triune God in the recent *Confession of Faith in a Mennonite Perspective* (Scottdale, PA and Waterloo, ON: Herald Press, 1995) accepted by two major Mennonite denominations.

23   Willard Swartley, *Slavery, Sabbath, War and Women* (Scottdale, PA and Kitchener, ON: Herald Press, 1983), pp. 218-219.

24   Note this verse on every piece of material in the *Foundation Series Curriculum*.

25   David Schroeder, "Discerning What Is Bound in Heaven," in A.J. Dueck, ed., *The Bible and the Church* (Winnipeg, MB: Kindred Press, 1988), p. 70.

26   Harry Huebner, "Christology: Discipleship and Ethics," in Erland Waltner, ed., *Jesus Christ and the Mission of the Church: Contemporary Anabaptist Perspectives* (Study Conference on Christology, Illinois State University, Normal, Illinois), August 4-6, 1989 (Newton, KS: Faith and Life Press, 1990), p. 56.

27   *The Priestly Kingdom: Social Ethics as Gospel* (Notre Dame, IN: University of Notre Dame Press, 1984, p. 36.

28   *Slavery, Sabbath, War and Women*, p. 218.

29   John H. Yoder, "The Authority of the Canon," in *Essays on Biblical Interpretation*, p. 279.

30   Ibid., p. 282.

31   Millard Lind, "Reflections on Biblical Hermeneutics," in *Essays on Biblical Interpretation*, p. 152.

32   Swartley, *Slavery, Sabbath, War and Women*, p. 218.

33   Yoder, *The Priestly Kingdom*, p. 9.

34   Waldemar Janzen, "A Canonical Re-thinking of the Anabaptist-Mennonite New Testament Orientation," in Harry Huebner, ed., *The Church as Theological Community* (Winnipeg: CMBC Publications, 1990), pp. 90-95.

35   Walter Klaassen, "Anabaptist Hermeneutics," in *Essays on Biblical Interpretation*, p. 7.

36   Harry Huebner, "Christology: Discipleship and Ethics," in *Jesus Christ and the Mission of the Church*, p. 65.

37   J. Denny Weaver, *Becoming Anabaptist* (Scottdale, PA and Kitchener, ON: Herald Press, 1987), p. 120.

38   "The Hermeneutics of Obedience," in *Essays on Biblical Interpretation*, p. 58.

39   *The Foundation Series Handbook*, p. 6.

40   "Christology: Discipleship and Ethics," p. 60.

41   Ben Ollenburger, "The Hermeneutics of Obedience," p. 58.

42   "Hermeneutics and Discipleship," in *Essays on Biblical Interpretation*, p. 44.

43   C. Norman Kraus, *Jesus Christ our Lord* (Scottdale, PA and Kitchener, ON: Herald Press, 1987), p. 106.

44   John H. Miller is a Mennonite who has asserted the importance of the "Father" name for God. See *Biblical Faith and Fathering* (New York and Mahwah, NJ: Paulist Press,1989).

45   John H. Yoder, "A People in the World: Theological Interpretation," in James Leo Garret, Jr., ed., *The Concept of a Believers' Church* (Scottdale, PA: Herald Press, 1969), p. 258.

46   J. Denny Weaver, "Perspectives on a Mennonite Theology," in *Explorations of Systematic Theology*, p. 17.

47   Yoder, *The Priestly Kingdom*, pp. 135-147.

48   Ross Bender, *The People of God* (Scottdale, PA: Herald Press, 1971), p. 93.

49   Swartley, *Slavery, Sabbath, War and Women*, p. 237.

50   "The Hermeneutics of Peoplehood," in *Essays in Biblical Interpretation*, p. 49.

51   "Biblical Interpretation in the Life of the Church," adopted by Mennonite General Assembly, June 18-24, 1977 (Estes Park, CO), reprinted in Swartley, *Slavery, Sabbath, War and Women*, pp. 235-249.

52   C. Norman Kraus, *Jesus Christ our Lord*, p. 158.

53   *Confession of Faith in a Mennonite Perspective*, p. 17.

54   "Biblical Interpretation in the Life of the Church," p. 237.

55   Yoder, "The Hermeneutics of the Anabaptists," p. 18.

56   Dyck, "Hermeneutics and Discipleship," p. 37.

57   "Biblical Interpretation in the Life of the Church," p. 237.

58   Yoder, "The Hermeneutics of the Anabaptists," p. 21.

59   "Discerning What Is Bound in Heaven," pp. 68-72.

60   Ibid., p. 72.

61   Marlin Jeschke, *Discipling in the Church: Recovering a Ministry of the Gospel* (Scottdale, PA and Kitchener, ON : Herald Press, 1972, 1979, 1988).

62   Ibid., p. 7.

63   *Confession of Faith in a Mennonite Perspective*, p. 19.

64   David Schroeder, "Binding and Loosing," *Seeds* 3, 4 (June 1984): 29.

65   A. James Reimer is one Mennonite theologian who has challenged this focus on the concrete, prophetic and ethical side of the Christian faith. He suggests that the lack of emphasis on man [women and men] as ontological being in Mennonite theology has expressed itself in a lack of emphasis on the mystical, sacramental side of life. See "The Nature and Possibility of a Mennonite Theology," pp. 33-55.

66   C. Arnold Snyder has summarized the struggle of the Anabaptists with the relationship between the flesh and the spirit during the time of the Reformation. He talks about the church as sacrament and the dangers in this notion as interpreted by certain Anabaptists, including Menno Simons. See *Anabaptist History and Theology: An Introduction* (Kitchener, ON: Pandora Press, 1995), pp. 350-363.

67   "A Canonical Rethinking of the Anabaptist-Mennonite New Testament Orientation," in Harry Huebner, ed., *The Church as Theological Community* (Winnipeg: CMBC Publications, 1990), pp. 90-100.

68   Ibid. p. 53.

69   Leander E. Keck, "Ethos and Ethics in the New Testament," in James Gaffney, ed., *Essays in Morality and Ethics* (New York: Paulist Press, 1980), pp. 30-31.

70   Nicholas Lash, *Theology on the Way to Emmaus* (London: SCM Press, 1986), p. 42.

71   *The Politics of Jesus* (Grand Rapids, MI: Eerdmanns, 1972). Though a second edition was published in 1994, it is this edition that has been influential in the Mennonite church. Generally the second edition, while updating some scholarship by including a brief epilogue at the end of each chapter, reasserts the main thesis of the first edition.

72   Ibid., pp. 13-15.

73   Ibid., p. 23.

74   Ibid., p. 62.

75   Ibid., p. 39.

76   Ibid., pp. 46-47.

77   Ibid., p. 134.

78   Ibid., p. 153.

79   Ibid., p. 179.

80   Ibid., pp. 181-182.

81   Ibid., p. 191.

82   Ibid., p. 190.

83   Ibid., p. 192.

84   Ibid., p. 199.

85   Ibid., p. 213.

86   Ibid., p. 231.

87   Ibid., p. 244.

88   Ibid., p. 187.

89   Mary Schertz suggests that different experiences of personal autonomy separate the experience of men and women from each other. If this is true we cannot assume a common experience in community arising out of a common vision of discipleship. See "Creating Justice in the Space Around Us," in Elizabeth G. Yoder, ed., *Peace Theology and Violence Against Women*, Occasional Papers 16 (Elkhart, IN: Institute of Mennonite Studies, 1992), p. 14.

90   John H. Yoder, "Sacrament as Social Process: Christ the Transformer of Culture," *Theology Today* 48, 1 (April 1991): 33-45.

91   Ibid., p. 44.

92   Ibid., p. 35.

93   John H. Yoder, "Binding and Loosing," in Michael G. Cartwright, ed., *The Royal Priesthood* (Grand Rapids, MI: Eerdmans, 1994), p. 344.

94   The story of the transformation of Mennonite peacemaking from quietism to an active witness includes the power of fraternal admonition. See Leo Driedger and Donald B. Kraybill, *Mennonite Peacemaking* (Scottdale, PA: Herald Press, 1994), pp. 134-145.

95   Yoder, "The Hermeneutics of Peoplehood," p. 48.

96   Loewen, *One Lord, One Church, One Hope, and One God,* p. 79.

97   Several examples can be given of this occurring in Mennonite history. Note the discussion by C. J. Dyck of the origin of the Reformed Mennonite Church and the schisms in the Old Order Mennonite Churches in *An Introduction to Mennonite History* (Scottdale, PA and Kitchener, ON: Herald Press, 1967), pp. 296, 300.

98   Melanie A. May, "The Pleasure of Our Lives as Text: A New Rule of Christ for Anabaptist Women," *Conrad Grebel Review* 10, 1 (1992): 36.

99   Ibid., pp. 33, 35.

100 Mary Schertz, "Creating Justice in the Space Around Us," p. 7.

101 "The Anabaptist Vision: Was It Visionary Enough for Women?" *The Conrad Grebel Review* 12, 3 (Fall 1994): 312.

102 Carol Penner points out that in the *Annotated Bibliography of Mennonite Writings on War and Peace: 1930-80* (Scottdale, PA: Herald Press, 1987), there is no reference to incest, child abuse, or wife battering, even though the editors do include other justice issues like "race" relations. Thus violence against women has not been seen as a peace issue. See "An Exploration of Mennonite Theology from the Context of Violence Against Women," in *Peace Theology and Violence Against Women*, p. 110, n. 27.

103 "Sacrament as Social Process," p. 39.

104 John H. Yoder, *The Fullness of Christ* (Elgin, IL: Brethren Press, 1987).

105 "Sacrament as Social Process," p. 36.

106 Lois Y. Barrett, "Women's History/Women's Theology: Theological and Method-ological Issues in the Writing of the History of Anabaptist-Mennonite Women," *The Conrad Grebel Review* 10, 1 (Winter 1992): 4.

107 Rodney J. Sawatsky, *Authority and Identity: The Dynamics of the General Conference Mennonite Church* (North Newton, KS: Bethel College, 1987), pp. 8-9.

108 (Scottdale, PA: Mennonite Publishing House, 1951), p. 358. See also the pamphlet written by Wenger, which justifies the need for women to wear a prayer veiling in order to symbolize this relationship between men and women. *The Prayer Veiling in Scripture and History: The New Testament Symbol of Woman As Glory of the Race* (Scottdale, PA: Herald Press, 1964).

109 *Separated Unto God: For Christian Simplicity of Life and for a Scriptural Nonconformity to the World* (Scottdale, PA: Mennonite Publishing House), p. 208.

110 Elmer A. Martens, "Adam Named Her Eve," in John E. Toews, Valerie Rempel and Katie Funk Wiebe, eds., *Your Daughters Shall Prophecy* (Winnipeg, MB: Kindred Press, 1992), p. 44.

111 A recent sociological study gives the following statistics. In 1972, 17 percent of respondents to a questionnaire favoured ordination of women. In 1989, this had increased to 44 percent. See J. Howard Kauffman and Leo Driedger, *The Mennonite Mosaic: Identity and Modernization* (Scottdale, PA and Waterloo, ON: Herald Press, 1991), p. 206.

112 Yoder, "The Hermeneutics of Peoplehood," p. 52.

113 Ibid., p. 47.

114 "The Silence of Women Is a Goal of Pornography," *Mennonite Reporter* 15, 13 (June 24, 1985): 11.

115 Magdalene Redekop, "Through the Mennonite Looking Glass," in Harry Loewen, ed., *Why I Am Mennonite* (Scottdale, PA and Kitchener, ON: Herald Press, 1988), p. 251.

116 Yoder, "Sacrament as Social Process," p. 36.

117 Ibid., p. 37.

118 Klaassen, *Anabaptism: Neither Catholic nor Protestant*, p. 18.

119 Magdalene Redekop, "Through the Mennonite Looking Glass," p. 240.

120 Yoder, "Sacrament as Social Practice," p. 38.

121 The age of baptism varies in Mennonite churches. Some churches encourage children in early adolescence to join the church while others discourage baptism until some time in the late teens. The "age of accountability" is not closely defined, but suggests a time when persons are ready to own their faith.

122 Donald B. Kraybill, "Modernity and Identity: The Transformation of Mennonite Ethnicity," in *Mennonite Identity*, pp. 153-172.

123 "Creating Justice in the Space Around Us," p. 14.

124 I am using the term hermeneutical circle in the sense of a circle that repeats itself again and again rather than in the sense of a spiral where ongoing transformation is expected.

125 See the second edition (1994) of the *Politics of Jesus*, pp. 189-191, where he questions one of his footnotes that has been particularly hurtful to women.

126 Yoder, *The Politics of Jesus*, p. 182.

127 Walter Brueggeman, *Interpretation and Obedience* (Minneapolis: Fortress Press, 1996), p. 120. His discussion of the relationship between canon and interpretive community is particularly helpful in explaining this notion of biblical authority.

128 Ibid. p. 120.

Chapter 3

Discipleship and Authority: Feminist Hermeneutic Community

Though the term discipleship is not used by all Christian feminist theologians, several women do refer specifically to this term as a way of claiming "biblical religion as an integral part of their own historical identity."[1] Elisabeth Schüssler Fiorenza, who identifies with the discipleship of equals both in the past and in the future, and Sandra Schneiders, who understands the world of the text as a world of discipleship in which readers are invited to dwell, in different ways affirm the importance of the notion of discipleship in articulating their relationship to the Bible. Others, like Letty Russell, Sharon H. Ringe and Rosemary Ruether, do not focus on the term itself. However, their writings reveal how important the vision and commitment connected with the discipleship movement created by the presence of Jesus is to their approach to the Bible.

These Christian feminists are part of a larger feminist hermeneutic community that consciously advocates for a hermeneutics of suspicion as crucial to the interpretive process. According to the *Dictionary of Feminist Theologies,*[2] the term feminist is suspect as a general designation because its use has been associated with the dominant perspective of white, middle-class, Western women. These Western women, whether Catholic, Protestant or Jewish, are the most influential in defining the term and continue to identify themselves by this name. In this chapter, feminist will be used for those women who claim the name for themselves, primarily Western white women. Specifically, the dialogue will be with Christian feminists, both Catholic and Protestant, since it is these women who initially formed the feminist theological discourse. Those who name their theology *mujerista* or womanist will be respected as distinct discourse partners who create new and different conversations.

It is feminist theologians who have moved the discussion most strongly towards an ideological critique of patriarchy. They have insisted that the oppression and domination of women within the interpretive process be acknowledged. In their challenge of traditional interpretations they have expressed their conviction that the biblical text must be liberated from its "patriarchal captivity," so that it can again exercise a liberating function in the Christian community.[3]

The writings of these women demonstrate the changing relationship to the Bible that has come about for white Christian women in North America with the rise of feminist critical consciousness in Western society. Barbara Brown Zikmund and Carolyn De Swarte Gifford describe and analyze this

63

history.[4] Three stages can be identified, each of which raises crucial questions about biblical authority.

Nineteenth century feminism. In the early nineteenth century, interpretation of the Bible in North America was largely in the hands of men, and its authority was usually not questioned by the churches. In the early part of the century, women's stories were assumed to be part of the larger male story. Whether a scholar was male or female was assumed to be irrelevant to the work of theology. However, as women became more aware of the importance of their unique experience as women they began to ask questions about their role in society and church. The resulting agitation for change made "women" a hermeneutical issue for churches that had assumed that the roles of women were divinely sanctioned by Scripture. Thus it was only natural that the Bible began to be searched for a definition of womanhood. For those attempting to uphold the status quo, this meant going to the Bible in order to define the differences between men and women using men as the norm for human nature. Even when the Bible was used positively, to glorify women's place, the secondary status of women was assumed.

By the 1830s and 1840s some women began to see the need for a different understanding of the Bible and its authority. At the same time, reformers like the Grimkè sisters began to question the way images of maleness and femaleness were linked to particular spheres of activity. The issue moved very quickly to the differences between the "male/public realm" and the "female/private realm."[5] By supporting this difference with biblical references, the clergy were able to challenge women who attempted to enter into public discussions on moral issues such as slavery. Women began to call for a distinction between those parts of the Bible that were essential and those that were culturally relative. They were seeking alternative interpretations to oppressive interpretations based on the patriarchal culture of the times in which the Bible was formed.

A crucial change was taking place in the approach to the Bible. This change had to do not only with how the Bible was interpreted but also with who interpreted it. Women began to see the need to do their own study of the Bible. For example, women under the leadership of Elizabeth Cady Stanton examined every major passage in the Bible in order to interpret it in ways that would counteract the oppressive power of the text. The resulting *Woman's Bible* presupposed not only that the Bible could be treated like any other book but also that it was limited by its historical context. Other women, such as Katherine Bushnell and Lee Anna Starr, produced extensive analyzes of the treatment of women in the Bible and gave alternative interpretations of woman's nature and sphere in the biblical texts. Though these women used their knowledge of biblical languages and scholarship, they were not part of the scholarly establishment that continued to dominate biblical studies. The few existing female biblical scholars did not produce self-conscious feminist scholarship during this period.

The over-all approach developed by women during this time was one that tried to compensate for the inequality and marginality that women found in society, church and theology. This approach, called "soft feminism" by Zikmund, glorified women's place. It gave women a special calling, it pointed out women's special strengths and it assigned women a special place of influence in church and society on the basis of the Bible. Biblical study focused on the unique role of women in the Bible or on those qualities that were considered feminine.

During this time, the Bible was used in a very similar way both by those who wished to protect the status quo and those who wished to raise women's status. Both used the Bible to define the differences between men and women in order to justify their position. However, an important shift had begun to take place that positioned women and their concerns in a more direct relationship with the Bible. The issue of how the boundaries of the hermeneutic community were established had begun to surface.

Women's studies. During the early twentieth century, women began to promote studies on women for egalitarian reasons. They argued that, ultimately, women and men shared a common history and that it was necessary to go behind the differences between women and men to find their common humanity. Human history was distorted if women's contributions remained unnoticed and unappreciated and therefore there was a need for women's studies programs to supplement the history of men that was better known. New courses and programs were introduced to add new information to the traditional fields by concentrating on "herstory." The new historical research was considered remedial work and therefore the information gathered was freely shared with other scholars working in the same fields and often was appreciated by them.[6]

Sometimes, scholars treated women as one among many minority groups and placed women's studies on the edge of the academic world or considered it a passing fad. The fact that women's studies tended to be consciously critical only in their concern about what was left out of traditional historical studies, however, made it part of mainstream studies. This allowed it to use methods similar to those used by the rest of the academic world.

Biblical authority received some new challenges with the advent of women's studies programs. New images of women were highlighted that did not conform to patriarchal roles. At the same time, orthodox assumptions about the inclusivity of tradition were being stretched and the issue of inclusive language began to be raised. However, not until the 1960s did professional female biblical scholars begin to raise the issue of male domination in the shaping of the Jewish and Christian tradition. Scholars, like Margaret Brackenbury Crook and Valerie Saiving, stimulated key theological issues with their questions about the androcentric nature of recorded history. The claim to equality in the historical record inevitably raised the crucial issue of the authority of a book that focused on male history, even though the book was considered normative by the church.

Feminist critical consciousness. Zikmund points out two important things that happened in the movement from women's studies to feminist studies in the 1970s and 1980s. First of all, the new materials and methods cultivated in women's studies became the basis for a critique of past assumptions and paradigms. Second, together with other liberation movements, a new interpretive framework began to be constructed.

This means that feminist studies is not concerned only with those aspects of life in which women play a primary part. A feminist consciousness asks inclusive questions about every text and every event in history. It is concerned to point out the injustices of history and to attack majority positions that are oppressive. If women are to be included in the total picture, everything must be rethought and reinterpreted.

This has implications for biblical authority. For not only are the understandings of the world under review, the convictions about God and God's relationship to humanity are also being critically assessed. Letty Russell calls this critical move the "feminist touch," that, like the legendary king whose touch turned everything into gold, turns every feminist theme into a discussion about authority.[7] Some feminists, such as Mary Daly and Daphne Hampson, have rejected biblical authority and patriarchal theological traditions and have sought to recover the religious insights of goddess religions or focused on feminist spirituality based on women's experiences of the sacred.[8] The women who, continue to see the Bible as crucial for their understanding of the Christian faith, struggle with articulating their convictions about the divine/human relationship and explaining how these affect biblical authority. They seek an interpretation that will "affirm women so that they are acknowledged as fully human partners with men, sharing in the image of God."[9] However, they question the traditional metaphors that have been used to speak about God.

For many feminists, the development of a new framework of interpretation is based on a new consciousness of their personal/communal identity as female Christians. Over against an identity formed by patriarchal and androcentric biblical texts, some of these feminists have named themselves disciples in order to speak of their full inclusion in the Christian tradition. New definitions have explained patriarchy, not only in a very loose sense as men dominating women but as a "male pyramid of graded subordinations and exploitations" that specifies women's oppression in terms of the class, "race," or religion of the men to whom women "belong."[10] A study of the way Christian identity continues to encourage feminist theologians to seriously engage the biblical text, while advocating a critical feminist methodology, can provide new insights into one particular framework for biblical authority.

This chapter will again explore two aspects of the hermeneutic community in order to allow a dialogue between Mennonite and feminist understandings of power and authority. The analysis will begin by demonstrating why feminist theologians insist on a hermeneutics of suspicion as the basic approach to biblical authority. A variety of Christian feminist writings will demonstrate how this approach is used when talking about the divine/human relationship. Second, particular discourse patterns will be illuminated by examining several writings of Elisabeth Schüssler Fiorenza as paradigmatic instances of the language of discipleship. She is not only a popular spokesperson for feminist theology but has also explicitly connected her notion of the discipleship of equals with her understanding of the political process of interpretation.

The focus will be on illuminating the relationship of the theological language to the social/political practice of biblical interpretation in the feminist hermeneutic community. The truth claims as well as the normative practice assumed by feminist theology in its use of the term discipleship, can then be named.

Theological Convictions

Feminists who refuse to give up on the liberating power of the Bible continue to root their approach to the Bible in their understanding of God and God's relationship to the world. Although feminist theologians exhibit great differences in their interpretations of particular texts and in their methodological assumptions, they also share a number of key convictions about their own activity and about the presence of God in the world. These assumptions will be illustrated from the writings of a number of women who identify themselves as feminist while continuing to name themselves as Christian. The examples given will show both the variety of expression and the unifying thread that allows these women to see themselves as part of the same theological enterprise.

In feminist writings, doctrinal convictions about the divine/human relationship are often intertwined with convictions about the shape of the hermeneutic community as a political movement and the power of the biblical text as both liberating and oppressive. The trinitarian framework, a traditional way to speak about God, has been particularly problematic for Christian feminists.[11] However, freedom to reimagine has been given by noting the metaphorical nature of all religious language about God and accepting human agency as part of the theological enterprise.[12] A number of systematic theologians have begun the work of reconstructing this language "from below," while at the same time using a triune framework for speaking about the God of the Bible.[13]

The particular shift made by many feminist theologians, a shift that expresses itself in a hermeneutics of suspicion, will become evident in this brief analysis.

God—The Creator/Liberator

> For the creation waits with eager longing for the revealing of the children of God. . . . We know that the whole creation has been groaning in labour pains until now; and not only the creation, but we ourselves, who have the first fruits of the Spirit, groan inwardly while we wait for adoption, the redemption of our bodies. For in hope we were saved.[14]

A central conviction shared by many feminists is that women are united in their "unfreedom" and that it is the contradictions of their present experiences that force them to struggle for a new vision of the future in which women will be fully human and fully equal. This lack of freedom is shared by many women, including Christian women. Letty Russell expresses the need for faith in God in this struggle. "The patriarchal structures of scripture, tradition, church, and theology are such that the process of reconstruction of women's place in man's world requires a utopian faith that understands God's future as an impulse for change in the present."[15]

These feminists are convinced that God intends women to freely and responsibly participate with God in a new creation. Though oriented to the future, this conviction is rooted in the solidarity of God with women who are created in God's image.

Feminists often begin their theology by pointing out the difficulty of identifying the creative activity of God. They insist that it is largely obscured by a patriarchal and androcentric world view. For example, the Genesis account of creation has been used to depict women as responsible for original sin thus effectively removing them as mediators and participants in God's creative activity in the world. Moreover, the naming of the Creator as Father emphasizes a worldview that has been used to justify a connection between human maleness and divine authority.[16] This idolatry is not easily countered with men as the official interpreters of the Christian tradition.

The struggle to understand God's creative activity must therefore begin with the struggle to affirm the creation of women in the image of God. This requires a total reorientation because the theological dualism of *imago dei*/fallen Adam often connects with sexual duality, as well as with other polarities of our western worldview. As Rosemary Ruether points out, there is a tendency to correlate "femaleness with the lower part of human nature in a hierarchical scheme of mind over body, reason over passions."[17] This dualism, that correlates maleness with reason and mind, and thus with spirit, is strongly rejected by feminists. Instead, the emphasis is on the original purpose of God in creating woman in the image of God. Elizabeth Johnson understands how crucial this identity is for theology when she declares, "This theological interpretation of female identity is the centre of gravity for feminist discourse about the mystery of God."[18] Feminists assert that women are not derivative of men, they are not the objectified other, but rather they are "fully human and need to be valued as such."[19]

A crucial aspect of the valuing for women is the valuing of women's own experience. Feminists recognize that women have understood their own experience primarily through male interpretation. The theology of women as created in God's image has been hidden and sometimes even denied in communities that confess God as Creator. Women's identity has also not been noted in the description of the people of God in the androcentric Bible. As pointed out by Sharon H. Ringe,

> in the biblical documents women are absent as subjects of their own religious experience. . . . for women the canonical function of scripture as a mirror of the identity of the community of faith breaks down, for the mirror does not reflect our own faces or the faces of our foremothers. Instead we see characters on the stage of a drama written for them by male authors: women of the biblical communities do not get to play themselves.[20]

Christian feminists therefore, cannot base their hope on God's past action in history, recorded in an objective text and interpreted by the people of God. A theology of God as Creator can only be liberating if it includes God's continued creative activity that can challenge the interpretations of the past. Therefore, women cannot separate God as a Creator from God as a Liberator who stands in solidarity with women as they struggle for a new world.

A guiding principle of biblical interpretation is understanding liberation as "an ongoing process expressed in the already/not yet dynamic of God's action of New Creation."[21] The biblical horizon of promise implies that the process of interpretation is dynamic and self-correcting, as God's ways and intentions are reinterpreted in light of the present historical situations. However, feminists insist that this horizon has become fixed and must be liberated by a hermeneutics of suspicion that will free the Bible from its patriarchal and androcentric bias.

Feminists therefore affirm their own experience and their own freedom to name reality by naming their own identity as women created in God's image. They emphasize their calling to be co-creators with God of the world as it should be. They resist exclusive male images of God, pointing to the idolatry involved in that naming. They are aware of themselves as autonomous beings who can become the subjects, rather than the victims, of history.

At the same time, many feminists stress relationality and mutuality as the basis of human solidarity. As Margaret A. Farley explains, feminists are convinced that persons, women and men, are centres of life, capable (without contradiction) of being centred more and more in themselves as they are centred more and more beyond themselves in one another. They are convinced, too, that in this mystery of autonomy and relationality, equality and mutuality, lie the clues we need for the relation of persons to the whole universe in which we live.[22]

Historically, this coming together of equality and mutuality happens in the community of struggle that seeks to overcome the domination and oppression of half the human race. This community of struggle cannot easily be equated with the institutional church that often supports the status quo and is itself oppressive to women and other marginal people. Feminists therefore are finding different ways of speaking about a community that is struggling to participate in the creative process in partnership with God. For example, Russell uses the phrase "household of God" as an alternative translation of the kingdom of God. In so far as church, in all its manifestations, "becomes a place where household of freedom is experienced, it also becomes a sign of God's household."[23] She wants women to understand themselves as participating in "God's *oikonomia* or householding of the whole earth." She insists not only that all theology is rooted in the experience of particular theologians and communities, but that rooting theology in the experience of those often considered "non-persons" is what God is all about in the world today.[24]

Schüssler Fiorenza speaks about the hermeneutical centre of feminist biblical interpretation as "women-church *(ekklēsia gynaikon)*, the movement of self-identified women and women-identified men in biblical religion."[25] Women-church, based on the prototype of a discipleship of equals found around Jesus, affirms liberation from all patriarchal alienation, marginalization and oppression. Both the symbols of the *basileia* and of new creation as they are used in the Bible focus on a different reality experientially available for women.[26] For her, "the common hermeneutical ground of past, present, and future is not 'sacred history' or 'sacred text' but commitment to the biblical vision of God's new creation." [27]

Schüssler Fiorenza insists that it is not hermeneutical identification with biblical texts and historical practice that is needed. Instead, it is a historical solidarity with the vision of the people of God in biblical history. For her, this means that there must be a testing of the self-understanding of all social/ecclesial groups in terms of the inclusivity of their vision as the people of God. This testing for democratic vision must include the communities of faith represented in the Bible. This calls for a critical methodology based on a hermeneutics of suspicion.

Ruether calls for a new hermeneutical centre, but locates it with the prophetic-messianic tradition, a critically conscious movement that recognizes its constant need for renewal. She emphasizes that "no liberation movement can speak the universal critical word about injustice and hope for all time; it always does so within the limitations of its social location."[28]

What is clear in each of these ways of speaking about the community of struggle is the hope and commitment to a vision of God's creation in which there is cquality and mutuality for all persons. This implies that those who have been invisible in the hermeneutic communities because of sex, "race", creed or class must become visible partners in creating a new future. As Russell suggests, it is then that these communities of struggle become "prisms through which God's action in the mending of creation is to be understood."[29] It is then that they realize that God the Creator continues to be in solidarity with the human community by sharing the creative gift with human persons and thus living in partnership with them. Schneiders agrees when she insists, "To affirm creation is to live in a new world, a world one shares with the Creator."[30]

In feminist theology, God as *Creator/Liberator* invites women to affirm their identity as co-creators of a new community of equality and mutuality. This new *identity* implies a suspicion of all mediations of God's authority (including Bible and church) that contradict this image in the way they name God. Instead, God is affirmed as being in solidarity with the movement of freedom and liberation, a movement of those committed to the discipleship of equals.

Spirit—The Mediator of Power

> with the energy of the Holy Spirit let us tear apart all walls of division and the culture of death which separates us. And let us participate in the Holy Spirit's economy of life, fighting for our life on this earth in solidarity with all living beings and building communities of justice, peace, and the integrity of the creation.[31]

For many feminists, the Spirit is the creative life-giving power that opens them to relating in a new way to each other and to creation. In speaking about the Spirit, the focus is on the immanence of God, pervading the whole of human existence. This power is actively freeing and releasing persons from alternative powers that would control and limit their participation in God's new world. Therefore, it is the Spirit who provides the connection between women's present experience and God the Creator. It is the Spirit who gives women a new sense of personal authority.

This life-giving, energizing characteristic is especially important for many Christian feminists, since the Spirit is also often connected with female images of God. The Hebraic traditions of the female *Sophia* (Wisdom), *Shekinah* (presence) and *Hokmah* (Spirit) have allowed the possibility for some female metaphors for God. Marginal groups, considered heretical by orthodox Christianity, were often more free to use female imagery, adapting characteristics of Greek goddesses to speak of God. This was particularly true for gnosticism. As Ruether has pointed out, traditions with a female side of

God "continue to ferment under the surface of Christian theology," creating the possibility of going beyond the traditional all-male concept of God.[32]

However, many feminists are questioning the "patriarchal split" between masculine and feminine that is often promoted by this connection of the Spirit with women.[33] Those feminists who continue to stress discipleship tend to focus on the relationship between the Spirit and new creation in such a way that God is not identified solely with one gender. For example, Schüssler Fiorenza notes the early missionary movement's identification of the resurrected Jesus with both the Spirit of God and the Sophia of God. She shows how the pre-Pauline hymns express this identification. As Christians enter the "forcefield of the Spirit," they become the new creation, women and men sharing equally in the Spirit of wisdom and power of God.[34]

Within feminism, theological thinking about the Spirit usually begins with the personal indwelling of the Spirit and then moves to the communal expression of the Spirit's power. The struggle to understand this communal dynamic arises out of the feminist struggle with the tradition of the established churches. Schüssler Fiorenza is clear that the movement of the Spirit is not limited to the institutional church. She insists that women throughout history have acted in the "power of the life-giving Sophia-Spirit."[35] It is the struggling church of women that is central to the movement of the Spirit. She insists on a political social church as the locus of the Spirit's work.

Elizabeth Johnson focuses on the symbols skewed by sexism embedded within the text and the tradition. She insists that these must first pass through the fire of critical feminist principles in the context of the liberating vision of a "community of equal and mutual disciples," in whose midst the Spirit chooses to dwell. It is this community that will use women's experience to shape new building blocks for emancipatory discourse about God.[36]

Though feminists differ in describing the relationship of the Spirit to the community, they are clear that the experiences of the Spirit are not limited to men or official representatives of the church. As Schneiders points out, the Spirit was handed over to each disciple as a Pentecostal gift (Acts 2:14-21). It is the personal indwelling of the Spirit that "grounds the union of members of Christ who corporately constitute his presence in the world."[37] Russell considers authority as a partnership in which there is no competition between persons but rather enrichment through the sharing of personal experiences.[38] This view of authority implies that the community of equals is not created for its own end, just as Jesus' ministry is not an end in itself. Instead, "disciples are sent to do what he did: to feed the hungry, heal the sick, liberate the oppressed, and to announce the inbreaking of God's new world and humanity, here and new."[39] Russell speaks about the community as a sign pointing to God's household of freedom. New dialogical possibilities come with a new humanity made possible through the Spirit. Therefore, she stresses "open ecclesiology" that puts the focus more directly on God's action in the world and only indirectly on the church.[40] The church does not have walls that separate it from the world. Instead, the church is characterized by Christ's presence through the Spirit, a presence that invites involvement in God's liberating movement in the world.

Suspicion is necessary in order to detect the presence of those elements that prevent an openness to the Spirit's work. This suspicion is directed most clearly at biblical interpretation, which has frequently justified the present oppressive and exclusive praxis of the institutional church and tradition and has contributed to a static theology. Feminists point out the destructive ideology found in the text and in community interpretation and appeal to the prophetic and renewing dynamic that characterizes the work of the Spirit. They thus identify with the dynamic energy that testifies to the "continued unleashing of the power of the Spirit within his circle of disciples."[41]

In feminist theology, the *Spirit* indwelling and empowering women connects the experience of women directly with a God, who can be imaged as female. This *empowerment* allows women to come to the Bible and to the church institution with suspicion, confident that the Spirit has authorized their effort to detect oppressive ideology. Women are thus liberated to live in relationships of equality and mutuality, in a new community of disciples embodying God's presence in the world.

Jesus Christ—The Embodiment of Liberation

Traditional Christology and its understanding of Jesus Christ as revelatory is particularly problematic for feminists because of the way the maleness of Jesus has been identified with both normative humanity and with the maleness of the divine Logos. Elizabeth Johnson states the problem this way: "As visible image of the invisible God, the human man Jesus is used to tie the knot between maleness and divinity very tightly."[42] One way that some feminists counter this, is by affirming that the risen Christ continues to be disclosed through women and men. As Ruether points out:

> Christ, as redemptive person and Word of God, is not to be encapsulated "once-for-all" in the historical Jesus. The Christian community continues Christ's identity. As vine and branches Christic personhood continues in our sisters and brothers. . . . Christ, the liberated humanity, is not confined to a static perfection of one person two thousand years ago. Rather, redemptive humanity goes ahead of us, calling us to yet incompleted dimensions of human liberation.[43]

The issue for feminists is therefore focused very much on the locus of the revelation of God and its relationship to salvation though Christ. For those feminists who continue to stress discipleship as a key term to describe Christian identity, the importance of Jesus in the New Testament cannot be ignored. However, for many feminists there is a "decentering" of the classical tradition of revelation in Jesus alone and a relocating of this doctrine in the salvation experiences of women in the community of struggle. This relocation happens in a variety of ways, often dependent on a particular theologian's methodological approach to the Bible and theology.

Ruether, for example, attempts to focus the issues of classical Christology on Jesus as a messianic prophet who critiques the structures and practices of oppression and domination. She rejects Jesus' maleness as normative and moves toward a spirit Christology in which Christ is understood as androgynous. Schüssler Fiorenza focuses on the praxis and vision of Jesus shared by the disciples of equals both past and present. She therefore does not equate revelation with the biblical text but sees Jesus as the Sophia/Christ who even today liberates women and men from domination. Schneiders stresses the proclaimed Jesus as the inclusive subject of the biblical text. This proclaimed Jesus is always an imaginative integration of the historical and faith experience of Jesus Christ by Christians who have experienced the transforming power of God. Nakashima Brock moves most radically away from Jesus as the Christ, to centring Christology in the "Christa/Community."[44] For her, Jesus is but one participant in the revelation of redemptive community. For all these theologians there is a shift in the locus of revelatory authority. The locus is moved from an exclusive emphasis on Jesus as portrayed in the historical biblical text, to include Christ as experienced by the present and past community of disciples. All of these feminist theologians attempt to go beyond a hierarchical approach to the authority of the Bible, to a partnership approach in which the readers participate in creating the meaning of the text. All stress the struggle involved in identifying revelation in the reading of the text and instead connect revelation with the experience of salvation in the past and present. All therefore stress the need for a hermeneutics of suspicion based on the present experience of liberation and salvation.

This suspicion can be illustrated more concretely by the feminist response to prevalent interpretations of the death of Jesus. Feminists such as Ruether and Daly have pointed out the authoritarian and punitive images of divine power connected with atonement theories. Johnson agrees when she affirms that

> feminist theology repudiates an interpretation of the death of Jesus as required by God in repayment for sin. Such a view today is virtually inseparable from an underlying image of God as an angry, bloodthirsty, violent and sadistic father, reflecting the worst kind of male behavior.[45]

Instead, feminists like Johnson see Jesus' death as an act of human violence committed against the will of God. Jesus' active acceptance of his death is understood as a challenge to the twisted relationships that exist between humans and as a testimony to the solidarity of love between people.

For Johnson, the cross becomes a "parable" that enacts Sophia-God's participation in the suffering of the world.

Though the exclusive focus on Jesus is often questioned and the prevalent theology of the cross is rejected, many feminist theologians continue to find the notion of incarnation important to their work. This is true because incarnation connects with the important emphasis in feminism on embodiment. Feminists want to insist that bodies and sexuality, the earth, the social, the economic and the material context of our lives, is good. This is a way of recognizing the particularity of each of our lives in history. Thus Wilson-Kastner describes the incarnation of Christ as God being manifest in the life of Jesus, complete with all the limitations implied in being human. McFague suggests that we come to know God through divine incarnation in nature, as well as in Jesus. Johnson suggests that incarnation opens up the mystery of God to the concrete conditions of history, including suffering and delight. All of these feminists move toward creating a more immanent understanding of God as demonstrated by Jesus. But they also insist that the incarnation testifies to a scandal of particularity that really matters, "the scandal of Jesus' option for the poor and marginalized in the Spirit of his compassionate, liberating Sophia-God."[46] Jesus, in his human specificity, can be confessed as Sophia Incarnate and therefore truly revelatory of the liberating grace of God imaged as both male and female.

The term discipleship has been used by feminists to relate the incarnation of Jesus in history to the liberating movement of God in history through the community that embodies liberation. In this interpretation, the biblical narrative of Jesus and his disciples is not only a factual historical text but becomes instead a historical prototype open to its own transformation.[47] Dynamic interpretation for the sake of concrete experiences of salvation replaces static doctrines used to justify the traditional secondary status of women. Women who follow Jesus' vision and praxis are disciples who embody God's movement on earth.

In feminist theology, it is *Christ* who relates the embodiment of God in the community of disciples of equals to the embodiment of God in Jesus as described in the biblical text. Therefore, the mediation of God is not located in the patriarchal text itself but moves from the vision and praxis of the Jesus within the text to the vision and praxis of the disciples both past and present. Suspicion is necessary in order to discern those interpretations of the text that do not bring salvation, in order to open the way for new *revelatory and saving communication* by God.

God's Authority in History

In the theological language of Christian feminists, authority rests with God and God's continuing presence and activity *in history*. Though there is diversity in the formulations and emphases among feminists, the primary identity of God that gives authority to interpreters of the Bible is that of God, the *Creator/Liberator*, who liberates persons to experience their own freedom and autonomy. This gift of a new identity as a valued person created in the image of God is experienced by those who open themselves to the transforming power of the indwelling Spirit of God. As a result, women and men are enabled to recognize Christ in the vision and praxis of Jesus in the biblical text and in the relationships among people in the community.

Discipleship in feminist theology emphasizes the new consciousness of women through their involvement in the embodiment of God's liberating activity in the world. The authority of God is mediated through a process in which God's liberating activity in the experiences of women and men is expressed in the ongoing *relationships of mutuality and equality in the community*. The centre of biblical interpretation is therefore moved from the text itself to the conscious *identity* of those who claim liberation and to the *process* of the movement of God in history. The primary direction of interpretation is from the experience of the interpreter to the biblical text.

Feminists are suspicious of traditional mediations of God's authority, the church and the Bible, which justify biblical authority. They are critical of those human mediations that do not convey God's liberating, salvific presence as experienced by the marginal and oppressed in the community. A hermeneutics of suspicion describes the *suspicion of all mediations of God's authority that do not give freedom and autonomy to individuals and therefore do not promote relationships of equality and mutuality in the community.*

Salvation or liberation is defined as a social and political process that gives women the autonomy and freedom to participate in the movement of God to liberate all peoples. This social and political definition of salvation is rooted in the internal experience of a new identity and a new power. The *ekklēsia* is envisioned as a dynamic movement in harmony with God's liberating activity in history. Biblical interpretation that is suspicious of patriarchal traditions becomes one aspect of this liberating movement. Feminists thus insist that the immediate experience of God in women-church conflicts with the mediated experience of oppression that comes with a patriarchal reading of the Bible. Therefore, a critical hermeneutical approach must liberate the Bible so that the process of God's liberating action can continue.

However, an implicit assumption that is easily associated with a hermeneutics of suspicion can lead the community into an entirely different direction. By assuming the close identification of women's experience of liberation and God's salvific activity in the world, feminists locate divine authority in their own experience and in their own hermeneutic community. This shift to the community of feminists for the locus of revelation and salvation may lead to a rejection of others' claims of truth, without necessary dialogue about the substantive content of revelation. Prejudices against another hermeneutic community may be affirmed, thereby blinding the community to its own limitations. As Susanne Heine has pointed out, "One of the greatest problems of feminism and feminist theology seems to me to lie in the fact that women form a negative theory out of their hurt and their negative experience and claim universal validity for it."[48]

One example of this kind of prejudice is the way that some feminists have attacked the apostle Paul in the New Testament, making him the chief example of patriarchy. Paul becomes the scapegoat who has turned the "good" Jesus tradition into a bad one. Jewish scholars have pointed out how the same kind of prejudice produces an anti-Judaism that allows Christians to separate a Christian Jesus from the Hebrew Scripture and the Jewish context in which he was raised. Both of these approaches do not acknowledge the limitations of the present community to adequately analyze the past.

In addition, the focus on experience in the feminist community can hinder the recognition of those orthodox traditions and biblical texts that have mediated and contributed to their own feminist visions and experience of God. Feminist theologians also need to become conscious of how much they participate in the larger worldview of both church and society, in order to move beyond their own interpretations of the Bible that can also become static. They need to understand that their own harsh judgements of institutions and persons outside of their own movement is not always rooted in God's revelation.

A hermeneutics of suspicion, therefore, can hide a naive, uncritical acceptance by feminists of their own authority, disguised as personal experience of God. This would move the feminist hermeneutical process away from ongoing transformation by God, to a static acceptance of the status quo in the feminist community. It would permit suspicion of the experience of those outside of the community who also speak of God's salvation, while at the same time giving uncritical acceptance to experiences within the community that are said to be of God. Thus there is an ambiguity in the authority that supports a hermeneutics of suspicion. This ambiguity needs further clarification.

Discourse Patterns

In this section a shift is made to a discussion of patterns of language and to hermeneutical practice in order to illuminate how a hermeneutics of suspicion functions in the discourse of a feminist hermeneutic community. The ethos of authority that emerges will illustrate the customary, habitual ways in which feminists structure their dialogue.

Feminists begin biblical interpretation within the context of an ethos of liberation and empowerment given through a new identity of autonomy. Interpretation of biblical texts is influenced by a conscious decision to be suspicious of patriarchy and androcentrism and of the community that has controlled biblical interpretation in the past. At the same time, many Christian feminists do accept the possibility that some texts offer new insights that can be resources of liberation to persons and communities. Therefore, they stress a "critical evaluative hermeneutics" of the Bible, one sustained not so much by the "community of the forgiven," as by the community "always in need of reform."[49]

Elisabeth Schüssler Fiorenza's book *In Memory of Her* is a good illustration of this kind of contextual biblical interpretation.[50] Her interpretation of the *basileia* movement around Jesus has become persuasive for many feminist theologians, thus helping to define a particular feminist view of discipleship. Because she focuses on the political function of New Testament texts in the Christian church of the past and the present, she includes a brief discussion of the discipleship practices that she sees as important for the present women-church. Her book can therefore serve as a concrete example of "a performance" of scripture in the feminist hermeneutic community.

A summary of the ethos of authority that emerges from this exploration of discipleship language will be followed by a critical analysis from the perspective of women in the broader theological and church community.

Discipleship as Subversive Memory

For Schüssler Fiorenza, discipleship includes both the remembering of the suffering and oppression of early disciples, as well as the acceptance of responsibility for shaping the future in line with the vision and praxis of Jesus. Schüssler Fiorenza speaks of this as the challenge to "incarnate" the vision of Jesus in the community of moral discourse.[51] The emphasis is not on the substantive *content* of the biblical texts. Rather, the focus is on the political *function* of the particular texts in the community. This means that Schüssler Fiorenza's approach begins with the narratives and the historical actors, rather than with the sayings and teachings of Jesus or the apostles.[52] The framework that emerges is then used to evaluate the various teachings of the New Testament.

Schüssler Fiorenza's approach to the gospels, as well as to the moral directives of the household codes will illustrate how a subversive memory evaluates every claim to truth in terms of the tensions and conflicts it creates in the dominant cultural ethos.[53] A focus on these conflicts illustrates how the dynamic movement of liberation continues in a community.

The Jesus movement. In her study of the gospels, Schüssler Fiorenza emphasizes that the texts are "paradigmatic remembrances not comprehensive accounts of the historical Jesus." They are "expressions of communities and individuals who attempted to say what the significance of Jesus was for their own situations."[54] The gospels are thus theology, a critical appropriation of the memories and stories about Jesus by disciples who embody this understanding and invite others to join as disciples.

Schüssler Fiorenza recognizes that the Jesus movement could appeal to Israel's own tradition in the Hebrew Scriptures to counter the dominant lifestyle of the Jewish people. It was a movement of renewal that sought to embody God's *basileia* as good news to the marginal and impoverished within the Jewish community. Thus it was a Jewish movement *in tension* with the dominant patriarchal ethos of the culture of Judaism.

Schüssler Fiorenza characterizes this dominant ethos or life-praxis of Israel in the first century CE as determined by the key symbols of Temple and Torah, expressing the notion of Israel, as God's holy people, committed to living in covenant with God.[55] The followers of Jesus shared with other groups in Palestine a vision and hope for the *basileia,* or kingdom of God, a vision that included the political existence and holiness of Israel in the midst of the other nations. In this context, Jesus proclaimed and lived the message of the kingdom as already present. The eschatological salvation and wholeness of the nation of Israel, as the elect people of God, was already experientially available. This emphasis on both the present and the future *basileia* marked Jesus' preaching and ministry, thus creating a tension between brokenness and wholeness. A critical reinterpretation of the primary Jewish symbols of Temple and Torah placed them in the context of the people as the "locus of God's power and presence."[56] The Jesus movement therefore "refused to define the holiness of God's elected people in cultic terms, redefining it instead as the wholeness intended in creation."[57] Schüssler Fiorenza points out the tension created by this redefinition:

> Everyday life must not be measured by the sacred holiness of the Temple and Torah, but Temple and Torah praxis must be measured and evaluated by whether or not they engender the wholeness of every human being. Everydayness, therefore, can become revelatory, and the presence and power of God's sacred wholeness can be experienced in every human being.[58]

Schüssler Fiorenza does not focus primarily on the teachings of Jesus but on the followers of Jesus, in order to see the people, the historical actors for whom the *basileia* is claimed. She focuses on the narrative texts, allowing them to inform her understanding of the movement initiated by Jesus. It is then that the subversive character of this movement can be recognized and the crucial role of women can be seen.

She notes first of all that the *basileia* includes several distinct groups: the destitute poor, the sick and crippled and the tax collectors, sinners, and prostitutes. This demonstrates that God's will was an inclusive *basileia.* This vision was already spelled out in the wisdom traditions of the Jewish people and continued to be spelled out in the parables and wisdom sayings of Jesus as recorded in the gospels. It was embodied by both female and male disciples, who had a primary role in the mission of healing, preaching and inclusive table fellowship. This "intrusion" of Jesus and his movement into the dominant religious ethos of the people opened up access to God for everyone, but especially for those who had little chance to experience God's power in Temple and Torah.[59] Schüssler Fiorenza's interpretation of several specific discipleship texts illustrates that the teachings of Jesus, as well as his actions, challenged the patriarchal structures of the time in the name of the *basileia* that   he represented.

The household codes. In her discussion of the household codes, Schüssler Fiorenza begins by pointing out how these prescriptive texts have functioned to influence Christian ethics throughout the centuries by describing the relationships between those deemed superior and those deemed inferior. In a chapter of her book *Bread Not Stone*, Schüssler Fiorenza explicitly connects suspicion based on an ethic of discipleship to her analysis of the household codes.

Schüssler Fiorenza places these texts into a context of struggle between the dominant cultural ethos of the patriarchal household and the new ethos of equality found in the discipleship household of God. She also places them in the context of the "multiformity of biblical ethos and ethics" in the Bible and stresses the need for "critical evaluative hermeneutics" of these passages.[60] Her exegesis rests on the assertion that the Bible has been death-dealing as well as life-giving in the history of the church. She realizes that these particular passages have legitimated oppression and maintained the status quo of a patriarchal church that marginalizes and silences women. She therefore begins with a suspicion of texts that have such "formative power" in the life of the church. She assumes that these writings and the contemporary interpretations of exegetes are political and must first of all be evaluated according to the function they serve in the community.

For Schüssler Fiorenza, the most accurate picture of first century Christianity is of a movement that was subversive in its critique of societal values and destructive of patriarchal household structures. This subversive character was especially important for women and slaves, who were disengaged from their traditional roles and limitations by the new experience of God. With this assumption, Schüssler Fiorenza then asserts:

> The prescriptive household code trajectory attempted to ameliorate this subversion by asserting the congruence of the Christian ethics with that of patriarchal house and state. This trajectory did not continue the ethos of the house-church, with its voluntary and collegial structures, but sought to modify it and bring it into line with the structures of patriarchal family and society.[61]

Schüssler Fiorenza points out that the household codes were written in a social context where the emancipation of women and slaves from patriarchy was already part of the public discussion. In this context, the household codes could be seen as humanizing and modifying patriarchal ethics by obliging the patriarchal head of the household to exercise love, consideration and responsibility. However, in Schüssler Fiorenza's analysis both of these functions, whether reinforcing patriarchal submission or adapting the Christian community to its context, open the community to "political co-optation" by the Roman Empire. Therefore, "submission and obedience, but not equality and justice, are institutionalized by the patriarchal ethos" of the Epistles.[62] The vision of *agape* is reduced to a "mere moral" appeal. The transforming power of the gospel in history is hindered by the faith and praxis taught by these codes. A structural-political alternative to the dominant patriarchal culture is not given.

Schüssler Fiorenza is suspicious of the apologetic arguments that theologians have given when they argue for the Christian character of this early pattern of patriarchal submission. She suggests that these "arguments affirm the patriarchal character of biblical revelation and of the Christian church as well as document the ideological function of biblical theology and ethics." [63] She therefore asserts the need for a transformative biblical hermeneutical approach, based on an identity as a "self-identified" woman and a Christian that will not discard the personal, cultural and religious history within biblical religion. She focuses on the struggles of all members of the believing community, particularly women and others oppressed by patriarchal household structures.

Schüssler Fiorenza places the "common historical experience of women as an oppressed people, collaborating with our oppression and at the same time struggling for our liberation in patriarchal biblical history and community" into the centre of the hermeneutical discussion.[64] She emphasizes a "dangerous memory" that can keep alive the sufferings of patriarchal submission and subjection. She challenges patriarchal religion to both personal and structural conversion in several different ways: (1) She names the preference of interpreters for the patriarchal ethics of the household codes over against the egalitarian ethos of Jesus. This preference is based on "theological-political presuppositions and social-ecclesial interests," rather than on an evaluation derived solely from the New Testament itself.[65] (2) She construes the biblical text not as a timeless archetype, but as a historical prototype that is open to theological transformation. (3) She points out how the Aristotelian political ethics still operates to justify a structure in which the male is the head of the family, the basic political unit. In this way, Schüssler Fiorenza can point to the early Christian ethos of coequal discipleship in community as a way to restructure the patriarchal household of God into a "kinship community without clerical fathers and spiritual masters, a community not patterned after the patriarchal family."[66]

Schüssler Fiorenza insists on her freedom to interpret the Bible on the basis of her own identity and convictions. She accepts the responsibility of evaluating the ethical tradition as found in the household codes. Her interpretation concentrates on remembering the oppressive character of these texts. She does this by comparing the tension within Judaism, produced by the new ethos of inclusive wholeness as envisioned and practised by Jesus, to the lack of tension within Roman society that the moral teachings on subordination and superordination produced. She concludes that in the early church the household codes functioned to justify the dominant values of the larger society.

However, she also realizes that the biblical text continues to be powerful in the Christian community in the areas of ethics and morality. Because the Bible contains both an ethos of coequality and a patriarchal pattern of submission, she turns her attention to the community of interpreters and their responsibility. "The moral authority of the Bible is grounded in a community that is capable of sustaining Scriptural authority in faithful remembrance, liturgical celebration, ecclesial governance, and continual reinterpretation of its own biblical roots and traditions."[67] This authority can be dangerous if morality and worship are shaped by the remembrance of the historical winners, while the subversive memory of innocent suffering and of solidarity with the victims of history is abandoned.[68] The moral authority of the text must be adjudicated by a responsible community capable of naming those biblical passages that reflect a community in tension with the dominant patriarchal culture. This community consists of those in solidarity with the marginal and oppressed in society.

Schüssler Fiorenza therefore insists that biblical ethics is an exercise in "evaluative hermeneutics of biblical traditions and of Christian communities they have shaped and are still shaping."[69] It is an ethic that emphasizes remembering the suffering of those struggling for liberation and accepting the responsibility to evaluate both text and community on the basis of the liberation and equality that they promote. This ethic is congruent with the example of the early disciples of Jesus, who produced tension in the dominant ethos by remembering his vision and practice of inclusive wholeness.

To summarize, the interpretation of the gospels and the household codes by Schüssler Fiorenza alerts the community to two important functions that the notion of discipleship can have to empower women. (1) The notion of discipleship can be subversive of the dominant tradition. This produces a tension that can be recognized in the vision and praxis of Jesus and in the liberating experience of the early egalitarian households. (2) The notion of discipleship can affirm the experience of inclusive wholeness in a new community of God's people. This inclusivity can be recognized as central to the *basileia* as proclaimed by Jesus and experienced by those whom Jesus healed and included in his table fellowship.

Schüssler Fiorenza's concern is the wholeness of all who have been excluded from the community. This exclusion has been based on an uncritical acceptance of a dominant text. She therefore rejects the ethic of the household codes as the ethic of the historical winners. However, she accepts the *basileia* vision and praxis of Jesus as a resource for women today because it has liberated women and men from the time of its first proclamation by Jesus.

The hermeneutics of suspicion that is evident in her approach to the biblical texts is based on her identification with the experience of the oppressed and marginalized. She is suspicious of an ethic that would ameliorate tensions between the larger society and the vision of inclusive wholeness represented by the *basileia* movement. This means that she cannot accept the household codes as being in any way congruent with the vision and praxis of Jesus. She denies any potential the household codes may have had for challenging the powerful in the community with a strong ethic of servanthood. Her concern is for those who feel dominated by the powerful, whether in the past or present.

This raises the question as to whether Schüssler Fiorenza's definition of discipleship continues to challenge the feminist community to an ongoing practice of biblical interpretation that will transform the community. The continuity between oppression in the past and oppression in the present may not be entirely accurate for all members of the feminist community. At times, the tension between the feminist community and those outside its boundaries may not be entirely due to a new vision of equality and mutuality. Issues of power and authority may also arise within the feminist community. Schüssler Fiorenza's interpretation avoids criteria outside of the feminist experience of liberation for adjudicating when tension is healthy, arising out of the experience of God, and when it is unhealthy because it is not true to the gospel. Her more functional approach may not be adequate to provide criteria to determine God's revealing presence in history.

Authority and Power in Discipleship Practice

Another way of looking at authority patterns in the discourse of a community claiming to be a discipleship community is to look carefully at those practices that it considers essential for its identity. Schüssler Fiorenza has named some of these practices in her discussion of feminist spirituality. She sees them as "the central embodiment and incarnation of the vision of church."[70] These practices are reclaimed by Christian women in order to realize their own ideal of a discipleship community as a responsible community of liberation. They present a vision of the church as a community committed to a process that begins with a hermeneutics of suspicion. Central to this new vision of church is the struggle to bring inclusivity and wholeness to all of society.

In her discussion of spirituality, Schüssler Fiorenza assumes that the reconstruction of biblical religion that she has done can be embodied in a feminist community committed to the discipleship of equals. She suggests that the "vision and praxis of our foresisters must be allowed to become a transformative power that can open up a feminist future for women in biblical religion."[71] With this suggestion, she acknowledges a movement from the interpreted text to the community, a movement that empowers women. She thus indicates a relationship of authority. At the same time she assumes that this movement is distinctive, but not separated, from the so-called secular women's movements. She therefore speaks of her experience in women-church as both a "bonding in sisterhood for empowerment" and a reclaiming of the "baptismal call to the discipleship of equals."[72] The ambiguity of authority that comes with this focus on both inclusivity and a claim for the Bible as a crucial resource for disciples needs further exploration.

In this movement from the language of reconstruction to the language of spirituality, Schüssler Fiorenza attempts to move from the language of ethics in the biblical text to the language of performance in the present day. Her work can illustrate an ethos of authority in a community that assumes that resources from the text can still be obtained in the midst of a hermeneutics of suspicion.

Ekklēsia, the assembly of free citizens gathering to decide their own spiritual-political affairs. Schüssler Fiorenza has emphasized the importance of this gathering in order that women and other marginal persons can claim their own religious powers in a practical way.[73] She insists that freedom is concrete, as women participate fully in the decision-making process of the church, deciding matters affecting their own welfare and being accountable for their own decisions. She has named this assembly *ekklēsia gynaikon,* or women-church, a "political-oppositional term to patriarchy." These assemblies oppose patriarchy by the way they structure their political organization. They are dialogical communities of equals, in which critical judgement takes place and public freedom becomes tangible. She therefore has accepted the responsibility of naming when church happens and the conditions under which an assembly can be called church. In her later book, Schüssler Fiorenza has specifically stressed the radical democratic-political meaning of the Greek term for church.[74] This identification of church is based on an opposition to patriarchy and the institutions and structures that it represents.

The notion of *ekklēsia* has therefore been used by feminists to emphasize liberation from both societal and ecclesial authorities and to insist that a more inclusive community be formed to replace the present structures and institutions that embody patriarchy. Equality in decision making has been a way of including women who have been made marginal by the domination of patriarchal structures. This practice subverts both societal and church values and therefore Schüssler Fiorenza wants no separation made between the so-called secular feminist movement and the Christian feminist movement. Both are concerned with radical changes to the authority of these institutions and their practices. She stresses that the structural-patriarchal dualisms that have so determined women's reality be overcome in the *ekklēsia* of women. She specifically names a series of dualisms, between Jewish and Christian women, between married and single women, between the church and the world and between the sacred and the secular.

But a number of women point out problems with this focus on equality in decision making as the defining characteristic of *ekklēsia*.[75] By relating church so closely to an identity of liberation defined by white American females, feminist theology can be perceived as denying an identity of church and discipleship to those with different experiences and convictions. In fact, white American feminism may be more continuous with white male liberal democracy than with church or discipleship as experienced in a variety of times and places. Christian feminists may thus be excluding many communities of disciples who have expressed inclusivity in different ways.

Feminist theologians have responded to the complaints of women of other "races," social classes, statuses, and religions and attempted to form a sort of "rainbow coalition" by broadening the base of feminist thought and theology. But this has also made it necessary to establish feminist consciousness as the basic category of thought on which all can agree. As pointed out by Francis Martin, the result has been that feminist consciousness or spirituality has become the genus, and Christian, Jewish, Muslim and other religious groups have become species whose specificity is governed by the outlook and demands of feminism.[76] The autonomy to name and describe oneself is then taken away and feminist thought can itself become dominating.

The use of the term *ekklēsia* or women-church to name this coalition of women and men creates additional questions. The long tradition of using *ekklēsia* to speak of the Christian church cannot be totally ignored, even though Schüssler Fiorenza attempts to use it to speak of a public space open to all. Susannah Heshel suggests that there may be a hidden anti-Jewish tendency in biblical interpretation by Christian feminists, which attempts to hide differences under an assumed commonality. As she points out, "in feminist writings there are subtle indications of an attitude that all Jews are male, and all feminists are Christians."[77]

Criticism of the supposed common understanding of freedom and inclusivity also comes from black women. Delores S. Williams points out that the use of the term patriarchy hides certain forms of oppression by linking it too closely to males. She points out that a certain group of women possess power and authority because of their relationship to white-controlled American institutions. She therefore calls for an analysis of what appears to be a positive side of patriarchy, with regard to the development of white American women. It is this positive side that also distinguishes white women's privilege from black women's oppression. She emphasizes the failure of white feminists to point out the "substantial difference between their patriarchally-derived-privileged-oppression and black women's demonically-derived-annihilistic-oppression."[78] She goes on to speak about the experience of church in the black community, an experience that exhibits its own unique connection between the spiritual and political dimensions of life and history.

Women who come from a different denomination than Schüssler
Fiorenza may discover that their assumptions about the relationship between
church and society are different from hers. Mary Ann Tolbert speaks about the
difficulty that Protestant women have in appropriating the proposals for
women-church into their praxis. She suggests that the differences in theology
between Catholic feminists and Protestant feminists need further analysis.[79] For
denominations like the Mennonites and the Quakers, this is not the first time
that a different theology has resulted in nonconformity to the dominant
churches. How do the radical perspectives of these communities of faith
connect with the notion of women-church?

Differences in experience between those who have been part of
established churches and those who have been part of marginalized churches
can also be noted. Denominations differ in their social and political status in
society. This creates differences in the interpretation of the power of the
church. For example, Mennonite women who have been part of a church
designated as a sect, may have different experiences from women who have
been part of a mainstream church. Those who have experienced persecution for
their faith may also not easily see their own church as powerful.

A social and political analysis of oppression must therefore include an
analysis of differences in ecclesial experiences, as well as differences in the
theology of the church. The notion of church as described by Schüssler
Fiorenza easily assumes that society and church overlap completely, as has
historically been assumed in the notion of Christendom. These distinctions
need to be explored more fully so that feminist discourse does not just accept
the perspectives of the majority hidden in the language of a dominant
Christianity that fails to respect the integrity of minority positions.

Other differences between women, such as differences in education,
also affect discourse patterns. These are not easily acknowledged in the notion
of *ekklēsia* as defined by women in the academy. Katie Funk Wiebe, reflecting
on a conference of Mennonite women, writes about the many ways in which
domination can exhibit itself, even when people are gathered together to decide
their own political affairs. For example, she points to the separation that
happened during a conference of women because of a particular use of
language. created separations. She protests this type of domination:

> Theological jargon separated the academicians from the lay women at times.
> . . . Can women do theology without shifting to a language that sounds as if
> it comes from an alien country, which act is in itself a sign of intimidation? A
> little power is always appealing, regardless of what form it comes in.[80]

This issue of domination by the academy needs further exploration in feminist
theology in order to counter the intimidation felt by many women.

The issue of domination within the feminist community raises questions about the accountability of the community for its definitions and practices of discipleship and of church. Is there an accountability to God and to the larger community of disciples that goes beyond a general feminist experience of oppression? How is accountability, as well as freedom, concretely demonstrated in hermeneutical practice? How can the contested truth claims as well as the political function of these claims in the community, be included in the discussion of what constitutes church.

Various feminists have acknowledged that they too use a "canon within the canon" to identify those passages and themes in the Bible that inform their understanding of God and therefore their criteria for judgment in moral situations. As Trible points out, "Like many other interpreters, they [feminists] use scripture to judge and correct scripture for appropriation in their lives."[81] Other feminists point to the dialogue in the larger Christian community as a way to ensure broader accountability. Gayle Gerber Koontz calls for a hermeneutics of generosity to complement a hermeneutics of suspicion. She acknowledges her situation as a "North American, white, relatively wealthy, inadequately committed disciple" and suggests that:

> Precisely because of our already strong suspicion of difference, and given the warning in Jesus' reference to motes and beams, our particular task might be to practice a hermeneutics of generosity. If we have eyes to see and ears to hear, the gathering together of different selves and communities may well become an occasion for God's words of justice and grace to break forth. A genuine struggle to understand and respect one another's historical situations, situations that give rise to differing interpretations of Scripture and differing theological convictions, may well become a means of transformation, new insight, deeper faith and unexpected action.[82]

These acknowledgments by some feminists encourage dialogue with those who read the Bible differently. They suggest that there are assumptions held by Christian feminists that may be continuous with communities outside of feminism. These assumptions have not been clearly articulated and therefore need to be explored. Recognizing the diversity within feminism encourages dialogue about substantive issues, as well as further exploration of the function of these truth claims in the community.

The emphasis on an assembly of free citizens deciding their own affairs through feminist discourse can therefore function in two ways in the community. By asserting continuity between the early church and the present community of women, it can empower women to be actively involved in women-church. It can open the community to further critical dialogue with all who claim a vision of equality and inclusivity. However, this emphasis can also close the community to further dialogue, by limiting its discussion partners to those who claim an identical political stance. It can hide the differences in truth claims, thus allowing a subtle domination of others under the guise of equality and openness.

Breaking the bread and sharing the cup. Equality is demonstrated in women-church through a practice of eating and drinking together. According to Schüssler Fiorenza, breaking the bread and sharing the cup is a means of expressing in tangible form the common vision of wholeness that binds the community together.[83] It is a specific approach to solidarity, an approach characterized by the sharing of sustenance. This practice is open to everyone, crossing the boundaries created by the particularity of "race," creed or nationality. The challenge is not only to the church, but to all of society. This practice intends to bind all feminists together in a common struggle against a dualism that places women on the periphery of the community.

Sharing food and drink is a practice particularly focused on human bodily existence, emphasizing the importance of taking the physical nature of human existence into account in any understanding of human relationships. It is not only the mind or spirit that is important, but the very material existence included in the identity of each person. No duality between spirit and body is allowed to determine the relationship between people. Spirituality and economics therefore can not be separated. Physical violence against women cannot be justified the supposed superiority of the male, who represents spirit and mind, over the female. As Schüssler Fiorenza points out, "How can we point to the eucharistic bread and say 'this is my body' as long as women's bodies are battered, raped, sterilized, mutilated, prostituted, and used to male ends?"[84]

Sharing bread and drink are symbolic of coequality and wholeness, expressed in concrete ways in the community. By practising this ritual as women-church, women and men remember their present full inclusion in the community. However, they also remember the past exclusion of many people from the community, an exclusion based on women's physical identity.

Schüssler Fiorenza considers this practice of eating and drinking together as a receiving of each other, an experiencing of God's presence through each other. In this act, the gospel as God's alternative vision for everyone is proclaimed, especially for those who are poor, outcast and battered. Those on the boundaries of the church are placed into the centre and allowed to participate in this symbol of wholeness.

However, in Christian tradition the symbol of the bread and the cup points not only to the universal invitation to all to participate in God's vision for humanity, but also more particularly to God's self-giving love and grace that is poured out through Jesus' death on the cross. The experience of inclusion and relatedness symbolized by the breaking of the bread and the drinking of the wine is dependent on the grace of God, mediated through the life and death of Jesus. For many Christians, it is this continuity with the death of Jesus on the cross that accounts for the power of the symbolic action.

Many feminists struggle to redefine the connection to Jesus symbolized in the communion cup. Schüssler Fiorenza does not elaborate on the difficulties that do not allow an easy sharing of bread and cup, even in a community in which everyone shares the feminist vision of equality. She assumes that it is both the negative experience of patriarchy, as well as the positive integrating image of the people of God, that can move women to act to overcome the patriarchal-structural dualisms inherent in society. However, for many women a deeper dialogue about the meaning of the cross in their own tradition will be necessary before this sharing of the cup and bread can happen with integrity.

Moreover, Schüssler Fiorenza's approach does not deal adequately with the material and economic differences between women in the feminist community. It does not take into account the way sharing of the bread and the cup are hindered by identities that have been internalized, such as feelings of inferiority, superiority, strength or weakness, based on economic and other social differences. Gayle Gerber Koontz has pointed out that categories, such as "powerful" or "weak" are relationship specific and do not intrinsically characterize a group or a person.[85] Power relationships are therefore complex and most people feel both powerful and weak in various relationships. These feelings tend to be socially constructed and reflect the particularities of the many different communities in which each person participates.

The sharing and communion to which Schüssler Fiorenza points reflects a vision that is powerful in bringing persons together into a community of relationships. The complexity of these relationships can however be hidden by speaking only of gender differences or by assuming that a feminist identity will be enough to bring about equality and mutuality. Other continuities and discontinuities within the Christian tradition need to be admitted and evaluated in order that dialogue can deal with the substantive nature of these differences.

Initiation into community. Schüssler Fiorenza speaks about religious initiation to emphasize the fact that no special religious vocation or lifestyle is needed in order to be part of the movement for liberation.[86] She wants to stress the calling of all people to become the people of God. One does not need to be clergy or in a religious order to qualify for this calling. There is no separation between the private sphere of family and home and the public sphere of work and politics. Initiation into the religious life is there from the moment of baptism as an infant. The nurturing of children must be the responsibility of not only the parents but of the whole community. She thus stresses coequality in terms of an initiation into the movement. All are called to participate. In this way, she honours the memory of all who were marginalized in the religious community and challenges the exclusivity of the calling to participate in God's work.

Schüssler Fiorenza's discussion of initiation, however, assumes a particular understanding of the church that depends on infant baptism as an initiation ritual. It does not take into account more marginal Christian communities, such as Mennonites, who consider believers' baptism as the formal induction into a Christian community. The Mennonite understanding of baptism is more in tune with Schüssler Fiorenza's emphasis on commitment, accountability and solidarity, qualities that mark the voluntary response of only some people to the calling to wholeness. For Mennonites, baptism is connected to a specific commitment to God, to accountability in the Christian community and to solidarity with the people of God. It is not primarily connected to the socialization of people from infancy but rather to confession of sin and to conversion.

Initiation, as discussed by Schüssler Fiorenza, seems to assume an identity that is not chosen but given by birth. The baptism ritual is associated with the gift of creation, not with the choice to be a disciple. Though it is important to point out this gift of grace, many Christian groups would also need to know how freedom of choice can be given to persons as they enter adulthood. Questions must therefore be raised about how initiation into the feminist movement is related to an adult choice of Christian faith.

This again raises questions about the assumptions that lie beneath the meanings that Schüssler Fiorenza assigns to these various Christian rituals. Pamela Dickey Young points out that the term "Christian" as used by Schüssler Fiorenza can only be self-descriptive. If persons see themselves as part of the Christian tradition, then they may name themselves as Christian. She points out that this may mean that "if there is nothing that can be derived from the tradition itself that can be used normatively to argue that this is what Christianity is all about, then others can use the tradition in less liberating ways."[87] She therefore wants to point out the need to admit the normativity of the particular tradition that is informing the positions that one is taking.

A discussion of initiation can therefore be used to speak about the calling of all people to be the people of God. However, it can also be used to minimize the specific choices and commitments that women make in terms of their entry into a particular community, whether that community is feminist or Christian.

Ministry of divine wisdom. Schüssler Fiorenza speaks about the ministry of divine wisdom as the announcement of the inbreaking of God's new world and humanity here and now.[88] She realizes that there have always been the wise, who have guided the community. It is these people who can unmask and set people free from the structural sins that enslave them. They do this by feeding the hungry, healing the sick, liberating the oppressed and announcing the inbreaking of God's new world. The emphasis on divine wisdom allows a connection to be made between God's new world as envisioned in the gospel and the new world as envisioned by feminists.

Feminists tend to use the notion of divine wisdom to emphasize the movement from the feminist vision to the Bible. They stress the way the Bible, as historical prototype, can be shaped by the wisdom of women today who have discovered their own identity and are announcing the inbreaking of a new world. They stress how the notion of wisdom encourages them to be suspicious of all knowledge that does not bring about freedom and liberation for women.

However, other women are pointing out that there is another movement that is equally important. Contemporary wisdom must also be shaped by the Bible. As pointed out by Toinette M. Eugene, the Scriptures have

> provided authorization and legitimization for women who have rejected slavery, racism, anti-semitism, colonial exploitation, and misogynism as unbiblical and against God's will. . . . The biblical vision of freedom and *shalom* still energizes women in all walks of life and from entirely different cultural conditions and pre-understandings to continue to struggle against poverty, slavery, dehumanization, and denigration.[89]

This raises the issue of whether and how to use biblical scholarship by men that often unconsciously assumes a patriarchal world view. Mary Schertz is clear about her stance in this regard. "Truth is not gender specific and truth is of paramount importance. While it is vital to take seriously questions of context, such as the gender and power of the speaker, it is also vital not to ignore questions of content and truth."[90] She assumes that claims to truth will be part of every interpretation and that this search for truth will include a critical use of the interpretations of other hermeneutic communities. She hints that acceptance of authoritative claims are also dependent on the persuasive power of truth, which may be mediated through unexpected channels.

Feminists can use the tradition of wisdom to assert their own connection to wisdom in every age. They can insist that this ministry of divine wisdom includes the wisdom that comes from the personal and communal experience of women. However, feminists can also deny their indebtedness to the resources outside of the feminist community, which have mediated their access to wisdom. They can hide truth claims under the guise of personal experience. They can be closed to the wisdom of others by asserting their own wisdom as the final criterion of truth.

To summarize, the practices of discipleship as envisioned by Schüssler Fiorenza have two functions in the feminist community. (1) These practices have been used to promote solidarity between women and to relativize patriarchal claims of truth. In this way they have promoted freedom and liberation from the domination of texts that were interpreted to oppress women and other marginal groups. They have fostered supportive relationships between people in the community. They have encouraged women to claim their own religious authority and power and advocated a hermeneutics of suspicion towards all patriarchal truths that claim universality. This has meant that the feminist community sees itself as living in tension with the rest of society in its proclamation of inclusivity and in its practices of equality and mutuality. (2) These practices have also been used in the community to hide relationships of authority based on mediations of truth that were not acknowledged. The overarching framework that is produced when particular truth claims are disguised as universal experience can create a kind of domination within the community that can easily be denied. Suspicion of power when connected to gender relationships has sometimes not carried over to a suspicion of the hidden agenda within the feminist community. This agenda may deny differences between people and inhibit wrestling with issues of substantive truth raised by the biblical text. A hermeneutics of suspicion can lead to static interpretations within feminist theology that close feminists to the critical dialogue with others.

These different functions of suspicion in the feminist hermeneutic community are possible because of the ambiguity in the definition of experience. While patriarchal experience is clearly acknowledged as mediated by text and community, feminist experience tends to be understood as more directly related to God's movement in history. This sets up a claim that liberation and inclusivity are the will of God, without always acknowledging how Bible and tradition have contributed to this experience of liberation. Sometimes, an attitude of suspicion will cut off broader dialogue about truth claims that undergird the experience of liberation. Moreover, because of the way that text and experience are connected in this approach, feminists too easily assume a continuity between themselves and the marginalized in the biblical text, while ignoring the possible continuity between the dominant characters in the text and women in the feminist community.

The commonality between salvation as proclaimed in the biblical text and liberation as proclaimed by the feminist community needs further exploration. At the centre of this exploration must be an acknowledgment of the crucial difference between those feminists who acknowledge God as ultimate Source of the experience of salvation and those who do not.

Authority in the Interpretive Process

Feminist discourse tends to connect *experience* with the biblical *text* in a hermeneutical circle that is in danger of becoming closed. Christian feminists who begin with a hermeneutics of suspicion usually insist that critical biblical interpretation is authorized by personal and communal experience of freedom from domination. This leads to evaluating all biblical texts in terms of their subversive effect on the present patriarchal structures of society and church. These texts then become the basis for discerning other liberating texts and rejecting those that create a tension with the feminist vision of equality.

The attitude of suspicion in feminist theology therefore does more than detect patriarchy. It can also serve to justify feminist definitions of liberation as well as cut off dialogue prematurely with other hermeneutic communities and their definitions of salvation. A static approach to the Bible can easily be created that closes the feminist community to claims to truth that would challenges the status quo. However, a dynamic process can begin again, when those who were outside or marginal in the feminist hermeneutic community begin to articulate their discomfort with unexamined assumptions within the community. This subversion of feminist conversation creates an opportunity for a broadening of the hermeneutic community and a rereading of the biblical texts in search of deeper truths. Though this encouragement to state particular truth claims produces differences, it also serves to further the process of dialogue about substantive theological issues. Moreover, the function of truth claims within the feminist community can then also be examined.

Schüssler Fiorenza's interpretation, in her book *In Memory of Her,* illustrates an approach to biblical interpretation that could easily become circular, thus closing itself off to interpretations that would challenge her definitions of discipleship. By stressing the role of subversive memory in the interpretive process, she begins by remembering those who have been marginalized and dominated by the biblical texts. This leads to a suspicion of many texts in the Bible, which connect with domination as defined by modern feminism. But Schüssler Fiorenza also finds texts that define liberation and texts that empower those who are marginalized. She discovers texts that connect discipleship to a democratic process within women-church that is linked to God's Sophia. She notes that the particular remembering done by the early writers of the gospels alludes to disciples, both women and men, who glimpsed a vision of inclusive wholeness. She chooses to interpret the texts in such a way that the movement toward equality is justified and legitimated.

By focusing on the political function of the texts in the community, Schüssler Fiorenza does not have to identify explicit truth claims associated with the Christian tradition. She does not have to differentiate between those truth claims that are connected to the ethos of the larger society in which she lives and those that are connected to the gospel of Jesus Christ as mediated through the Christian tradition in which she stands. The danger of different truth claims being subsumed under the over-arching framework of equality or women-church is present also for Schüssler Fiorenza. Her desire for inclusivity may lead to the subtle domination of those whose convictions differ from the majority of the feminist community. Inadequate definitions of wholeness and salvation may become static definitions that determine both the conversation partners in community discourse and the interpretation of the texts.

Feminist authority, articulated through a hermeneutics of suspicion, can therefore also become powerful and dangerous when it is connected to divine revelation and salvation. It can justify a misuse of power by those within the feminist community and discourage those with different convictions about God to remain silent.

A Feminist Ethos of Authority

The critical redescription of the shape of biblical authority in the feminist community has focused on both the tradition (as embodied in theological convictions), and community discourse (as embodied in biblical interpretation and community practice). It has demonstrated how an identity of discipleship has encouraged feminists to read the Bible with suspicion in order to detect oppressive texts and interpretations that promote domination. The notion of the discipleship of equals has been useful in subverting those interpretations that have functioned authoritatively in the past, creating dominating structures and unjust and oppressive practices.

The notion of discipleship has been important for Christian feminists in asserting a connection with the Bible while maintaining a critical stance. It has allowed feminists to understand the hermeneutical process as an ethical and political approach dependent on theological convictions and a human process empowered by God. Any authoritative use of the Bible in the Christian feminist community is dependent on maintaining this close connection between the hermeneutic process of suspicion and an *ekklēsia* of disciples. Convictions about God that affirm women's identity as created in God's image and assure women's liberation have been most important to feminists. These convictions have brought the *ekklēsia* and the Bible into a dialectical relationship in which the newly empowered community of equals dethrones the authority of a patriarchal church.

Within this ethos of authority, the Bible has lost its status and authority as an objective basis for certain knowledge about God. In the words of Walter Brueggeman, a hermeneutics of suspicion has shattered "canonical interpretation which itself has become canonical."[91] The monopoly of power held by the established interpreting community has been overturned. The church is no longer seen as representative of God's revelation. Instead, the counter-voices in the biblical literature, interpreted by those on the margins of church and society, receive new authority.

However, the analysis has also shown that two alternative directions may be taken by feminists based on these convictions. Some feminists universalize their experience of oppression, suggesting that non-oppressive interpretation happens only from an attitude of suspicion of the tradition and the established church. They therefore make their own alternative communities new centres of authority by insisting that the criteria for revelation and salvation are contained in their own experience. The focus on the oppressive function of certain texts blinds them to any possibility that these texts could be interpreted differently. An unacknowledged monopoly of power is created, based on truth claims that have often not been explicitly stated. The process of interpretation becomes static and exclusive based on an assumed continuity between the oppressed in the Bible and the feminist community. In this process, choices are taken away from women because the community ethos allows no questioning of those interpretations that are dominant in the community. In this approach, suspicion is interpreted as suspicion of any revelation embodied in the experiences of persons outside of their own feminist communities.

A second direction is possible. This direction would move the feminist community into an ongoing process of self-analysis, as well as into a creative dialogue with other communities. It would acknowledge its own truth claims and become aware of the power that comes with a claim based on experience. Particular attention would be paid to the voices of those who feel marginalized in the feminist community. This direction would allow room for the disruptive voice of God, as mediated through the tradition and embodied in other hermeneutic communities. The dialectical relationship between text and community would remain open, allowing the truth claims of the Bible to engage the interpreter critically and creatively. In this direction, suspicion would be seen as suspicion of all human mediations that usurp God's power and authority.

This redescription of a feminist hermeneutics of suspicion has allowed me to see that an analysis of power and power claims alone cannot ensure interpretation that expresses God's vision for humanity and the world. Suspicion of others does not deal adequately with the temptations of power that are there for all humans, including those who were formerly on the margins of the community. The political, more functional, approach of feminist theologians does not give convincing reasons for continuing to read the text and to wrestle seriously with the truth claims of others. A hermeneutics of suspicion is therefore inadequate to function authoritatively as a mediator of God's revelation and salvation for the disciples of Christ.

What then does this mean for my own search for an understanding of biblical authority? Do I recognize within myself the two directions that a hermeneutics of suspicion can take me? What choices does this open up for me? The feminist claim that biblical interpretation must be subversive of all human claims to divine authority is a crucial reminder for me of the need for critical discernment of all truth claims. However, critiques of other interpretations are not enough. Decisions about authority have to be made even when domination is rejected. In fact, suspicion functions best if it gives freedom to make constructive choices about truth claims.

Because I too am easily blind to my own use of biblical interpretation to justify my actions, I must open myself to the critique of an enlarged hermeneutic community. At the same time, I will listen to the text as closely as I can, acknowledging both the strengths and limitations of my context. Neither obedience nor suspicion alone will define my approach to the Bible. Instead, I will make deliberate choices within the dialectical process that describes the relationship of text and interpreter. My hope is that this will lead to a reading open to God's disruptive voice in the text and in the broader interpretive community.

Endnotes

1   Elisabeth Schüssler Fiorenza, "The Will to Choose or to Reject," in Letty M. Russell, ed., *Feminist Interpretation of the Bible* (Philadelphia: Fortress Press, 1985), p. 126.
2   (Louisville, KY: Westminster/John Knox Press, 1996), p. xiii).
3   Letty M. Russell, "Liberating the Word," in *Feminist Interpretation of the Bible*, p. 12.
4   Barbara Brown Zikmund, "Feminist Consciousness in Historical Perspective," *in Feminist Interpretation of the Bible*, pp. 21-29; Carolyn De Swarte Gifford, "American Women and the Bible: The Nature of Woman as a Hermeneutical Issue," in Adela Yarbro Collins, ed., *Feminist Perspectives on Biblical Scholarship* (Atlanta, GA: Scholars Press, 1985), pp. 11-34.
5   Gifford, "American Women and the Bible," p. 15.
6   Richard Coggins, "The Contribution of Women's Studies to Old Testament Studies: A Male Reaction," *Theology* 91, 739 (1988): 5-16.
7   *Household of Freedom* (Philadelphia: Westminster Press, 1987), p. 12.
8   Mary Daly, *Beyond God the Father* (Boston: Beacon Press, 1973); *Gyn/Ecology* (Boston: Beacon Press, 1984); Daphne Hampson, *Theology and Feminism* (Cambridge, MA: Basil Blackwell, 1990).
9   Letty Russell, "Liberating the Word," p. 13.
10 Schüssler Fiorenza, *Bread Not Stone: The Challenge of Feminist Interpretation* (Boston: Beacon Press, 1884), p. xiv.
11 Marjorie Hewitt Suchocki, "Trinity," in Letty M. Russell and J. Shannon Clarkson, eds., *Dictionary of Feminist Theologies* (Louisville, KY: Westminster/ John Knox, 1996), pp. 304-305.
12 Sallie McFague, *Metaphorical Theology: Models of God in Religious Language* (Philadelphia: Fortress, 1982).
13 Elizabeth Ann Johnson, *She Who Is: The Mystery of God in Feminist Theological Discourse* (New York: Crossroad, 1990).
14 Romans 8:19-24a NRSV.
15 Letty M. Russell, *Household of Freedom: Authority in Feminist Theology* (Philadelphia: Westminster Press, 1987), p. 18.
16 See Mary Daly for a devastating critique of male language for God *(Beyond God the Father: Toward a Philosophy of Women's Liberation* [Boston: Beacon Press, 1973]). For a probing of the Father-based language of God that moves to reconstruction, see Ruth C. Duck, *Gender and the Name of God* (New York: Pilgrim Press, 1991).
17 Rosemary Radford Ruether, *Sexism and God-Talk: Toward a Feminist Theology* (Boston: Beacon Press, 1983), p. 93.
18 *She Who Is*, p. 62.
19 Margaret Farley, "Feminist Consciousness and the Interpretation of Scripture," in *Feminist Interpretation of the Bible*, p. 44.
20 "Reading from Context to Context: Contributions of a Feminist Hermeneutic to Theologies of Liberation," in Susan Brooks Thistlethwaite and Mary Potters Engel, eds., *Lift Every Voice* (San Francisco: Harper and Row, 1990), p. 287.
21 Russell, "Liberating the Word," p. 17.
22 "Feminist Consciousness and the Interpretation of Scripture," p. 47.
23 *Household of Freedom*, p. 26.
24 Ibid., p. 31.

25 "Continuing Our Critical Work," p. 126.
26 *In Memory of Her* (New York: Crossroad, 1983), pp. 103-104.
27 *Bread Not Stone*, p. 149.
28 "Feminist Interpretation: A Method of Correlation," in *Feminist Interpretation of the Bible*, p. 119.
29 "Authority and the Challenge of Feminist Interpretation," in *Feminist Interpretation of the Bible*, pp. 142-143.
30 *The Revelatory Text* (New York: Harper San Francisco, 1991), p. 49.
31 Chung Hyun Kyung, "Welcoming the Spirit: Hear Her Cries " (Council of Churches Publication, July 15, 1991), p. 223.
32 *Sexism and God-Talk*, p. 60.
33 Ibid., p. 61.
34 *In Memory of Her*, p. 199.
35 Ibid., p. 350.
36 *She Who Is*, p. 103.
37 *The Revelatory Text*, p. 73.
38 "Authority and the Challenge of Feminist Interpretation," pp. 144-146.
39 In *Memory of Her*, p. 345.
40 "Human Liberation in a Feminist Perspective," pp. 158-159.
41 *She Who Is*, p. 169
42 Ibid., p. 35.
43 *Sexism and God-Talk*, p. 138.
44 *Journeys by Heart: A Christology of Erotic Power* (New York: Crossroad, 1992).
45 *She Who Is*, p. 158.
46 Ibid., p. 167.
47 "Continuing Our Critical Work," p. 136.
48 Susanne Heine, *Women and Early Christianity: A Reappraisal* (Minneapolis: Augsburg, 1988), p. 3.
49 *Bread Not Stone*, p. 66.
50 Schüssler Fiorenza has recently published a collection of her essays in *Discipleship of Equals: A Critical Feminist Ekklesia-ology of Liberation* (New York: Crossroad, 1993). She has also further elaborated on feminist practices of biblical interpretation in her book *But She Said: The Rhetoric of Feminist Interpretation for Liberation* (Boston: Beacon Press, 1992). However, her earlier books have been the most influential in setting forth a feminist approach to biblical interpretation and thus they provide a concrete example of embodied interpretation.
51 *Bread Not Stone*, p. 91.
52 *In Memory of Her,* p. 152.
53 Ibid., p. 100.
54 Ibid., p. 102.
55 Ibid., p. 110.
56 Ibid., p. 120.
57 Ibid., p. 113.
58 Ibid., p. 120.
59 Ibid., p. 141.
60 *Bread Not Stone*, p. 66.
61 Ibid., p. 77.
62 Ibid., p. 78.
63 Ibid., p. 83.
64 Ibid., p. 86.
65 Ibid., p. 89.

66   Ibid., p. 91.
67   Ibid., p. 65.
68   Ibid., pp. 66-67.
69   Ibid., p. 70.
70   *In Memory of Her*, p. 344.
71   Ibid. p. 343.
72   Ibid. pp. 343-344.
73   Ibid., p. 344.
74   *But She Said*, p. 128.
75   Schüssler Fiorenza, as well as other feminists, has attempted to move beyond her own white feminist context, especially in her later books. She has invited conversation by other minority voices and has stood in solidarity with those who suffer. However, she, too, finds it difficult to name her own power as a respected white theologian.
76   Francis Martin, *The Feminist Question* (Grand Rapids: Eerdmans, 1994), p. 163
77   "Anti-Judaism in Christian Feminist Theology," *Tikkun* 5, 3: 96.
78   "The Color of Feminism," *Journal of Religious Thought* 43 (1983): 50.
79   "Protestant Feminists and the Bible," in Alice Bach, ed., *The Pleasure of Her Text* (Philadelphia: Trinity Press, 1990), p. 6.
80   "Responses," *The Conrad Grebel Review* 10, 2 (Spring 1992): 213.
81   Phyllis Trible, "Postscript: Jottings on the Journey," in *Feminist Interpretation of the Bible,* p. 149.
82   "Freedom, Discipleship and Theological Reflection," in Daniel Schipani, ed., *Freedom and Discipleship: Liberation Theology in an Anabaptist Perspective* (New York: Orbis Books, 1989), p. 175.
83   *In Memory of Her*, p. 345.
84   Ibid., p. 350.
85   "The Liberation of Atonement," *Mennonite Quarterly Review* 43, 2 (April 1989): 192.
86   *In Memory of Her*, pp. 344, 349-350.
87   *Feminist Method/Christian Theology* (Minneapolis: Fortress Press, 1990), p. 74.
88   *In Memory of Her*, p. 345.
89   "A Hermeneutical Understanding for Womanists: The Interrelation Between the Text and Our Experience," in Gayle Gerber Koontz and Willard Swartley, eds., *Perspectives on Feminist Hermeneutics*, Occasional Papers, 10 (Elkhart, IN: Institute of Mennonite Studies, 1987), p. 24
90   "Creating Justice in the Space Around Us," in Elizabeth G. Yoder, ed., *Peace Theology and Violence Against Women,* Occasional Papers, 16 (Elkhart, IN: Institute of Mennonite Studies, 1992), p. 22, n 4.
91   Walter Brueggeman, *Interpretation and Obedience* (Minneapolis: Fortress Press, 1996), p. 125.

Chapter 4

Discipleship and Authority: The Gospel of Mark

Recent Marcan scholars can rather easily be divided into two groups according to their interpretation of the language of power and authority in the text. Most agree that power issues are prominent theological concerns in the gospel.[1] Many recognize the power/powerlessness theme in the gospel as part of a larger "theme/counter theme pattern" within the text.[2] They agree that the ethos of authority pervading the gospel is related to how the disciples are pictured in the narrative. However, interpreters begin to diverge as they reconstruct the history of the composition of the text and as they begin to look at the possible effect of these texts in the early community. Redactional scholars have not been able to agree whether particular passages represent a theme or a counter theme, a claim or a counter claim, a confession or an anti-confession, because they cannot agree on which parts of the gospel are the work of the redactor and which are the work of the community tradition. But more importantly, interpreters differ as to how they see the language of power functioning in the community to which the gospel was directed.

Interpreters tend to resolve this apparent paradox in either of two ways. The first way sees power and authority as creative or formative of a new community and its way of life. It celebrates the potential that the powerful presence of Jesus brings to the community of disciples. Salvation through the death and resurrection of Jesus, and the call and commissioning of disciples, are keys to this view of power. These readings are based on an assumption of divine power and authority working through the event of Jesus. Several books by Ernest Best on discipleship illustrate this approach to the text.[3]

The second direction sees power and authority as dangerous to a community. It assumes that the language of power and authority functions to combat a false understanding of Jesus and the kingdom of God in the community. This false understanding has to do with a theology of triumph built on the tradition of miracles and resurrection, a theology that denies the cross and suffering. The gospel was written to refute these understandings and to affirm a theology of the cross in which salvation comes through following the crucified Jesus. These readings focus on human interactions and point out the misuse of power in the community. Theodore Weeden is representative of the scholars who move in this direction.[4]

These two approaches are similar to the ways in which the presence of women in the gospels is interpreted. For example, Elizabeth Struthers Malbon sees Mark as emphasizing the reversal of expectations in the early church and society by presenting the women as the first to know about the resurrection.[5] Mary Ann Beavis also concludes that women are seen as models of faith.[6] In contrast, Winsome Munro sees Mark as suppressing the historical presence of women in the history of Christianity.[7] Susan Lochrie Graham emphasizes the silence of the suffering, serving women in the gospel.[8]

As I began to reread and study the book of Mark for myself, I was tempted to resolve the conflict between the various interpretations by choosing one of these directions to orient me in my study. I could, with some justification, assume that the author had one of these purposes in mind as he wrote the gospel. In that way, I would not have to live with the tensions that seemed to be inherent to the text itself. I could move quickly toward an interpretation that would give me a clear definition of discipleship.

My commitment to a dynamic interaction with the text led me in another direction. I soon realized that making this choice at the beginning of my study, as both the Mennonite and the feminist hermeneutic communities would urge me to do, would jeopardize any openness to hearing what the text itself had to say. My analysis of the two hermeneutic communities that form my primary context cautioned me against this easy solution. I could now more easily see how the definition of discipleship as obedience, which came primarily from the Mennonite hermeneutic community, moved me in the direction of the first stream while the feminist definition of discipleship as subversive of human authority moved me into continuity with the second stream. I became aware of the need to respect the integrity of the text itself as a critical dialogue partner. Therefore a new approach was needed, an approach that would allow the ancient text to challenge modern thinking while accepting the pre-judgements that arise from my particular context of interpretation.

The approach that I chose admits my self-involvement in the inter-pretative task. My prior assumptions did influence what I could see in the text. However, by accepting the tension that came about because I was aware of the conflicting positions of authority that my context gave me, I could more easily accept the tensions and conflicts present within the text itself. I could postpone the resolution of the tensions until after I immersed myself in the world of the text. In this way, I was able to be more self-conscious about some of the choices about authority that I was making as I read and reflected on the possible meanings of the text. These choices in turn suggested to me some specific challenges for each of the hermeneutic communities of which I am a part.

One implication of this approach was that I had to pay attention both to the truth claims that the text was making and the function that the specific text had within the larger narrative. I needed to be aware when I was assenting to the text and when I was disagreeing with the text. I had to note my own critical responses to the text's claims. In the process, I began to be suspicious of a quick sense of continuity between my own convictions and the text and noted instead those places where alternative interpretations disrupted my easy assurances. This allowed me to see how these interpretations functioned for me in each of my interpretive communities.

The rereading of the text therefore became focused on the places of tension, on the contradictions with my own assumptions. I began to identify with the real struggle that readers of the Gospel of Mark face—readers who reject the authority claims of the gospel, as well as readers who wish to name themselves disciples in continuity with the description of the disciples given by the gospel writer. I also became aware that simple historical distance from the text created space for differing interpretations and shades of meaning.

Authority and Power: Definitions and Directions

Several working assumptions and interpretive directions arose out of my commitment to respect the integrity of the text as asserting truth claims of its own and having its own rhetorical purpose.

The Construal of Power and Authority

Respecting the integrity of the text implies that the historical distance between the gospel writer of the first century and the reader in the twentieth century will be respected.[9] This can prevent a premature identification of data in the text with present day authority issues that may have been foreign to the hermeneutic community of Mark. Therefore, I do not begin by choosing one of the conclusions that other scholars have come to about the role of women in the community. In fact, the tension between the scholars warns me to leave this hermeneutical decision until I have studied the gospel more thoroughly. I also do not begin by choosing between the divine authority of Scripture or the human nature of the Bible. Though in a study of biblical authority this decision is central, it will not be made until after I listen carefully to the text itself. Instead, my analysis will ask about the *ethos of authority* that surfaces in the plot and in the characterizations in the book. Only after that pattern has emerged will the matter of the relationship between male and female authority be addressed, as well as the issue of the authority of the Bible in history.

Historical distance will be taken into account in the attempt to understand the vocabulary used by Mark. Walter Wink has written a book in which he attempts to comprehend power language within the context of the Hellenistic and Hebrew culture of the first century. He points out that a primary assumption for the writers of the New Testament was the close association of spiritual and material factors in the notion of power.[10] Our modern, sociological categories describe power and authority within a cause-and-effect framework that looks primarily for human, non-spiritual causes for any exercise of power in the world. For example, if someone destroys another life in a ruthless murder, sociologists look for reasons for this senseless action in the family background or in the emotional and psychological state of the murderer. Power as understood in the worldview and religious system of the century that produced the Gospel of Mark included the spiritual, mythic world in its descriptions.

This can be illustrated by examining the vocabulary used in the Gospel of Mark. It includes terms such as *exousia* (authority), *dynamis* (power), *archon* (ruler) and *basileia* (kingdom). Each of these terms indicates the larger cosmological framework of spiritual and material forces that is assumed to be present in the world. In the New Testament, *exousia* usually has the sense of the right or the authority to exercise power and is used primarily to speak of human arrangements or "legitimations, sanctions, and permissions that undergird the everyday exercise of power."[11] However, it is also used to speak of the authority of God. In Mark it is used to describe Jesus' teaching (1:22, 27), his exorcisms and healings (1:27) and his forgiveness of sins (2:10). It is also used to describe the "authority or power" that Jesus transmits to his disciples (3:15, 6:17); it also denotes the authority that is recognized as a threat by his opponents (11:28, 29, 33). *Dynamis* refers not so much to the right but to the ability or power to act and so is used to describe the powerful deeds or miracles of Jesus (6:2, 5) and also the powers in the heavens (13:25, 14:62). In Mark, both *exousia* and *dynamis* are associated with Jesus and his ministry, a ministry in which the ambiguity of divine/human power is most evident.

Variations of the terms *arche* and *archon* are used to describe human power arrangements (10:42), but are also used to speak of the ruler of the demons (3:23). *Basileia*, a term that can be defined as the reign of a king, as well as the sphere in which the king is acknowledged, is used in the phrase "kingdom of God," again bringing together the spiritual and material realms that often become separated in modern thinking.

Wink summarizes the language of power and authority by noting its two dimensions.[12] Power and authority are seen as heavenly and earthly, divine and human, spiritual and political, and invisible and structural. Power and authority can be experienced as good or evil. The conflict between good and evil power encompasses both the material and the spiritual realm. A careful look at the language of power and authority in Mark must therefore be marked by an approach that does not assume a deep division between sociological and theological categories.

The Construal of the Text

One way of respecting the integrity of the text is to focus on its final form, rather than on certain redactional variants of the text or on the possible oral sources of the text. This is not to deny the variations that there may have been throughout the textual history of the Gospel of Mark or the complexities of its compositional history. Rather, it is to assume that the final form has been carefully put together by an author or editor in order to transmit a message.[13] It is to assume that the contradictions that we see may not have seemed contradictory to that author or editor. Much care must therefore be taken to first try to understand the text as it now stands. This includes paying attention to the particular literary form of the gospel. Because the narrative form gives some clues as to the larger rhetorical purpose of the gospel, the greatest attention in this analysis will be given to a narrative reading of the gospel as a whole.

In Mark, theological teaching and narrative are intertwined in the plot. Truth claims are made while characters interact and struggle with the presence of Jesus. A study of how the parables become part of the larger story-line gives us some clues as to how theological teaching and narrative interact. For example, it soon becomes clear that when the gospel writer places a parable or saying into the mouth of Jesus, he highlights a teaching or vision that he probably understands as important for his community. These claims to truth are not proved rationally so that no doubt can remain in our minds. Nor do they attempt to be universal in the sense that they claim to be true in every situation imaginable. Instead, these claims are rooted in the narrative itself. The parables seem to be placed in crucial places in order to serve as sources of orientation to the truth as experienced by characters in the gospel narrative.[14]

Mary Ann Tolbert has named two parables natural "plot synopses" of the gospel narrative in the manner of early Hellenistic literature.[15] Her study suggests that the gospel uses rhetorical devices similar to those used by popular Hellenistic literature of the times which allowed the hearers to follow the narrative as it was read aloud.[16] This literature was intended to persuade hearers and readers, to communicate using literary patterns and conventions shared by author and audience. The parables are markers or signposts, intended to act as guides in the interpretation of the story. They are not intended to be confusing, misleading or obscure for the reader. Instead, as stories told by Jesus, the central character in the narrative, the parables carry the authority to describe the reality of the situation in which the community finds itself.[17] They allow the audience to interpret correctly the various episodes that make up the narrative. They provide us with some of the presuppositions in the narration of the story.[18]

It is interesting to note that issues of power and authority are at the heart of these parables. One group of parables, the seed and soils parables, focus on the potential power or energy of the new reality of the kingdom (4:1-32). These parables show the divine initiative in sowing seed and the various human responses that limit the actual growth of the seed. These parables are suitably placed in the first half of the gospel, where the authoritative proclamation of good news and the powerful healing practices of Jesus are described. A parable in the later part of the gospel, the wicked tenant/beloved son parable, focuses on the human misuse of delegated authority and power and the divine response to that misuse (12:1-12). This parable is placed in the context of questions about Jesus' authority and the growing conflict leading to the death of Jesus. These parables can be read retrospectively as well as prospectively and therefore each of them summarizes the plot of the whole narrative from its particular point of view.

These parables can therefore provide a unique perspective in a rereading of the narrative, a perspective that is inherent rather than foreign to the text itself. This perspective encourages us to focus on two functions of authority and power—the creative function of power and the subversive function of power—before asking how these perspectives are brought together in the gospel itself.

The Construal of the Community

In recent years there has been much speculation about the geographical and historical identification of the community for whom Mark wrote the gospel. Considerable debate has been created about the geographical setting, whether in northern Palestine or Rome, and the exact date when the gospel was written. Because the context is not specifically named in the text, a number of different places and times have been suggested.

These differing reconstructions of the community context can result in distinct perspectives on the function of the authority language in Mark. In this analysis, the decision about a specific community context will be bracketed until after the text is more carefully studied. At the same time, the work of social historians will provide some necessary background that will allow a reading of the text with some knowledge about the general social, economic and political milieu of that time.

The functions that the narrative could have in a community can be imagined by studying the text itself to see what hints it gives. However, the functions that are imaginable for any scholar may be more closely related to the experience of the scholar than to the intent of the author. This ambiguity in reading practice again emphasizes the need to articulate the particular construal of the hermeneutic community that influences the interpretation of the text.[19] By embracing both the Mennonite and feminist communities as crucial contexts for my interpretation, I am acknowledging the variety of ways in which power and authority can be understood in a community. In this broader conversation about the meaning of the texts, I must pay attention to both directions that are indicated by recent studies on the Gospel of Mark. This will be done by studying the meaning of the two parables within their narrative context.

The Creative Function of Kingdom Power

The seed and soils parables in Mark 4 point to the capacity of some soils to bear fruit, as well as the failure of other soils to produce a harvest. These are simple stories, easily understood in the context of an agricultural economy. However, by connecting these parables so closely to the kingdom of God, the author relates them to understandings of kingly power, political realities and political relationships. It is the relationship to the kingdom that is ambiguous and needs interpretation. Attention will therefore be given to how the characters in the narrative are identified with the power of the kingdom.

Insiders and Outsiders

In the group of parables about seed and soil, the power that comes with vision and insight is connected to knowing the secret of the kingdom. The ability to grow and bring forth fruit is promised to those who "hear." As a result, insiders and outsiders to the secret are created. This polarity is clearly stated in a summary statement in Mark 4.

> To you has been given the secret of the kingdom of God, but for those outside everything comes in parables; in order that "they may indeed look, but not perceive, and may indeed listen, but not understand; so that they may not turn again and be forgiven." (4:11-12)

In these seed and soil parables, perceiving and understanding is connected to fruit-bearing and harvest, to an image of power or energy that can transform the seed into fruit, thirty, sixty and a hundredfold (4:20). Those inside have been given the secret that will lead to fruit bearing. Those outside look and listen but do not perceive and understand. Thus they do not bear fruit. Insiders are created by the ability to understand the parables. Outsiders continue to hear the parable but they do not understand.

The narrative that precedes chapter 4 gives some help in identifying the two groups that are named in these verses. A contrast between those "around him" and those "outside" can be noted (3:31-35). Mark seems to have deliberately refused to name "the twelve" as the inner group. Instead he teaches the meaning of the parables to "those who were around him along with the twelve" (4:10). These were the ones he named mother, brother and sister. Significantly, this group is not limited to either male or female members. Instead, the group included all who did the will of God.

A further identification comes at the end of chapter 4. In this incident, Jesus is teaching them in parables "as they were able to hear it" (4:33). The narrative goes on to say that he spoke in parables to the crowd, but that "he explained everything in private to his disciples." The disciples, which here includes the broader category of followers, are identified as that group that is gaining inside knowledge, but only as much as they are able to absorb. The expectation is created that they will bear fruit.[20]

Throughout the gospel there are hints that Mark assumed this basic division between insiders and outsiders. The various sayings that are scattered throughout the gospel add to this impression. A number of short pithy statements are placed in the mouth of Jesus, serving as authoritative promises to the insider and warnings to the outsider. John Donahue has pointed out that these gnomic sayings are divided fairly equally between those addressed to the twelve and those addressed to a wider audience.[21] He has pointed out that many of these gnomic sayings involve concrete instances of the crucial division hinted at in chapter 3—between doing God's will or not doing God's will. These instances include:

> respect for God's creative intent in marriage (10:11); losing ones life "for the gospel" (8:35); forsaking riches (10:43-44); enduring persecution (13:13); welcoming the powerless children (9:36-37); living a life of service (10:43-44); performing the duties of hospitality (9:41) and trust in the power of prayer (11:23).[22]

The sayings often include a promise of a reward, such as the saving of one's life (8:35), the last being first (10:31) or prayer being answered (11:23). However, these promises are usually juxtaposed with warnings directed to the outsider. Doing the will of God is juxtaposed to blaspheming against the Holy Spirit and thus not receiving forgiveness (3:29, 35). Losing life is juxtaposed to saving life, being last to being first (8:35, 10:31).

This pronounced dualism has proved to be a difficult hermeneutical problem for many interpreters.[23] The condemnation seems severe and unwarranted. Suggestions have been made that these words were placed into the mouth of Jesus by later redactors who wished to use Jesus' authority to further their own views. It is Mark's muddled redaction that has produced the dualism in Mark 4.[24] A use of that approach is not helpful, however, if one assumes that the actual words of the historical Jesus can never be conclusively separated from the views of the community. Instead, these assertions must be seen in the context of the larger narrative in order to see what function they have rhetorically for the author.

Mary Ann Tolbert suggests that in a narrative reading, parables are not told *so that* some will not understand. Rather "the parables like Jesus' healing and preaching ministry in general, do not force people outside or pull people inside; they simply reveal the type of ground already present."[25] The typology used here is thus one of disclosure and interaction, rather than one of conversion and dominance.[26] What is made very clear in the gospel is that the kingdom of God is a secret that will be revealed (4:21-22). Hearing the parable will affirm for the readers and listeners of the gospel that they can be insiders who bring forth fruit because they understand. Though there are warnings to the outsider, the effect is to point to the promise.

This promise frames the whole gospel and is hinted at in both the beginning and end of the gospel. "The beginning of good news" implies that there will be new understanding that comes with Jesus (1:1). "There you will see him, just as he told you" implies that the promise given through the life time of Jesus continues after his death (16:7).

This suggests that the dualistic language functions to point to the reality of what happens when the kingdom is proclaimed. The Word of God divides the listeners by creating a new vision and a new possibility of being. With the presentation of the new reality of the kingdom comes the need to make a choice. Jesus is the catalyst that interrupts previous commitments and requires new allegiances.

The Ambiguity of Jesus' Power

There have been a variety of opinions about the primary emphasis in the parable of 4: 1-9, often called the parable of the sower. Is it the soil, the seed or the sower that carries the most weight in the story? Does authority and power lie in the sower, the word that is sown or the soil which may or may not bring forth fruit? This, however, is not the concern of the parable. Rather the parable points to the limitations created by certain kinds of soils and the possibility of an incredible harvest in the right kind of soil. Thus there is an ambiguity about the actual source of power.

The other parables in the chapter carry on the ambiguity. "The kingdom is as if *someone* would scatter seed on the ground" (4:26), "the *earth* produces *of itself* first the stalk, then the head, then the full grain in the head" (4:28), it is like a mustard *seed*, which, when sown upon the ground. . . . becomes the greatest of all shrubs" (4:31-32). The metaphor shifts and changes, creating nuances that bring about ambiguity and paradox.

The ambiguity surrounding the power and authority of the sower in the parable is parallelled by the way Jesus' authority is described in the narrative. Jesus seems to be identified primarily with the sower in the longer narrative. Though he is pictured as powerful, he is not pictured as having final control of the results of his ministry. As Tolbert points out: "Jesus can exorcise demons, calm the waters and the winds, and overcome death, but he cannot force those he heals to obey his admonitions or give faith and understanding to his disciples."[27] This irony pervades the narrative as told by Mark. Jesus is connected to both divine power and human vulnerability.

Literary critics have pointed how the narrative affirms a strong connection between divine authority and Jesus. Jesus is pictured as functioning with abilities normally reserved for the public narrator. He is established as the "evaluative centre" of the story in the prologue (1:1-13), through a series of reliable witnesses including scriptural quotations, prophetic announcements, a voice from heaven, cosmic and apocalyptic signs.[28] The most direct affirmation comes from God who, as a speaking character, enters the narrative at the baptism and the Transfiguration. Throughout the story, the demons immediately recognize Jesus' divine authority and when they are told to be silent they obey.[29] Thus the readers are never led to question the inevitability of the link to the divine and the cosmic triumph of Jesus over Satan.

    Throughout the gospel it is made clear that the power of the kingdom is exercised through Jesus' words and actions. Already in the prologue John proclaims that the one coming is more powerful, for he will baptize with the Holy Spirit (1:8). The power of Jesus is immediately demonstrated by the authoritative way in which Jesus calls disciples, teaches, casts out the unclean spirits, heals and interprets the law. The miracles of Jesus are called deeds of power (6:2), rather than signs and wonders as are the deeds of false messiahs and false prophets (13:22). The teaching is authoritative, not like that of the scribes (1:21). Jesus does not permit the demons to speak and they obey. The term *exousia* is explicitly connected with Jesus' teaching, his exorcisms and healing, and his forgiveness of sins. He enters Jerusalem as a king and occupies the temple, the ultimate authoritative centre of worship for the community.

    As pointed out by Senior, Mark's overall portrayal of Jesus and his mission is a

> vigorous, powerful onslaught of the rule of God, signalled at the very outset of his ministry (1:14-15), demonstrated in his acts of exorcism, healing and teaching, brought into sharp relief in his conflicts with opponents, shared with his disciples (3:15;6:7), and whose consummation "in power (*dynamis*)" will be manifested at the coming of the Son of Man (14:62, 13:26).[30]

There is no doubt that Jesus is identified as the "strong man" who will break the power of Satan. Thus Jesus represents both divine authority and divine power in the plot and drama. This leads the readers to align themselves with Jesus and the authority that is claimed for him.

    Though Jesus is pictured as divinely empowered in the gospel, he is not identified completely with God, nor depicted as an all-powerful divine being in his ministry among the people. Though the readers know of this divine authority, the characters in the story struggle with Jesus' authority, as with that of a human person. The humanness of Jesus is communicated in a variety of ways.

    First of all, Jesus is pictured as part of the community, just as other members would be. He is the carpenter from Nazareth, the son of Mary and the brother of James, Joses, Judas, Simon and several sisters (6:3). He gets angry and sad (3:5), speaks sternly (3:12), seeks to avoid the crowd (7:24) and is amazed at the unbelief of people (6:6). Jesus relates to God as other humans do. He prays to God (1:35, 6:45, 14:32-41), has beliefs based on the traditions that only God is good (10:18) and that the Lord our God is one (12:29). He participates in synagogue and temple worship (6:2, 12:35). In a very human way, he challenges and accuses the religious authorities in terms of their interpretation of the law (7:1-12), he argues with a Syrophoenician woman (7:24-30) and he rebukes his disciples (8:33). At the prospect of arrest and death, Jesus is distressed and agitated (14:33) and in his dying moment his only words are a cry that witness to his feelings of being forsaken by God (15:34).

The ambiguity of Jesus' authority is highlighted at those times when the crowd or individual characters in the story are faced with the choice between various human authorities (e.g., Mark 2:1-12, 15:6-15). These characters are well aware that the question of authority is a crucial one because it is overtly discussed throughout the story. Sometimes, the discussion focuses on the legitimation of Jesus' authority. There are arguments about the origin of his authority—being from Beelzebub or from the Holy Spirit (3:1-28), being human or from heaven (11:27-33) and whether he is a prophet or the Messiah (8:27-30). His home town struggles with the question of how someone born and raised in Nazareth could have such wisdom and power (6:1-6).

However, increasingly the question of authority becomes a question of power. As pointed out by Rhoads and Michie, "In the story, the portrayal of Jesus changes from the powerful one who relieves suffering to the vulnerable one who is the victim of suffering."[31] This vulnerability is particularly poignant in the scenes of Jesus' arrest and death, where irony pervades the entire scene (14:53-15:39). Jesus, who is announcing the kingdom, is mocked as a King. Jesus, known as prophet, is blindfolded and told to prophesy by those who have just heard false testimony. Jesus, as teacher of the "good," is crucified between criminals. The taunts by the official leaders, whose power and authority had been previously questioned by Jesus, express the irony clearly. "He saved others; he cannot save himself. Let the Messiah, the King of Israel, come down from the cross now, so that we may see and believe"(15:31-32).

Though depicted as vulnerable, Jesus is not presented as weak. Though empowered by God, Jesus makes real choices. Tolbert has pointed out how the secrecy motif adds to a picture of a person who chooses to reject personal glory and honour.[32] His commands to silence and his attempts to stay hidden are choices he makes in order to avoid fame and give God the credit (1:34; 2:12; 3:12; 5:19,43; 7:24; 10:18, etc.). As Jesus moves to the cross, he continues to be described as someone who takes initiative and makes difficult choices. In Gethsemane, he is distressed and troubled, but in contrast to the disciples, he actively chooses a direction and takes the initiative to meet his betrayer and the enemy armed with clubs and swords (14:32-43). Jesus confronts those who arrest him by asking why they have brought weapons when he could have easily been apprehended at any time (14:48-49). During the trial, Jesus refuses to speak when asked to defend himself against false witness; yet he openly confesses his relationship to God and his kingship when it is extremely dangerous to do so (14:60-62; 15:2). Though his death makes him appear vulnerable, it is the occasion for two very powerful responses to his life. The first, a powerful ripping of the temple curtain is apparently an action of God. The second, a confession of Jesus as son of God by the centurion who had helped crucify him, is described as a human response to an authority visible to all, but acknowledged by few

In summary, Jesus' authority is described as legitimated by divine signs of approval. At the same time, his authority is most clearly revealed in the choices that he makes as a human person confronted with choices similar to those others make in their daily life. These choices include depending on God's power, as well as using the authority he has in healing, non-oppressive ways. His presence therefore becomes the catalyst for the unmasking necessary to create a new kind of kingdom on earth.

The Unmasking of the Soil

The various soils are not the same according to the parable in 4:1-9, just as the responses of the characters in the story to Jesus are not the same. It is the sowing of the seed that exposes the quality of the soils, showing some as unfruitful. It is the proclamation of the Word that exposes the limitations of the hearers of Jesus' words. If we place the parable beside the longer narrative, we can identify the various soils by the way the various listening groups are described.[33] Two of these groups, the insiders and the outsiders, are pictured in terms of "flat" characterization, thus pointing to their typological function in the narrative.[34] The third group is "round" with complex characterization. These are the ones who hear the word but various obstacles keep them from bearing fruit. A closer look at these three groups will point to the power of the presence of Jesus in the story. This power serves to unmask and disclose the identity of each of the soils, an identity that is often hidden under the guise of human status and power.

The insiders. The insiders that bear fruit can be identified because of the unexpected bounty of the harvest. Tolbert points out that since a fivefold to tenfold harvest was normal for Palestine in the first century, the yield suggested in the parable is beyond imagination.[35] The parables in 4:26-32 add further metaphors to clearly indicate that when fruit is produced, it is a mystery. The surprise lies both in the effortless way in which the growth happens as well as in the contrast between the small beginning and the great end result. Therefore, focusing on those parts of the story in which there is both unexpected response as well as surprising praise will help identify the insiders to the kingdom.

The four episodes following the parables are particularly important for identifying the unexpected good soil (4:35-5:43).[36] Jesus questions his disciples as they tremble in fear on their little boat in the midst of the storm. This points to the crucial characteristic that Jesus is looking for in the insider. "Why are you afraid? Have you still no faith?" he asks the disciples. However, it is not disciples, the ones expected to exhibit faith and overcome fear, who provide us with examples of good soil. Instead, we must look in unexpected places.

In the next incident, a man possessed by demons, lives among the dead in the tombs, and although self destructive and out of control, nevertheless recognizes Jesus as the Son of the most high God. He bows before him and shouts out his requests. Jesus responds to the man, sending the spirits into a herd of pigs. The townspeople are afraid when they see the powerful results of the exorcism. Surprisingly, this man who was healed is commanded to go to his own people and his own land to tell them what the Lord has done for him. The story ends with "and everyone was amazed" (5:20). The healed man produces an abundant harvest for everyone to see. The next episodes, which involve the healing of two females, are intercalated, with the number twelve providing a close connection between the stories. The woman with a haemorrhage illustrates the move from fear to faith. The courage to touch the garment of Jesus results in a healing before Jesus even actively responds to her. Jesus exhortation to Jairus not to fear, only believe, confirms the opposition between faith and fear. Only the parents of Jairus' daughter and his disciples were privy to the healing, presumably because they had faith. And again the response is "they were overcome with amazement." The result was even greater than expected, for even those presumed dead could be raised.

Healing and faith are closely related in these stories that describe the good soil that brings forth fruit. The people exemplifying faith are from a broad spectrum of society, including the outsider (the demoniac), the unclean (the woman) and the leader of the synagogue (Jairus). Often they overcome great obstacles in order to gain Jesus' attention. This is evident also in other stories in the gospel. The paralytic is healed when friends overcome the obstacles created by a great crowd. Here it is the faith of the friends that brings both forgiveness and healing. The Syrophoenician woman persists in asking for healing despite Jesus' rejection of her first plea. Jesus praises her insight and persistence, indicating that the healing of her daughter was the result of her words (7: 24-30). The healing of Bartimaeus concludes a section in which the question of who is first and who is last is prominent (Mark 10). Jesus' specifically commends Bartimaeus' faith. Bartimaeus becomes the paradigm or symbolic ideal of a disciple who does not seek honour and glory when asked what he wanted Jesus to do for him. In contrast to James and John, he asks "to see again." He is healed and follows Jesus "on the way."

It is interesting that in the Gospel of Mark, Jesus almost never initiates the healings. Instead, it is simply his presence that mobilizes people of faith to come to him and plead with him. Often, the crowds who observe these healings are amazed and glorify God. The ones who are healed are usually minor characters, often anonymous, who serve to exemplify the values of the kingdom rather than the values of this world. They are characterized as without human power or status and their fruit bearing qualities are therefore often hidden. Several episodes illustrate how these "little people" are deliberately associated with the kingdom of God.[37] In the first instance, Jesus places the child in the centre of the community (9:33-37). Here the disciples, who have been arguing about who is the greatest, are urged to welcome a child into the kingdom, "for whoever wants to be first must be last of all and servant of all."

A second episode about children is just as illuminating (10:13-16). When the disciples try to keep away those who are bringing children, Jesus sharply rebukes them and insists that children belong to the kingdom. This story is placed next to the story of the man who did not follow Jesus because of his many possessions. Children without status and economic power are unexpected participants in the kingdom.

Another clear example is the story of the widow's offering in which her contribution is viewed as greater than that of the many rich who put large sums in the treasury (12:41-44). The contrast between the widow who gives freely and the scribes who "devour widows' houses and for the sake of appearance say long prayers" illustrates the sharp contrast between the insiders and outsiders that is evident throughout the narrative.

Often these little people are shown as serving Jesus in special caring ways. The woman who anointed Jesus' head or the women at the tomb who wished to anoint Jesus become important examples of insiders. They are people with courage who risk something in order to serve Jesus. They exemplify those who are often seen as last but will be placed first, or those who lose their life but will gain it.

Thus faith versus fear and apparent powerlessness versus the reaching for status and honour characterizes the people who are seen as insiders to the kingdom. They are the ones who have heard and understood the word and have allowed the word to change their lives. They experience the presence of Jesus as an invitation for healing and participation in the kingdom.

The outsiders. There is a second group of characters who seem to be clearly identified as outsiders. These are the ones for whom everything comes in parables in order that "they may not turn again and be forgiven" (4:12). They are the ones who "have nothing" and "even what they have will be taken away" (4:25). They are not insiders to the teaching of Jesus because their hearts are already hardened.

This group can rather easily be identified by the listening audience because of the stereotypical way in which the group is pictured. These are the Jewish or Gentile authorities who are in positions of power and leadership. These are the ones opposed to Jesus from the beginning and the ones who do not change their stance throughout the story. They are the opponents to Jesus and are pictured as a group. Herod, Pilate and the High Priest are the individual representatives of this group.

Rhoads and Michie point out several consistent traits that characterize this group.[38] They are blind to the rule of God, they "lord over" people and they are anxious to save their own power, importance, wealth and lives. Though they are often in dialogue with Jesus, their questions imply accusations rather than openness to learning. They aim to trap Jesus, in order to get rid of him. Several examples point to the escalation of violence that comes with the attitudes and actions of these characters.

Chapters 2 and 3 of Mark show this escalation by the way the questions by the authorities become ever more intense and determined. The simple Greek term for why (*ti*) in 2:7 changes to *hoti* (16), *dia ti* (18) and *ide ti* (24), until the Pharisees conspire with the Herodians to destroy Jesus.[39] This odd coalition of leaders returns again at the end of the narrative, when religious leaders and political authorities, including Herod and Pilate, cooperate in ensuring the death penalty for Jesus.

The "why"questions continue throughout the gospel without any more openness to really hearing the word. Chapter 7 points out this hardness of hearts. The Pharisees come to ask Jesus why the disciples do not live according to the traditions of the elders. Jesus points out how the Pharisees' and scribes' concern with the tradition allows them to use the commandments of God in order to get away with not fulfilling their obligations to their parents. In other words, the commandments can be twisted for their own gain. In this story, the contrast is between human tradition and God's commandments. A similar contrast between the human and the divine comes in the direct discussion about authority in chapter 11.

Jesus' critique of these authorities is particularly devastating. Several times he warns the disciples to beware of their teaching (8:15, 12:38-40). They are pictured as seeking status and for the sake of appearance saying long prayers. The narrator adds to this picture how they feared both Jesus and the crowd that followed Jesus (11:18, 12:12). They are thus pictured as weak and impotent, catering to self-interest and popular opinion. The fruit of this kind of soil is the cruel death of Jesus, the one embodying divine authority. There is no doubt in the mind of the hearers as to the unfruitfulness of these outsiders to the kingdom, who cannot be forgiven because they refuse to hear the word. This group experiences the presence of Jesus as a challenge to their authority and a condemnation of their actions. Fear and violent anger characterize this group.

The potential fruitful followers. The strong dualism and stereotypical depiction that permeates both the narrative and the parables is mediated by an elaboration of the concrete obstacles that keep the potential followers from hearing the word. There are various characteristics of the soils that allow the sprouting of the seed, but that do not encourage its growth. It is these obstacles that make outsiders of insiders and that suggest that hearing the word is not easy and natural. Thus the main rhetorical purpose of the parable is to remind the listeners, the potential followers, to understand and to become the right kind of soil.

The clue that will help identify those in the narrative who potentially can become either productive or unproductive soil is the word "listen." This moves the focus to the ones who ask questions in order to learn, to those who are the recipients of special teaching in the gospel story. Their fruitfulness is not assured until their response is fully shown. This group of characters can most easily be identified as the group that Jesus corrects, reprimands and warns because the possibility of fruit is there. The final evaluation of these characters is kept open, thereby allowing the readers to identify with them in both their failures and their successes. These potential fruitful followers include the twelve but also individuals from the other groups, such as Joseph of Arimathea, the centurion, the women at the crucifixion and the tomb, and the "scribe who is not far from the kingdom." They include leaders and ordinary persons in the community. They may also include the family of Jesus who misunderstands him but who provide the occasion for an important teaching against exclusiveness in the kingdom (3:31-35).

The followers, as a group, constitute those persons who have conflicting traits and therefore those with whom the readers will most easily identify. The initial impression the readers get of these followers is that they are on the way, that they answer the call of Jesus to become members of the new family around him. Simon, Andrew, James, John and Levi provide these first positive examples. The mother-in-law of Peter, who serves, could also be included in this group. The twelve are appointed from this group to have authority to proclaim and cast out demons (3:13-16; 6:6-13).

From the beginning, the readers understand that the loyalty that characterizes this group is not ultimate, nor is it fully tested. Even more clear is that these followers are uncomprehending and misunderstand the kingdom of God. This is particularly shown in the two feeding miracles and the boat scenes in chapters 6-8. According to the parable in 4:1-20 the obstacles to hearing involve primarily three aspects. The followers illustrate all of these characteristics. (1) Satan comes and takes away the word that is sown (4:15). If we identify the "word" with Jesus' words we can see several instances that could be understood as Satan's blocking of the followers' ability to remember. Note that Peter's words of rebuke are identified by Jesus as Satan's word in 8:33. Peter has not understood Jesus' words about the cross. Instead he has accepted Satan's words. Note also how the women need to be reminded of Jesus' word promising resurrection when they are faced with Jesus' death (16:7). (2) The ones hearing the word lack root so that they endure only for a short time. Trouble or persecution cause these listeners to fall away. The followers all clearly illustrate this tendency as they desert Jesus and flee when he is arrested (14:50). Here the women seem to be an exception. (3) The cares of the world and the lure of wealth and the desire for other things come in and choke the word. The disciples certainly desire glory and honour (10:35-45) and the lure of wealth is a struggle for them as seen by their questions after the rich man leaves Jesus (10:17-31).

It is this group of listeners to Jesus' proclamation and teaching who are faced with decision. This is the group with whom the readers of the gospel can most easily identify. They can easily relate to the social expectations that dominate the identity of these disciples. They recognize that they too can be transformed as a result of the story that is being told, the "seed" that is sown by

Mark. The ending is therefore crucial because it speaks a word of hope to these disciples who often fail to be faithful. It reminds them to go back to Galilee, that place where healing and teaching occurred. There they can become soil that will bring forth fruit. These leaders thus experience the power of the kingdom in its challenge to them to return for greater transformation and instruction.

A New Identity

By using the parables of the seed and soil as plot synopses, the potential power of the kingdom that can transform seed into fruit is identified and named. Jesus, as the embodiment of divine power, enters the world, creating new choices for the people who meet him. Through the unmasking created by his presence and actions, Jesus exposes the identity and character of the people around him. The soil in which the seed is sown represents those who have the opportunity to experience his proclamation, his healing, his teaching and his confrontation. They become the primary field of struggle between the two alternatives— bearing no fruit and becoming outsiders to the kingdom or bearing fruit and becoming insiders who experience Jesus' transforming power. Faith and fear are alternative responses to this offer of healing power.

In this reading of Mark, the focus is on identity and embodiment. The terms *insiders* and *outsiders* are not used to describe the attitudes toward someone who excludes others, nor the feelings of someone who feels excluded. Instead, they describe the essence of a person or community in the eyes of God. Being inside or outside depends on our primary identity, as good soil or unproductive soil. This identity is revealed and disclosed as people meet Jesus. The power of the kingdom as embodied in Jesus' preaching, healing and exorcism exposes the identity of the people that he encounters. This exposure is often surprising. It can lead persons to further attempts to disguise their weakness and fear or it can lead persons to seek healing and forgiveness.

Jesus, with his authoritative presence, invites women and men to become insiders. He invites them to become vulnerable by admitting their weakness and seeking healing. Transformation is available through the presence of God embodied in Jesus. The choice is difficult because of the need for status and authority and the fear of a revelation of weakness and sin.

The sharp dualism between insiders and outsiders that is seen in the teaching of Jesus is also evident in the narrative of the gospel. However, the sharpness is somewhat lessened because the choice is clearly left to the hearer of the word. Because those around Jesus can become outsiders as well as insiders, they serve to introduce dynamic movement into the more static picture drawn by the sayings of Jesus. The choice is however not only a choice in terms of a truth claim about who Jesus is or an ethical stance about a way to confront evil. Instead, the choice has to do with one's basic identity. It focuses on hearing the revealing word and accepting the healing presence of God.

This reading of the gospel suggests that it is the presence of Jesus that brings about both the experience of unmasking and the experience of healing to a community of potential insiders. In Mark's telling of the story, the presence of Jesus becomes the catalyst for transformation. However, by the time that the narrative is told, hearers of the story could no longer experience that presence directly. In Mark's proclamation of the good news, another embodiment of Jesus is placed into their midst creating similar opportunities to reveal identities. The narrative about Jesus, in the same way as his historical presence, functions to unmask and to heal. In much the same way as Jesus did in his incarnation, the narrative also takes on the vulnerability of the human. In neither case will a connection to the divine be used to control the response. Instead, the good news will be proclaimed as beginning the story. Only the hearers can give the ending, whether that ending will bring forth fruit beyond expectation or produce only a small plant that shrivels and dies.

The Subversive Function of Kingdom Power

The parable of the wicked tenants/beloved son in Mark 12:1-12 centres on a conflict between the authority of a master and the power of the tenants. It begins with the tenants' misuse of the authority granted them. It ends with amazement at the Lord's doing. In between there is the story of the repeated effort of the master to collect his share of the harvest.

The occasion for the telling of this parable is different than that of the parables of the seed and soil because it is not told to the crowd or explained to the disciples. Rather, it is told against those authorities who were questioning Jesus about the source of his authority being from heaven or of human origin. Jesus has just finished telling the chief priests, the scribes, and the elders that he will not reveal the source of his authority to them (12:33). He then goes on to tell them this parable that they understood to refer to themselves, a parable that in some way was subversive of their authority and power. The result is a plot to get Jesus arrested. It is not surprising that this parable has been called the "central political parable" in the gospel.[40]

Ched Myers has pointed out that the social struggle between groups in a community is often articulated in terms of symbolic discourse. The clear allegorical character of this parable indicates that the hearers would easily be able to identify the various characters in the story that Jesus told. The parable is thus clearly ideological.[41] But the historical narrative too can be an ideological production. A number of questions about the narrative of Mark are therefore raised by this parable that seems so obviously ideological. On whose behalf does the narrative function? How does it subvert or legitimate the dominant order? Whose interests are included?

These questions can be answered more accurately by tracing the plot of the parable in the larger narrative. The focus of the parable is on the tension and conflict between powers rather than on the creative power of the kingdom. Both the characteristics of the master's power as well as the characteristics of the tenants' power will be illuminated by a reexamination of this storyline.

Divine Authority/Human Authority

Rhoads and Michie, in their account of the plot, point out that though Jesus is the immediate cause of the conflicts in the story, God is the ultimate origin of many of the actions and events.[42] They suggest that Mark 12 allows us to see the role of God in the plot, a role that is hinted at in other ways but is made most clear in this parable. The parable is a kind of synopsis of the history of God's actions in his vineyard that are not completely contained in the narrative itself but happen before and after the story that Mark tells.

The parable points out that violence and control characterize the actions of the tenants who have claimed the fruit of the vineyard for themselves. Though servants have been sent to reap the harvest they have been mistreated and killed. Human authorities have been ruling for themselves rather than for God. The climax of the parable comes when the master of the vineyard begins something new by sending his son to the vineyard. It is this new action of God that gives the thread of meaning to the events in the narrative and makes for both the conflict and the suspense of the story.

Throughout the parable, it is the owner who initiates the new responses by his action of repeatedly sending messengers. The parable ends with the statement "and this was the Lord's doing and it is amazing in our sight" (12:11). In the parable, God's actions are therefore seen as over against human actions that have been violent and controlling. The divine reign is understood over against human power and reign. A radical apocalyptic dualism is established, a dualism that has to do with allegiance to opposite authorities. This dualism is evident throughout the storyline, but is especially evident in the episodes surrounding the parable. A closer examination of these episodes will point out the polarization that is not only in the parable but also in the narrative.

In the episode immediately preceding the parable, Jesus reenters Jerusalem and is confronted by the chief priests, the scribes and the elders (11:27-33). These authorities can be identified as the Sanhedrin, the highest Jewish court of law and the chief political agency of Judea.[43] The anxiety of these leaders is highlighted through the repetition of the question in verse 28, "By what authority are you doing these things? Who gave you this authority to do them?" These leaders perceive themselves as representing the temple, an institution legitimated "from heaven." They thus challenge Jesus to present his credentials. Jesus counters this question by presenting them with an example of ambiguous authority in the preaching of John. His question is a loaded one because the preaching of John, like that of Jesus, had not been given recognition and authority by the religious leaders. Rather, the crowd of people who came to be baptized recognized John's authority as coming directly from God. The leaders are given an opportunity to demonstrate their sensitivity to God's movement in history by naming John's baptism as "from heaven." Instead, they refuse to publicly commit themselves. Jesus in turn will not answer their question.

In the incident immediately following the parable, the religious leaders from the above group conspire with two other groups, the Pharisees and the Herodians, in order to trap Jesus (12:13-17). The issue of taxes was one that divided collaborators with Rome from the subversive underground movement that refused to pay their dues to an oppressive government. The question, "Is it lawful to pay taxes to the emperor or not?" is a politically loaded one, a question that dares Jesus to commit himself to a political position. Again the question is repeated twice for emphasis. Myers notes the clear parallels between the previous challenge and this one. But more importantly, he notes how Jesus' response is also parallel, especially in the radical divine/human antithesis."Was John's baptism from heaven or from men? Pay back Caesar what is Caesar's, and God what is God's."[44]

What Jesus is doing here is challenging the authorities to act according to their allegiances, allegiances that are clearly stated as polar opposites. Jesus again turns the question back to the authorities. What position do they take on this issue? Jesus' own allegiance is not the question. What is at issue is the ultimate loyalty of the political leaders.

It is easy to see how the parable sandwiched between these two episodes also focuses on the issue of loyalty and allegiance. The tenants who do not give their first loyalty to the owner of the vineyard abuse and oppress the servants who come to collect the harvest. The servants who carry out the owner's wishes are beaten, insulted and killed by the tenants. Those listening to Mark's story will not have much difficulty identifying the allegorical allusions. In chapter 3, we have heard already about the collusion between the Pharisees and the Herodians who were conspiring to destroy Jesus. The story of John's death at the hands of Herod has been told in some detail. And Jesus' death has been predicted several times. It is not difficult to identify both the tenants and the faithful servants.

When the parable is studied in the context of these two incidents, Mark's ideological position is made much clearer. Mark is challenging the *appeal to God's authority* that is legitimating the religious and political actions of some of the leaders. He challenges this authority in the temple, the primary locus of religious authority. This false authority is further clarified in the next episodes. Here the debates between Jesus and his opponents focus directly on the issue of the hermeneutical authority of the ruling classes in the community.[45] Readers are reminded of other clashes over interpretation of the Torah described earlier (7:1-13, 10:2-10).

In Mark 12:18-27, the Sadducees, the more conservative religious group, enter the debate by asking his interpretation of the resurrection. Again, Jesus points out their lack of understanding of God's authority and power. He accuses them by saying, "Is not this the reason that you are wrong, that you know neither the scriptures nor the power of God?" (12:24). As Elisabeth Schüssler Fiorenza has pointed out, the central issue discussed here is not an abstract theological argument about the Resurrection, a favourite debate between the various groups of religious elites. Rather, the issue is the alternative world that God is creating to take the place of the patriarchal world in which marriage structures guarantee the blessing and promise of God.[46] The Sadducees have not been able to recognize this new world and its power. They thus continue to rely on human authority.

The next incident, in Mark 12:28-34, again brings up the issue of loyalty and commitment. A note of ambiguity is introduced, however. A scribe asks a question that could easily be interpreted as another trap to get Jesus to reveal his deepest commitments by articulating the greatest commandment. However, this time Jesus does not turn the tables on the scribe. Instead, he answers the question, bringing together traditions from Deuteronomy and Leviticus. What is even more surprising is that the scribe agrees with Jesus and alludes to further scripture passages to affirm Jesus' interpretation of the law. And Jesus sees the wisdom of the scribe, noting that he is not far from the kingdom.

The strong duality between divine and human authority that has been affirmed throughout these passages is mediated by the scribe who does not act according to the reputation that his profession has gained in the gospel thus far. His debate with Jesus shows some willingness to learn. This openness shows his nearness to the kingdom. The chapter ends with none daring to ask Jesus any more questions. Instead, Jesus continues teaching using the scriptures to make a point against the notion of imperial leadership in the tradition of David as often taught by the scribes.[47] He then goes on to use the opposite examples of the scribes and a widow to contrast the attitude and actions of oppressive authority with the attitudes and actions of a victim of oppression.[48] This final teaching is specifically directed to the disciples.

In this section of the narrative human authority versus divine authority becomes the central issue in the conflict between Jesus and the other religious authorities. This polarity was already hinted at in Mark 1:22, where Jesus is said to have taught as one "having authority and not as the scribes." The story ends with the death of the one who embodied God's authority at the hands of those who embodied human authority. The question is raised for the reader: Is all human authority condemned by the gospel writer?

The Alternative Politics of Jesus

In the parable of the wicked tenants/beloved son the conflict is over the share of the produce that belongs to the owner. Seizing what belongs to the owner for themselves, the tenants change the underlying agreement between master and tenant. Instead of accepting the terms of the lease in which both owner and tenant have certain responsibilities and rewards, the tenants attempt to seize the whole vineyard for themselves. The conflict is therefore between the valid claims of the owner and the false claims of the tenants. The parable pictures a power struggle taking place caused by the unjust way in which the tenants claim the vineyard.

In the narrative, this struggle is told in the context of the "socio-symbolic codes" of the language of a first century Palestinian community.[49] These codes are a complex network of assumptions that are accepted unquestioned by a community and that have great power to order the interactions of people with each other. Ched Myers' framework will be used to name the various aspects of this order that provides a context for understanding the activity of Jesus.[50] A simple portrait of the alternative politics that Jesus brought to this order will be drawn by using examples from the narrative to point out how it subverts both this dominant order and the various resistance movements.

The symbolic order of Palestinian Judaism. Myers builds his model on two interrelated and mutually reinforcing systems that regulate the life of the Palestinian Jew in the first century—those of pollution and those of debt. The pollution code has its basis in Israel's self-understanding, as a holy people called to be set apart from the surrounding cultures by worshipping only God. The debt code has its roots in the basic covenant with Yahweh expressed in Exodus and the Ten Commandments. This symbolic order was objectified or embodied in two main institutions: the temple and the Torah. It operated in every sphere or site of social life. Myers has named these sites the land/table (the production and consumption of goods), the village/home (the kinship and community relations) and the synagogue/sanctuary (the cultus). The elite in Palestine struggled for power and control in these arenas in order to increase their social and political standing. The dominated struggled for access to the redemption promised by the system, occasionally challenging the authority of the elite over them.

Pollution and debt codes ranked places, times and persons according to purity or holiness. Clear boundaries and divisions were assumed, boundaries that were almost impossible to comply with in the daily life of the poorer people. A number of ways of coping with these codes were recommended by the various groups competing for control of the system. The approaches ranged from the elitism of the Sadducees, who assumed that only the priestly caste could comply with the purity regulations, to the manipulative show of solidarity with the masses by the Pharisees, that only served to ensure their control of the system.

This order is complicated by the threat from the Roman Empire, an alternative political system that attempted to control this Jewish system for its own ends. Rome's strategy of allowing limited internal autonomy to the nations it conquered encouraged the cooperation of the elite of the colonized state with their Roman overlords. As pointed out by Myers, this strategy is "typified in many ways by the half-Jew Herod."[51] He built the magnificent Jewish temple in Jerusalem but placed the eagle, the symbol of the Roman Empire, above the entrance gate to the temple. A number of different resistance movements to this collaboration arose, which were brutally suppressed by Rome. Fear continued to haunt the elite, who walked a tightrope between the Jewish and Roman social codes.

Various strategies were used in the struggle to subvert the dominant power exercised by the Jewish elite in collaboration with the Roman political power. The Essenes and Pharisees could be classified as two groups who attempted to reform Judaism but in different ways. The Essenes focused on personal renewal, withdrawing as a community in order to nurture their own community ethos, an ethos that challenged some of the symbolic codes but did not directly engage the dominant order of the society. The Pharisees attempted to build up the synagogues as an alternative to the political base of the temple. The Pharisees were a diverse group that clearly tried to reform Judaism by extending the symbolic order to the masses in increasingly strict oral regulations. The Pharisees were however *not* a dominant group but one seeking to regain power in the community.

Various loyalist groups, who sought structural changes in order to restore traditional values, were also present. They were usually interested in supplanting collaborationist priests with patriotic ones in order to bring back the golden age of Jewish supremacy in Palestine. The Zealots, as well as other more moderate groups, represent this option.

A portrait of kingdom politics. Mark pictures the subversive activity of Jesus in the context of conflicting social and political options. He articulates this activity in terms of the symbolic code familiar to readers used to the dominating political presence of Rome. Mark's portrait of kingdom politics is not intended as mere historical description. Instead, it is strongly rhetorical and attempts to persuade listeners to adopt a particular approach to authority and power. For the gospel writer, kingdom politics consists of a political strategy closely tied to the embodiment of authority in Jesus. Three central aspects of the option presented by Jesus' approach can be explored.[52] Each aspect includes an invitation for humans to participate in the exercise of power. However, this invitation implies that the use of power by his followers would need to be in continuity with Jesus' use of power.

(1) Proclamation and teaching. In the narrative of the Gospel of Mark, the public proclamation of the kingdom is a subversive activity. This is indicated already in the programmatic announcement of the kingdom's nearness and the call to repentance and belief in the gospel (1:15). Repentance assumes a turning around, a radical change. This radical change is immediately shown to be incompatible with the scribal establishment and the social order that they represent. The subversiveness of Jesus' proclamation is also emphasized by its link to the preaching of John. Thus it also stood in opposition to the authority of Herod and his collaborative politics.

Perhaps one way in which the challenge to the dominant order is most clearly indicated is the way Jesus publicly uses and subverts the written traditions of the scribes, a group active both in the synagogues of Galilee and in the temple of Jerusalem. He does this in the context of a deliberate linking of the Hebrew scriptures with the "new" kingdom that he is proclaiming (1:1-2) Myers summarizes Jesus' appeal to the Hebrew Bible in this way:

> He deploys it offensively (11:7) and defensively (2:24ff.), and argues hermeneutics with the scribal theologians (12:24ff.) and Pharisees (10:2ff.). His challenge to the interpretive competence of his ideological rivals often has a bitter rhetorical edge: "Have you not read what David did . . . ?" (2:25); "Have you not read this scripture . . . ?" (12:10); "Have you not read in the book of Moses . . . ?"(12:26). This shows that Mark was very engaged in the battle over the redemptive medium of scripture with the other literate social groups of his time.[53]

Jesus' preaching and teaching is very much an appeal to the apocalyptic and prophetic traditions of Judaism.[54] His two longer sermons reflect the dualism that is characteristic of apocalypticism (Mark 4 and 13). But instead of the triumphalistic eschatological expectations of Jewish nationalism that characterized the various political interest groups, Jesus instructs his followers to hear and to watch, to listen and to interpret correctly. Mark 13 especially is focused on discernment of the political situation in order that they will not be deceived. Jesus' emphasis is on the suffering that will accompany the demise of the old order, symbolized by the demise of the temple.

Jesus' preaching condemns an order that abandons the commandments of God and holds to human tradition (7:6-13). This order uses the tradition and the authority of Moses as an excuse to act unjustly and to emphasize strict boundaries between the unclean and clean. Jesus challenges these boundaries, not because they are traditional but because they have become oppressive and do not really get to the heart of good and evil. This condemnation of injustice is in fact in continuity with the prophetic word of the Jewish tradition. The vineyard was a well-known metaphor for Israel and the parable uses imagery related to the lament of God in the Book of Isaiah. There too the Lord seeks fruit but sees instead bloodshed and the cry of the oppressed (Isa. 5:1-7). There too the lack of justice is related to a false seeing and understanding. There too evil was called good and good was called evil and the leaders were wise only in their own eyes (Isa. 5:20-21).

The condemnation of oppressive power in the past, however, does not preclude an invitation for humans to participate in the proclamation of a new kind of power. In chapter 5, the healed man is told to "Go home to your friends and tell them how much the Lord has done for you and what mercy he has shown you." The disciples are sent out on a mission to proclaim the message (3:14) and we read later that they "proclaimed that all should repent" (6:12). The gospel ends with the women being given the commission to go and tell.

In the directions to the disciples, the nature of the power that accompanies proclamation and teaching is clearly indicated. Instead of demanding authority, Jesus orders them to be dependent on the hospitality of the host to whom they are bringing the message (6:8-13). In the face of rejection, there is no retaliation. As pointed out by Myers, this "makes the missionaries completely vulnerable to, and dependent upon, the hospitality extended to them, and obviously precludes them from being able to impose their views by force."[55] Throughout the narrative, this approach is exemplified by Jesus in his proclamation. The disciples who participate in Jesus' mission must realize that if they depend on divine power as Jesus does they too will face rejection and will participate in the destiny of Jesus on the cross.

The preaching and proclamation of Jesus challenged the resistance movements of the times, as well as the dominant social group. In his use of the tradition, Jesus challenges the categories and boundaries emphasized by the chief interpreters of the tradition. In his public involvement and in his dependence on the welcome of the listeners to his message, he challenged those who resisted by violent means. The subversive preaching and teaching was intended to invite all to turn and hear the good news of God's kingdom. The proclamation was thus inclusive in its invitation but subversive in its effect.

(2) Exorcism, healing and feeding. From the moment that Jesus steps into the drama created by Mark, proclamation is linked with deeds of healing and exorcism. However, the authorities do not welcome these acts of compassion. Instead, they are interpreted as subversive, as an attack on the established authorities. Why is this so when healers and magicians abounded in the Hellenistic world? Kee points out the difference: "They were not intended, as was the case with the Hellenistic wonder-worker stories, to glorify the one who performed the act. They were told instead to identify his exorcism as an eschatological event which served to prepare God's creation for his coming rule."[56] The authorities recognized that Jesus represented something new that could not stand together with the old. As Myers points out, the powerful action of exorcism represented an attack on alternative authorities, whether these authorities are the scribes who thought they could define the Holy (1:24) or the Legion representing military might (5:9).[57] Exorcism

represented a liberation from social and political forces that dominated and oppressed people.

Jesus' healings and exorcisms were not only linked with diseases as scientifically defined but challenged the dominant symbolic definitions of order within the community.[58] The exorcisms and healings that are described were associated with the social process of defining illness. In the symbolic order of the community, illness was associated with impurity and sin, implying exclusion of the victim from the community. The healings by Jesus are linked with forgiveness (2:1-12), with restoration to social wholeness (5:33-34) and with empowerment to follow "on the way" (10:46-52). The rules of the "holy place" (synagogue) and "holy time" (Sabbath) are deliberately broken by Jesus in order to show how they have been used to legitimate injustice and oppression. In the same way, the feedings and healings on both sides of Lake Galilee imply the breaking down of the barriers between Gentile and Jew. Thus healing represents a freeing from boundaries that promote injustice and exclusion.

While Jesus condemns the human authorities who have controlled the defining of health and wholeness, he invites others to join with him in this healing, liberating ministry. He invites the disciples to participate in the exorcism, healing and feeding of the crowds. He locates the power to heal not in himself but in God and the faith of those who are healed (5:34,7:29, 10:52).

The healing, exorcism and feedings were subversive because they defined God's power as always there for the sake of other people. Those who wished to participate in God's mission must align themselves with this kind of power that does not impose boundaries between people in order to legitimate injustice or to justify exclusive or coercive community behaviours..

(3) Disruptive confrontation of the dominant order. The disruption and challenge presented by the activities of proclamation and healing have already been noted. However, the gospel writer also describes directly confrontational words and actions that symbolically denounce certain practices of the social system. These actions range from breaking the law by plucking grains in the field, to eating with unclean hands, to deliberately healing on the Sabbath, to the anointing of Jesus by a woman. Jesus' followers join with him in these actions. The height of such symbolic confrontation comes in the episode of the cleansing of the temple (11:15-19).

This show of resistance by Jesus comes after he enters the city in an ambiguous and paradoxical procession. The irony of Jesus riding meekly on an ass is in sharp contrast to the expected military parade for a Davidic king (Zech. 9:9).[59] However, Jesus does act in a powerful way as he enters the temple. His power challenges those who would exploit the poor. He drives out the money changers and those who were buying and selling. The story concludes with an accusation of robbery taken from the Book of Jeremiah. In Jeremiah, the temple is also under severe criticism (Jer. 7:4). For Jesus, the temple was to have been a "house of prayer for all people," an image taken from Isaiah 56:1-8, where the scriptures speak about God gathering the dispossessed and the outcasts to become part of the household. The temple has not fulfilled its function of drawing all people to God. Its power must therefore be resisted and an alternative household must be established.

This alternative is already indicated in Mark 3:31-35, where the true kindred are those who do the will of God. This alternative household, in the tradition of the remnant in Judaism, has the mission to heal, exorcise and proclaim. Its symbolic actions have to do with feeding the multitudes (both Jew and Gentile) from the abundance that is there in God's provisions. The disciples are reprimanded for their lack of understanding that there is enough bread for all (8:14-21). The disruptive confrontation by Jesus therefore points to both a new community and a new understanding of the stewardship of resources, both material and spiritual.

Jesus resists the power of the dominant Jewish and Roman authorities by breaking the law when it interferes with his actions of mercy. However, he does not use force to save himself when his actions result in arrest. His strategy does not change to one of domination when what he wishes to bring about is not accepted. Jesus will not continue the cycle of violence in which the oppressed become the oppressors. He becomes vulnerable, accepts arrest and abuse as the result of his powerful actions, and dies on the cross. The invitation to his followers includes this call to the cross, the ultimate symbol of resistance to a power that would dominate and oppress. The faithful servants in the parable receive a similar fate as the son because they are on a similar mission.

The politics of the kingdom can be summarized by the apocalyptic parable in Mark 3:23-28. The parable does not challenge the strong dualism between Satan and God that the scribes are using to denounce the authority of Jesus. Instead in the parable, Jesus, who is on God's side is entering the house and plundering the property of the "strong man." He is tying up the one deemed powerful. Therefore, it should be clear that he is not doing this with the authority of the strong man but with another authority, the authority of the Holy Spirit. It is a serious sin to mistake the power of the Holy Spirit as expressed in the healing and exorcism activity of Jesus and to name these deeds as blasphemous. The power of God must not be confused with the power of Satan. The politics of Jesus cannot be confused with the politics of other human authorities.

The Invitation to Subversive Politics

The parable ends with a subversion of power. The owner of the vineyard will come and destroy the tenants who had seemed so powerful and will give the vineyard to others.[60] The power to inflict death through which the human authorities had ruled is broken. The death of the son is not a triumph for the tenants, but an opportunity for the master to bring about the reversal that is inherent in kingdom politics. It is the master who has the ultimate authority over life and death.

This amazing subversion is indicated in the quotation from Psalm 118:22. The rejected stone has become the cornerstone of a new building with new tenants. What kind of power can turn a failure into success? What is the significance of the rather ridiculous story of a master who continues to send servants and finally a beloved son to a group of people who continue to mistreat and kill these messengers? How is this related to the reversal promised in the Hebrew tradition?

The invitation to participate in the subversive power of the kingdom can be looked at from the positions of the various character groups in the story. Each of these groups is described as experiencing the subversive power of God in a unique way. Each is invited to participate in a new kind of political action. Three groups can be pointed out, each providing a kind of subplot in the story.

The authorities. This group of people represents the dominant socio-symbolic order and can be seen as the stewards of that order. In the narrative, they experience the subversive power of the kingdom as a threat to their own power. They therefore fear Jesus and the crowd that follows Jesus and use whatever means they have to destroy the servants of the owner of the vineyard. They collaborate with each other, for they see in Jesus a threat to the loyalties they have chosen.

Throughout the story the authorities form a united front against Jesus. The image that the reader gets is of people with but one over-riding concern, their own authority and power. Most of the interaction of Jesus with this group is focused on exposing the origin or nature of their authority. As pointed out by Kingsbury, all the character traits of the authorities stem from one root trait: characteristically these leaders are hypocrites, because they imagine that they are on the side of God when in reality their hearts are far from God (7: 6-8). They are "without divine authority" and therefore are on the side of Satan.[61]

In the narrative, the authorities do not yet experience the full destruction of which the parable speaks. However, there are symbolic actions and words by Jesus that point to this destruction. In chapter 11, the cleansing of the temple intercalated into the episodes of the fig tree suggests that the temple, as it now functions, is condemned because it is not fruitful.[62] In Mark 13, Jesus is speaking to those who marvel at the wonderful stones and wonderful buildings of the temple, and predicts that "not one stone will be left here upon another." The time of judgement will come.

Though a central theme of the parable is the destruction of the power of the tenants, this does not happen immediately or in the expected way. The owner patiently continues to send servants and finally his son. It is this final action of the owner that brings about the reversal. As pointed out by Clevenot, the subversive dynamism of this action "forces violence to show its hand," to "exteriorize itself and to become objective" thus showing its inner nature.[63] It is after oppressive power has done its work and is at its most evil that the reversal happens. The tenants do not control this new action of the owner of the vineyard. Their power is taken away and given to others.

These others can include members of the ruling class who act and speak according to a new understanding of the kingdom. A centurion recognizes and is a witness to Jesus as the Son of God. Joseph of Arimathea, a respected member of the council, asks for Jesus' body and buries him wrapped in a linen cloth. The authority and leadership has been given to those who recognize divine authority and are willing to serve and suffer because they embrace a new kind of power. Malbon summarizes the subversion this way: "The Marcan Gospel does indeed schematize the Jewish religious leaders as foes of Jesus, but it refuses to absolutize that schema. Being a foe of the Marcan Jesus is a matter of how one chooses to relate to him, not a matter of one's social or religious status and role." [64]

The dominant ruling class experiences the authority of Jesus as subversive in two ways. First of all, they experience it in the way their own power, supported by divine authority, is challenged, exposed and destroyed. Second, subversion happens in the narrative when members of this group are invited to become God's servants. They are given the choice to change and be transformed.

The servants of God. These servants are characterized by the way they carry out the mission of the owner in the spirit and power of that owner. In the narrative, these servants include not only the prophets of the Old Testament but also John the Baptist and Jesus. The disciples of Jesus too are invited to participate in this mission. The story ends with the invitation to the women to participate as well.

This mission is already indicated in the imagery of the "way" in Mark 1:2. The reference is ambiguous and thus could include both Jesus and John as messengers.[65] Preparing the way is a metaphorical way of speaking about the role of a messenger who proclaims the coming of the king. Throughout the narrative, Jesus becomes the model messenger who proclaims the kingdom and prepares for the gathering of the harvest by the owner. He speaks and acts in the name of the owner, calling for repentance and belief in the good news.

In the second half of the narrative, the emphasis is primarily on the sufferings that the servants and the son must endure. This is already indicated by the sufferings of John the Baptist, whose forthright preaching brought about his death. The sufferings and death of Jesus are described as the inescapable result of challenging the authority of the tenants, the rulers of the dominant social order.[66] Jesus' death is depicted as the final provocation before the owner acts anew. The Resurrection becomes God's greatest subversive action, for it turns apparent powerlessness into the most powerful action in the story.

The invitation to become a servant of God includes the way of the cross (8:34), a way that the disciples who join Jesus in his mission find difficult to

walk. The confessional crises about Jesus' identity and the issues of leadership
and authority that plague the small group of followers create a larger question
that permeates the gospel: how does kingdom power and authority work? Why
does suffering inevitably follow? The disciples demonstrate their misunderstanding most clearly in Mark 8:22-10:52. Clearly they do not understand the
kind of service that Jesus modelled.

These incidences take place during a time of popularity for Jesus, when
many people recognize him as a prophet and when the disciples, with Peter as
their spokesperson, are witness to him as the Messiah. Yet Jesus sternly orders
them not to tell anyone and goes on to teach the disciples the necessity of his
suffering as son of man (the Human One). Peter rebukes Jesus, however, for
the way of suffering does not fit his understandings of the way of the Messiah,
the way of a servant of a powerful owner of the vineyard.

The harsh rebuke of Peter by Jesus in this section reminds the readers
of the rebuke that Jesus gave to the demons (1:25, 3:12). Jesus' words
explicitly reiterate the sharp opposition between divine and human things that
permeates the entire narrative. The following teaching by Jesus emphasizes this
opposition by pointing to other oppositions like life/death and first/last. Even
though the disciples have recognized Jesus as having divine authority, they
have much to learn about what divine power really means.

There is another moment in this section that also points to the need for
more learning. Several disciples experience the truth of Jesus in a marvellous
vision. This vision brings to the fore Moses and Elijah, representative of the
law and the prophets, two figures who have been implicitly present in the
gospel story thus far.[67] Peter becomes the spokesperson again, addressing Jesus
as Rabbi. But when he attempts to build a memorial honouring this moment,
a voice from heaven reminds them that Jesus, as beloved son, embodies the
Word of God in their day. It is Jesus' words that they must honour. And again
there is a warning not to tell anyone about what they had seen. The discussion
ends with Jesus again speaking about suffering, using Elijah as an example.

It is particularly at such moments of powerful revelation that the
disciples fail completely in understanding the politics of Jesus. Recognizing
Jesus as Messiah in his power and glory does not seem to automatically ensure
that the disciples will understand the way of the kingdom. They do not realize
that kingdom strategy means a dependence on God for any healing ministry
(9:28-29). They argue about their own status and fail to welcome the healing
activity of others (9:33-41). They rebuke those who are bringing children to
Jesus and are perplexed that the rich find it difficult to enter the kingdom
(10:13-27).

The climax of misunderstanding the strategy of Jesus comes in the
episode in which James and John ask to sit at the right and left hand of Jesus
in his glory (10:35-45). Jesus has just taught the renunciation of power in his
response to the rich man and in his prediction of his death. Yet here the search

for status is linked directly with participation in Jesus' mission. James and John are using their link with Jesus as an opportunity for gaining more power and authority. They seem to think that the power given to them to proclaim, heal and exorcise will be rewarded by greater rank in the kingdom of God. The other disciples are indignant, perhaps because James and John have unfairly taken advantage of an opportunity to gain status that they would all have liked to have. This gives Jesus the opportunity to give one of his clearest teachings on power and authority. Leadership as domination is denounced. Instead, the disciples are to follow in the steps of Jesus, who came to serve and give his life as a ransom for many. Servanthood may lead to suffering but this suffering can serve as a ransom, a freeing of servants (slaves) who are dominated.[68]

The disciples seem unable to understand Jesus' teaching. Though they are committed to Jesus, they think that they can rely on their own strength to stand by Jesus during his arrest, trial and death. Again, Peter demonstrates how greatly he overestimates his own power (14:29). But the other disciples show this same lack of understanding, both at the Last Supper and in the garden of Gethsemane. Though they do not wish to betray or deny Jesus, they do not stay awake to pray for the power that they will need (14:32-42). It does not take long for them all to desert Jesus.

Again, it is Peter who recognizes his weakness (14:72). At the end of the narrative it is to the disciples and Peter that the message of hope is to be given. Jesus will go ahead into Galilee. There they will see him, just as he told them. It was in Galilee that Jesus healed and taught and they discovered his power. Will they be open to healing so that they will see him as Bartimaeus did and follow on the "way"?

There is another group of followers whose story is told in the narrative. This group is not as prominent as the twelve and enters the story directly only in the last pages of the narrative (14:40-41). These are the women who had been following Jesus from the beginning, who were probably present at the healings and feedings. The account says that they served him, thus showing greater comprehension of Jesus' political message than did the twelve. Throughout the narrative, there are hints that women seem to comprehend the mission of Jesus in a unique way but their story is not told. However, here they enter the story at the time of great danger. They courageously go to the tomb to anoint Jesus. The test of their courage comes with the mandate to tell the story of the Resurrection to the other disciples. It is then that terror and amazement seize them. Their first response is fear. After all, who would believe a group of women with a fantastic tale such as this? They too must be empowered in order that the good news of kingdom power will be proclaimed. The story ends on this note of fear, though the longer endings probably appended to the narrative by the early church, assure us that the women responded to the invitation to enter into the political arena with their story.

The servants are those in the narrative who recognize that Jesus has power and they are the ones who give him their allegiance. However, these same followers confuse the power dependent on status and coercion with the power given to them by God. Therefore, they are afraid and lack the courage to confront evil. They have trouble recognizing their own need for healing and empowerment. At other times, the followers misunderstand the kind of power that Jesus gives. They assume that the power to proclaim, heal and exorcise is related to the power to dominate and oppress or to the power that is rewarded in terms of social status and economic and social power.

These servants of the owner also experience a subversion of power. This subversion comes just at the point when they become enamoured with the great power and authority that is given to them through their call to be servants of God. They must therefore be taught that only dependence on God's power will give them the strength they need when suffering and death comes. Jesus, as the son of God, demonstrates this dependence on God in his refusal to use oppressive power. His death becomes the opportunity for God to show his healing power. The message of Resurrection spoken by the young man at the tomb calls the women to also live in this hope. They are asked to return to Galilee where they will again see Jesus. There they can find the healing and teaching that they need in order to follow the way of the cross.

The narrative hints at the servants being the "others" to whom the vineyard is given. However, it also points out how easily servants can become tenants who think they own the vineyard. The followers are forced to make a choice that will make them evil tenants or faithful servants.

The "others" who receive a new mandate. The "others" are those to whom the mandate is given to care for the vineyard when the unfaithful tenants are removed. Clevenot has pointed out that in the structure of the narrative, the tearing down of the oppressive authority structure around the temple is replaced by something new.[69] The scenes of the Last Supper in Mark 14:12-25 relate to the scenes in which Jesus enters Jerusalem and throws out the tenants in that house (11:1-25). Note how both scenes begin with the sending of two disciples with specific instructions. In these scenes, a new household is formed around a common meal in which Jesus' giving himself "for many" is celebrated. This new authority is not over another but to serve another, as modelled by the woman who anointed Jesus at the meal in Bethany.

The theme of food permeates the Gospel of Mark. Jesus eats with tax collectors and sinners. He pronounces all food clean. Both Jewish and Gentile crowds are fed in the wilderness with a meal creating abundant leftovers. The theme of food also points to the reversal that is experienced by those who become willing servants of God. These are the persons in the narrative who did not expect an important role because they were on the margins of society. The disciples, when they were called, came from many different professions, but none were considered leaders or powerful according to the dominant social code. These people form the crowd around Jesus and come for healing and teaching. They are the disabled, the ritually unclean, the socially marginalized, the women, the children and the Gentiles. They are received unconditionally by Jesus as belonging to the kingdom and willingly serve as called upon (e.g., 1:31, 5:20, 14:6-9).

In the parable, this group takes little initiative or action. However, their story is included as representative of the new order. These are the people who have experienced the healing, feeding and forgiving power of God in their lives. They have eyes to see and ears to hear and therefore will be aware of the "yeast of the Pharisees and the yeast of Herod" (8:14-15). These "others" will now take over the work connected with the vineyard that is freely given to them to administer. They will become servants of the owner, gaining the power that "can move mountains" (11:23-24). But they will also face the temptations of that power and will therefore need to learn to forgive as they have been forgiven (11:25).

The subversion that the powerless experience is the unexpectedness of the call to serve and the miracle of powerful healing, liberation and feeding in their own lives. Like the Syrophoenician woman, who had learned to receive only the crumbs thrown to the dogs, these powerless persons experience the full measure of God's power in response to their faith in God's grace (7:24-30). They are thus invited to embody this new political way in their lives. The importance of their story is therefore not dependent on being dominant in the narrative. Instead, they best represent the subversiveness of the kingdom.

A New Ethic

The use of the parable of the wicked tenants/beloved son as a plot synopsis has illuminated human power and authority by placing it into the broader context of the cosmic battle between God and Satan. In the narrative of Mark, there are clearly two kinds of power and authority at work. Both of these can be embodied in human communities and in individuals. These two kinds of power are radically opposed to each other, creating a polarity or dualism in the narrative world. This polarity reaches its climax as the oppressive power of evil authority makes its ultimate move by killing Jesus. The tension in the story, focuses on the various characters who must choose what kind of power to embody. The narrative challenges the human characters to discern the power and authority of God and to align themselves with it.

This duality produces conflict between those who believe that they represent the authority of God and those who truly express divine power in their words and actions. It is only the subversive action of God that allows the reader to see Jesus' death as the opportunity for God to act powerfully in a moment when Jesus seems most powerless. This creates the opportunity for a new call to the followers to experience God's power to heal and forgive in their lives and to walk the way of suffering, confident in God's power of resurrection.

The ending of the gospel, with its challenge to proclaim this power of God, is not surrounded with a great show of authority. Instead, the women are seized with terror and are afraid. This fear can lead the followers to the source of their strength. This source is not in Jerusalem, the centre of the dominant social power, but instead in Galilee where the healing and teaching takes place. The followers are invited to return to the beginning and to follow the way Jesus leads. If they are open to healing, liberation and teaching they will know real power. This kind of power will inevitably take them back to confront the oppressive powers in Jerusalem. Suffering may follow but the challenge is to watch out for deception because human oppressive power can easily be confused with the power of God embodied in human authority (13:5). To see Jesus will mean to be able to recognize a power that forgives, heals and feeds those who do the will of God as faithful servants.

In the parable, the sharp dualism between the two kinds of power is expressed in the contrast between the tenants, who misuse the authority given them, and the others, to whom the vineyard is now given. In the narrative, this dualism is most clearly demonstrated in the opposite ways in which the official authorities and Jesus use the power given them as servants of the owner. The crowd around Jesus, which includes the disciples, are given the choice. They are the ones who must decide their ultimate allegiance and align their lives according to the logic inherent in the source of their power. God, who invites rather than forces faith, who heals rather than oppresses and kills, is the source of power that brings new life where there is death. Ultimately, this is the power that will triumph.

The central emphasis of the narrative, when read in the light of this parable, is the temptation faced by those called to be servants of God. The division between people in the story depends on their recognition of God's power and their willingness to live by the implicit rules of that power. The Gospel of Mark thus makes the radical claim that Jesus embodied God's way of confronting evil. This calls for a new ethic based on a new truth claim—a claim that Jesus both revealed and empowered God's way of life.

This reading of the story legitimizes an authority that embodies God's alternative politics by confronting oppressive power. It exposes authority that justifies its use of violence and oppression by an appeal to God's power. Therefore, this reading empowers those who, as God's servants, rely on God's power in the midst of their suffering. It does this by explaining why it is so difficult to see God's power in what seems like failure and promising that God's power will subvert this false show of power in the final hour.

There is also a strong warning inherent in this reading of the narrative. It is easy to confuse the powers of God and Satan at a time when oppressive power becomes dominant and when fear becomes overwhelming. It is when the disciples see death and destruction that they need to have faith and pray for God's power to subvert the false powers. They must admit their need for divine power when their way of love makes them very vulnerable. Readers are therefore urged to be alert, to watch and to pray.

The Marcan Ethos of Authority and Power

The language of the Gospel of Mark is specifically concerned with authority and power issues. My retellings of the gospel have concentrated on two aspects of this power: creative power and subversive power. The themes and counter themes that have surfaced in each of these readings are interwoven in the narrative.[70] There is a relationship between the themes that cannot be captured if they are seen as opposite readings. The two readings converge in a common pattern of authority language, a pattern that includes the unique emphasis that each parable illuminates.

The Pattern of Authority Language

The similarity of the metaphorical language used in the parables in Mark 4 and 12 points to ways in which they come together in a common pattern of authority and power. Both parables begin with planting and contain the promise of harvest. In both parables, the harvest is dependent on divine power being embodied in the world. Both parables tell the story of the obstacles that hinder the recognition and embodiment of the power of God in the world. Therefore, both readings challenge the community to recognize this divine power and invite the readers to participate in this powerful movement of God in the world. However, both readings also warn of the temptation to use divine authority to conceal structures of domination and to hide a personal craving for status.

The ending of the gospel is important for both readings. Fear and terror, the primary obstacles to faith in Jesus, are prominent in the ending. Both the male followers who thought they were strong and the female followers who felt weak and afraid are represented in the ending. The promise by the young man at the tomb that they would see Jesus in Galilee points both of these groups of followers back to the beginning of the gospel where the stories of the proclamation, healing and teaching of Jesus are told. Here they can be healed and liberated from false power and can again be invited to follow Jesus on the way.

The ending, with its focus on the women followers, also illustrates the subversiveness of the narrative. While the male disciples may have dominated the narrative plot, they do not dominate the "punch line." This subversive ending challenges the women to retell the story by including the radical reversal that is proclaimed by the young man at the tomb. Note that this challenge is first of all given to the women and only secondarily to the other disciples. But the stories of healing and teaching include stories of women and men. Thus the call to proclaim is given to both women and men.

Though there are strong convergences in the readings, it is important not to subsume the differing emphases under a common theme. Several crucial differences can be pointed out that illuminate distinct aspects of the ethos of authority that are evident in Mark.

(1) Though there is a dualism or polarity that is created with the presence of Jesus in both readings, the emphasis is different. In the constructive reading, the focus is on personal identity and character as seen by God. Persons are exposed as being insiders or outsiders to the kingdom. They can be healed and become soil that bears fruit or they can remain as they are, without fruit-bearing capabilities. In the second reading, the dualism is presented as a choice between opposite kinds of power and authority. The human structures of authority are unmasked in their relationship to the politics of God. The focus is on ethical and political choices based on an understanding of the nature of God's power as embodied in Jesus.

(2) Both interpretations point to Jesus as the primary embodiment of divine authority. The first considers Jesus in his power to heal and liberate individuals and communities from their own inner impotence and poverty. The second focuses more strongly on Jesus as the embodiment of an alternative political strategy. Liberation or salvation is a strong theme too, for in order for individuals and communities to be whole they must be liberated from the false social codes that want to determine their actions.

(3) Both interpretations point to the choices that persons have to make as the story of Jesus confronts them. The first unmasks personal weakness and invites persons to accept the healing and liberating power of Jesus. The second unmasks the power of the structures that dominate persons. It subverts any use of divine authority to bolster the human need for domination over others. It thus invites persons to participate in an alternative way of confronting evil.

(4) Both interpretations invite all who hear to participate in the mission inaugurated by Jesus through proclamation, healing, teaching and confront-ation. The first speaks more to a new personal identity that can bring wholeness by its very presence. The second seeks to provide an alternative political strategy for subverting the dominant powers and proclaiming healing for all.

A Discipleship Ethos

The writer of the gospel has written the narrative in such a way that the readers begin to identify with the disciples in the story. Elizabeth Struthers Malbon describes the disciples as the "fallible followers" of Jesus. She thus identifies the strategy of the gospel writer as twofold: "With both disciples and the crowd depicted as followers, as fallible followers, the Marcan narrative message is plain: discipleship is both open-ended and demanding; followership is neither exclusive nor easy."[71]

There seems to be a deliberate ambiguity about the identity of the disciples that allows the reader to see them as both outsiders and insiders. In the story, these disciples are easily tempted to become part of the false authority structures that need subversion. However, sometimes they become part of the crowd that needs healing and feeding. This creates the real choices that face the characters in the story and thus mirrors the real choices that face the readers. This strategy allows the unmasking and subversion of would-be disciples, whether characters or readers, at the same time as it allows the affirmation and empowering of those who are weak and fearful.

Discipleship in the gospel represents all those who are faced with choices because they are faced with the embodiment of divine authority in the words and actions of Jesus. The ethos of authority that discipleship represents in Mark is therefore dependent on an *embodiment of divine authority* in the community, whether this community is the early church or a contemporary community of readers. This embodiment both unmasks the personal identities of the members of the community and subverts oppressive human authority structures. This allows an alternative power to emerge in the community that can heal persons and empower the community to choose the way of divine power—a way of being in the world that combines power with vulnerability, authority with marginalization.

The presence of Jesus, with his authority and power, is therefore risky for a community. It will expose a person's core of being. It will reveal structures of oppression. It will force persons to choose between God's kind of power and their own need for control over others. It will therefore be a temptation to send Jesus out of the community. Disciples therefore struggle to allow the freeing and healing presence of Jesus to remain in their midst. Accepting liberation and healing is no easier than rejecting the use of coercive power and domination.

The Function of a Discipleship Ethos of Authority

The narrative form of the Gospel of Mark invites the readers to identify with the various characters and make choices about the various situations facing the characters in the story. However, it may be difficult to know with whom to identify in this narrative. In the beginning of the gospel, the readers naturally identify with the disciples in their struggle to recognize and name divine authority. This identification creates tension in the reading process, because the fallibility of the disciples becomes more and more evident. The reader is therefore easily persuaded to identify with the hero of the story, Jesus. This, however, means identifying with the cross and with a non-violent approach to oppressive structures. This becomes a difficult choice and involves believing that God's power can heal and restore the dead. It is the readers who must decide. Will they continue to identify with the "fallible followers" in their failure? If they choose to identify with Jesus will they also be willing to identify with his choice to go to the cross?

The answers that interpreters give to these questions is often influenced by the ethos of authority in their own hermeneutic communities. Therefore, a look at the communities in which the gospel is read will help place these choices into a more specific context.

The community of Mark. Because of the historical distance between the hermeneutic community in which the writer of the gospel stood and the present community we have to rely on a somewhat speculative reconstruction of the original context. However, there are some aspects of the Gospel of Mark that point to a certain kind of community:

(1) The community probably assumed a dualistic framework for assessing the world. This framework placed a deep gulf between good and evil, between God and Satan. This is reminiscent of the apocalyptic literature of the first century especially popular in minority communities.

(2) The community saw itself as gathered around the Hebrew Scriptures and around faith in Jesus as Son of God. This is evident in the kind of legitimations in Mark that place Jesus at the centre of the narrative.

(3) The community has probably experienced the misuse of power both from within and from without. Both the unmasking of personal power and the subversion of structures of power point to the need in the community for a deeper understanding and experience of God's power.

(4) There are hints that authority struggles within the community could include conflicts where power is based on gender. Yet Mark speaks from within the unreflective patriarchal worldview of his century and does not identify these struggles directly. He accepts the view that women are generally representative of the other, the poor and the weak. This makes the presence of the women at the end of the gospel disruptive. At the same time, Mark does not identify either gender with one of the poles of his dualistic framework. Jesus' maleness does not become a legitimating factor for the authority that he is given. Neither does the femaleness of followers become the primary problem to be overcome in representing God's kind of authority in the mission of the followers of Jesus. Instead, it is the openness of both women and men to God's healing that is affirmed by the stories. It is the false use of authority by women and men that is exposed in the narrative.

(5) The ethos of authority in Mark intrudes and interrupts not only the ethos of authority in the discipleship community but also that of the larger society. Both the parables and the narrative open the story outward to a broader group of people beyond the community and challenge them to respond to the truth that is proclaimed. Malbon has pointed out the pattern of movement in the gospel from the disciples to the crowd to the hearers/readers of the narrative.[72]

Can these assumptions about the community help us identify the particular geographical and historical community to which Mark addressed the gospel? Senior suggests that a specific historical context for the kind of theology dealing with external power could be found in a number of places and times in early Christianity.[73] He suggests that on both internal and external grounds, this context could be Rome in the aftermath of the persecution by Nero. Both the nature of the kingship of Jesus and the kind of subtle inversion of power that is suggested by Mark would be suitable for a community in Rome around 70 CE. Myers suggests a town such as Capernaum, in Galilee, as a more probable location. He feels that the gospel was written to encourage a social group alienated by the dominant culture but engaged in alternative political action.[74] In either case, the Gospel of Mark relativizes and subverts human political authority in the interest of proclaiming a new way of discipleship, rooted in the confession of Jesus as the authoritative presence of God.

The choices that were made by the original community that responded to the Gospel of Mark are largely hidden in history. However, we can guess that the gospel message was controversial for the followers of Jesus, as well as for the larger Jewish community in the first century. By clearly showing Jesus as the embodiment of divine power and authority, while presenting him in his human vulnerability, Mark's gospel subverts notions of dominance and status. Moreover, like Jesus, the Gospel text itself is vulnerable, open to misinterpretation and abuse. It can be understood as another human witness that embodies or represents divine authority in history. As the story was read in various locations in the first century, the ethos of authority of each reading community would be revealed and exposed, forcing would-be disciples to make important choices.

A Mennonite/feminist hermeneutic community. The interpretation of the gospel that I have made places several challenges before readers whether they stand within a Mennonite or a feminist hermeneutic community. Aspects of the interpretation can function either to justify one of the communities in its present social/political life or to unmask the false authority and power present in one of the communities. In my dialogue with each community, I must therefore choose between speaking critically and constructively or speaking affirmatively, justifying the dominant ethos of the community.

These choices are not easy. The external ethos of each community creates authority paradigms within me that have the power to influence the direction I will choose. It is therefore important to articulate the specific way that the interpretation of Mark challenges each hermeneutic community. Several of these challenges seem clear to me after this study of Mark:

First, Mark's gospel claims that Jesus, as an embodiment of God's authority and power, created certain ultimate choices for his disciples by his very presence in history. But even more than that, Mark presents his gospel in such a way that these same choices are placed before readers in every age. His gospel therefore suggests that God's authority and power can continue to be embodied in various human witnesses in a community, including the witness

of the narratives themselves. Readers must make choices about God when they
read Mark's witness to God's presence in history.

These choices becomes complex when the dominant construal of the
Bible in a particular hermeneutic community is examined. According to Mark's
narrative, Jesus is recognized as an embodiment of God's presence by his
disciples, not primarily because of his overpowering authority but rather in
spite of his vulnerability to misinterpretation and abuse.[75] It is the ambiguity of
Jesus' authority and the vulnerability of Jesus' as human that exposes the
sensitivity of the people to divine authority. Both the Mennonite and feminist
communities struggle with the unpretentious nature of the human witness to
divine authority embodied in the narrative of Jesus. Mennonites would like to
strengthen the authority of the Bible by naming the Bible and the church as the
only witnesses able to represent divine authority. By making obedience the only
possible response for those who name themselves disciples, they fail to
understand the vulnerability that is necessary because these witnesses to God's
authority are human.

Feminists are less clear about the Bible as an embodiment of Jesus in
the community. They question its authority, placing more weight on their own
ability to discern Christ in their midst. They fail to see how a kind of obedience
to their own self-interests may jeopardize their response to God.

Mark's claim that Jesus embodies God's authority challenges both
communities to state their truth claims in a way that will acknowledge both the
empowerment that God gives to disciples through the presence of Jesus and the
vulnerability that comes because this claim is embodied in a human-authored
book and in human-created institutions. Mark's claims also challenge me to
find a way to speak about biblical authority that opens me to God's authority
as I continue to read and interpret the Bible, while at the same time encourages
me to remain vulnerable because of my humanity as an interpreter of a human-
authored book.

Secondly, the strong dualism or polarity in the Gospel of Mark is
particularly challenging for someone who has been attempting to describe and
illuminate relationships, rather than surrendering to the more prevalent
dualistic or polarized thinking. It is clear that the gospel writer differentiates
between two alternatives in his understanding of power. He suggests that those
who hear God's message and bear fruit are the opposites of those who do not
hear and understand and therefore do not bear fruit. He implies that the
authority of God and the authority of coercive and oppressive human structures
are polar opposites.

What has become striking to me in my study is that these opposites are
presented as choices facing the readers of the gospel. They are not primarily
presented as a way to characterize those outside of a particular hermeneutic
community, but rather as possibilities for those inside the community. The
absolute identification of some people with God's authority and others with

human authority is subverted by a narrative that turns the usual categories upside down.

This produces tension within both Mennonite and feminist communities who have been tempted to disown one or the other alternative as foreign to their own identity and ethic. Mennonites have placed strict boundaries around the community, attempting to disown all those who understand God's message differently, since they see themselves as being obedient to God's authority. Feminists have claimed the right to define salvation and liberation and have been suspicious of the experiences and definitions of others. Both obedience and suspicion can easily lead to an exaltation of one's own interpretation and an exclusion of the views of others.

The polarity in Mark suggests that the primary duality that must be maintained for disciples is the difference between human and divine power. This presents all humans with the same choices and does not allow disciples, whether Mennonite or feminist, to fully identify themselves with the divine. Practically, this implies that suspicion of self must stand side by side with suspicion of others. Therefore, I must be open to critical dialogue that will allow others to question my conclusions, just as I sometimes question the conclusions of others. I must be ready to obey the voice of God whether it comes to me through my own experience or through the dialogue with others.

(3) The two readings of the gospel point me to the choices that are involved both in gaining healing and in using authority and power. A minority status, whether as a Mennonite or as a feminist, does not protect me from these hard choices. There is a choice involved in gaining healing and in receiving strength as well as in the use of that power. The message of Mark challenges both communities to go beyond their own past experience, in order to seek healing and empowerment. A minority status does not mean weakness when there is a new identity and a new empowerment possible through the gift of God.

There is a danger with this emphasis. This challenge could be used in a negative way within the community to insinuate that the victims of abuse and oppression are responsible for their pain and abuse. Women and children have had the gospel used against them in this way throughout history. A focus on the readiness of Jesus to heal, together with his confrontation of all types of abuse, could be helpful in avoiding the negative use of the emphasis on autonomy and choice.

The temptation to deny the power and authority that comes with education, economic security, denominational identity, race or gender is there within both the Mennonite and the feminist community. The gospel would challenge the community to expose any use of political and social power to dominate or control and encourage the community to discover the nature of divine power to heal and save. It would also suggest that the invitation to fully become part of a community should be made to all who feel marginalized and

outside of the community. This would affirm some of the efforts that Mennonites and feminists have already made in this direction.

(4) The truth claims associated with discipleship challenge me in a
variety of ways, especially since the struggle of authority is both an external
social and political struggle and an internal struggle of identity and character.
This struggle changes depending on the community with which I identify most
strongly in any particular situation. The focus on healing and liberation is
especially important for Mennonites, who have stressed servanthood and self-
giving as key to discipleship. A broader ethos of salvation would make
servanthood a choice rather than a role that is assumed. The focus on
vulnerable confrontation may be especially important for feminists as they seek
ways to confront domination. There is a need to define the ethics of
communication and confrontation in line with Jesus' approach.

(5) This study has affirmed for me that the personal and the social-
political must not be pitted over against each other. This may be especially
important for Mennonites who have emphasized community and failed to
recognize the personal dimensions of healing and identity. It would affirm the
relationship of the personal and political that is already within feminism.
However, the emphasis on the household of God would urge both communities
to be more strongly aware of the larger Christian community that represents the
brother, the sister, and the mother of Jesus. This urges me toward more
dialogue and conversation.

(6) The strong sense of mission that pervades the gospel challenges me
to define my central goals and aims as an interpreter. This challenge is also
there for Mennonite and feminist hermeneutic communities. They must begin
to see themselves as rhetorical and political communities. For Christians, these
goals can be critically assessed in terms of an identity of discipleship that
focuses on a relationship to Jesus, and an ethic of discipleship that does not
dominate but invites the other into the community.

In summary, Mark's gospel recognizes both the potential and the danger
that comes to a community of disciples with the promise of divine power and
authority. Because the power of liberation can quickly lead to domination, God
continues to subvert the political and social codes that are set up to give status
and authority. God invites all to choose healing and liberation and thus to serve
God in a vulnerable way.

The authority that the Gospel of Mark has for persons standing in a
Mennonite or feminist hermeneutic community will be demonstrated by the
way in which their vision and praxis is transformed by the reading of the text.
The kind of authority that is exhibited by the gospel, however, cannot be
established merely by affirming the Bible as a mediation of God's word. It can
more fruitfully be shown by the way God's revealing and saving presence is
experienced by persons and communities reading the Bible. When biblical
interpretation is experienced as powerful in its ability to heal yet remains

vulnerable in the way it functions in the community, a kind of authority is experienced that resembles the authority of Jesus in the first century.

Endnotes

1   E.g., Fernando Belo, *A Materialist Reading of the Gospel of Mark* (Maryknoll, NY: Orbis, 1990); Ched Myers, *Binding the Strong Man* (Maryknoll, NY: Orbis, 1990); Herman C. Waetjen, *A Reordering of Power* (Minneapolis: Fortress, 1989).
2   Werner H. Kelber, *The Passion in Mark: Studies on Mark 14-16* (Philadelpia: Fortress Press, 1976), pp. 167-168. For another reading that recognizes two levels of meaning, see Mary R. Thompson, *The Role of Disbelief in Mark* (New York: Paulist Press, 1989). She concentrates on belief and disbelief, rather than power and powerlessness as key to the narrative reading of the gospel.
3   Ernest Best, *Following Jesus: Discipleship in the Gospel of Mark* (Sheffield, UK: JSOT Press, 1981) and *Disciples and Discipleship: Studies According to Mark* (Edinburgh: T&T Clark, 1986). Other examples of a similar understanding of the Gospel of Mark in its focus on the power of Jesus to create a community of disciples would be John R. Donahue, *The Theology and Setting of Discipleship in the Gospel of Mark* (Milwaukee, WI: Marquette University Press, 1983), and Jack Dean Kingsbury, *The Christology of Mark's Gospel* (Philadelphia: Fortress Press, 1983).
4   Theodore J. Weeden, *Mark—Traditions in Conflict* (Philadelphia: Fortress Press, 1971). Several other interpreters who would concur that the major thrust in Mark is corrective theology would include Werner H. Kelber, *Mark's Story of Jesus* (Chico, CA: Scholars Press, 1980), and Etienne Trocme, *The Formation of the Gospel According to Mark*, trans. Pamela Gaughan (Philadelphia: Fortress Press, 1975).
5   "Fallible Followers: Women and Men in the Gospel of Mark," *Semeia* 28 (1983): 29-48.
6   "Women as Models of Faith in Mark," *Biblical Theology Bulletin* 18, 1 (January 1988): 3-9.
7   "Women Disciples in Mark?" *Catholic Biblical Quarterly* 44 (1982): 225-241.
8   "Silent Voices: Women in the Gospel of Mark," *Semeia* 54 (1992): 145-158.
9   I will be assuming that the author is male as the tradition has done, realizing however that women may have been involved in the oral or even written stage of the narrative.
10 Walter Wink, *Naming the Powers: The Language of Power in the New Testament* (Philadelphia: Fortress Press, 1984), p. 3.
11 Ibid., p. 17.
12 Ibid., pp. 11-12.
13 Robert C. Tannehill stresses the importance of recognizing the narrative unity of the gospel because it allows the function of any one part in the story to emerge with greater clarity. He insists that the rediscovery of the story element is a discovery of power and significance previously unrecognized. "Reading It Whole: The Function of Mark 8:34-35 in Mark's Story," *Quarterly Review* 2, 2 (Summer, 1982): 67-68.
14 James G. Williams agrees with the importance of the relationship between story and parable. However, he emphasizes the "richly ambiguous" nature of that relationship and the way in which a parable implies potential meanings beyond its immediate context *(Gospel Against Parable* [Sheffield, UK: Almond Press, 1985], pp. 155-199). Note also Tolbert's discussion of the gospel as a "concrete universal" in *Sowing the Gospel: Mark's World in Literary-Historical Perspective* (Minneapolis: Fortress, Press, 1989), pp 129-130.

15   *Sowing the Gospel*, pp. 121-124. In her study Tolbert suggests that the parables speak to the identity of Jesus and clarify the role and actions of the various characters in the story.

16   Ibid., pp. 48-79.

17   Ibid., pp. 105-106.

18   Tolbert suggests that the parables of the sower consist of a generalized and universal typology while the parable of the tenants is a more limited, quasi-historical typology (*Sowing the Gospel*, p. 129). The narrative setting suggests to me that both parables are used allegorically and are connected both to the larger narrative and to the historical situation of the readers as disciples who were attempting to understand themselves as God's people. The first answers the question of why not every Jew became part of the new community, the second focuses more on the conflict of the new community with the old.

19   Reader response literary theories have helped create methodologies that focus on the function of particular language patterns for various kinds of readers. A good example that combines reader response methods with historical methods is the study of Carol Schersten Lahurd, "Reader Response to Ritual Elements in Mark 5:1-20," *Biblical Theology Bulletin* 20 (Winter 1990): 154-160.

20   Tolbert, *Sowing the Gospel*, p. 101. Tolbert interprets Mark 4:33-40 as situational irony in which the readers expect some degree of understanding because of v. 34. Instead the story reports that the disciples were fearful and had little faith. She therefore assumes that the disciples are the rocky ground. It seems to me however, that the disciples are still named as insiders, though insiders who can become outsiders because of their fear.

21   John R. Donahue, "A Neglected Factor in the Theology of Mark," *Journal of Biblical Literature* 101, 4 (1982): 584.

22   Ibid., p. 585.

23   Frank Kermode focuses on the arbitrary way in which the outsider is kept outside of the mystery of the gospel, dismayed and frustrated by the inability to enter the door of understanding. See *The Genesis of Secrecy* (Cambridge, MA: Harvard University Press, 1979), pp. 27-28.

24   E.g., Jeremias, *The Parables of Jesus*, S. Hooke, trans., 2nd rev. ed. (New York: Charles Scribner's Sons, 1972), pp. 13-18.

25   Tolbert, *Sowing the Gospel*, pp. 160-161.

26   Ibid., p. 163.

27   Ibid., p. 113.

28   Ibid., pp. 108-113.

29   Kingsbury points out that the cries of the demons serve the positive purpose of reminding the reader who Jesus really is. By alternating the cries of the demons with the questions of the human characters in 1:14-8:26, the knowledge of the demons is juxtaposed with the ignorance of the human characters who do not understand who Jesus really is. See Kingsbury, *The Christology of Mark's Gospel*, pp. 86-87.

30   Donald Senior, "With Swords and Clubs. . . . Mark's Critique of Abusive Power," *Biblical Theology Bulletin* 17 (1987): 14.

31   *Mark as Story* (Philadelphia: Fortress, Press, 1982), p. 112.

32   *Sowing the Gospel*, p. 227.

33   Character portrayal is an important literary device of Hellenistic writers in which villains or heroes were created in order to serve as models of human virtues and vices. See Elizabeth Struthers Malbon, "The Jewish Leaders in the Gospel of Mark: A Literary Study of Marcan Characterization," *Journal of Biblical Literature* 108, 2 (1989): 277-280. Malbon suggests that in terms of form rather than content Mark's typological characterization has two extreme types with the followers constituting a third type

described more subtly and with greater complexity. This more complex group is *both* good and bad while the extreme types are *either* good or bad. The parables of the seed and soils are in line with this general approach by including both a strong dualism and a more complex understanding of the difficulty of really hearing the word and bearing fruit.

34 Literary critics use the terms "round" and "flat" to contrast characters who are depicted as having changing and conflicting traits (therefore complex and unpredictable) with characters who have fewer, usually consistent traits (therefore stereotypical and predictable). See Rhoads and Michie, *Mark as Story*, p. 102.

35 *Sowing the Gospel*, p. 152, n 40.

36 *Sowing the Seed*, pp. 164-172. Tolbert emphasizes the contrast between the good soil and the rocky soil in these stories. I see the contrast more between good soil and unproductive soil in these verses, with the disciples representing the middle ground between unproductive soil and productive soil. Throughout the story the disciples are seen as insiders or perhaps even potential sowers in the kingdom who can become outsiders if fear overcomes the initial faith. The events following these chapters continue the typology by developing more strongly the various kinds of unproductive earth and thus the dangers facing the disciples.

37 *Mark as Story*, p. 129.

38 Ibid., pp. 117-122.

39 Willard Swartley, *Mark, the Way for All Nations* (Scottdale, PA: Herald Press, 1979), pp. 50-51.

40 *Binding the Strong Man*, p. 308.

41 Ched Myers views Mark as an ideological narrative, "the manifesto of an early Christian discipleship community in its war of myths with the dominant social order and its political adversaries" (*Binding the Strong Man*, p. 31). His interpretation has been especially helpful in noting the function of the narrative in light of the second parable.

42 *Mark as Story*, p. 74.

43 *Binding the Strong Man*, p. 307.

44 Ibid., p. 312.

45 Ibid., pp. 314-318.

46 *In Memory of Her*, pp. 144-145.

47 Ibid., p. 319.

48 Ibid., p. 321.

49 Ibid., p. 70.

50 Ibid., pp. 73-87. Myers relies on Belo in constructing his particular model and on various social scientists in describing the various ideological and social strategies. I will only give Myers' syntheses in this brief summary.

51 Ibid., p. 82

52 Ibid., p. 436.

53 Ibid., p. 97.

54 Ibid., pp. 101-104.

55 Ibid., p. 214.

56 Howard C. Kee, "The Terminology of Mark's Exorcism Stories," *New Testament Studies* 14 (1967, 1968): 255.

57 *Binding the Strong Man*, pp. 142-143.

58 Paul W. Hollenbach, "Jesus, Demoniacs, and Public Authorities: A Socio-Historical Study," *Journal of the American Academy of Religion* 49, 4 (1982): 569-572; John H. Pilch, "Healing In Mark," *Biblical Theology Bulletin* 15, 4 (October 1985): 142-145.

59 Ibid., pp. 290-297.

60   Aaron Milavec points out that in the parable the vineyard is not destroyed as it is in
      Isaiah 5. Rather the problem of the use of power by the tenants who have been placed
      in charge of the vineyard is the central concern of the parable. They are the ones who are
      destroyed. Therefore the others cannot be identified as the Gentiles who are now the new
      Israel. See "The Identity of 'the Son' and 'the Others': Mark's Parable of the Wicked
      Husbandman Reconsidered," *Biblical Theology Bulletin* 20, 1 (Spring 1990): 35. A
      supersessionist theology common in traditional exegeses of this passage is foreign to
      Mark who included all who were considered marginal, both Jew and Gentile, in his
      invitation to become the others to whom the vineyard is now given.
61   *Conflict in Mark* (Minneapolis: Fortress Press, 1989), p. 14.
62   Tolbert, *Sowing the Gospel,* pp. 192-193.
63   Michel Clevenot, *Materialist Approaches to the Bible* (Maryknoll, NY: Orbis Press,
      1985): 82.
64   Malbon, "The Jewish Leaders in the Gospel of Mark," p. 276.
65   *Sowing the Gospel*, pp. 139-148.
66   I am in agreement with Tolbert that in Mark's gospel, Jesus' death is not the innocent
      sacrifice demanded by a righteous God *(Sowing the Gospel*, p. 262).
67   *Binding the Strong Man*, p. 250.
68   Ibid., p. 279.
69   *Materialist Approaches to the Bible*, pp. 80-81.
70   Joanna Dewey, "Mark as Interwoven Tapestry: Forecasts and Echoes for a Listening
      Audience,"*Catholic Biblical Quarterly* 53, 2 (April 1991): 231-236.
71   Elizabeth Struthers Malbon, "Disciples/Crowds/Whoever: Marcan Characters and
      Readers," *Novum Testamentum* 28, 2 (1986): 123-124. Though Malbon has studied
      Mark with different questions, her study of Marcan characters has come to similar
      conclusions as I have in my study.
72   Elizabeth Struthers Malbon, "Fallible Followers," *Semeia* 28 (1983): 45.
73   "With Swords and Clubs" p. 18.
74   *Binding the Strong Man*, pp. 85-87, 414.
75   William Placher has also noted the vulnerability of the biblical narrative in his recent
      book, *Narratives of a Vulnerable God* (1994). See especially chap. 4.

Conclusion

An Invitation to Further Experimentation

"We do not simply accept the tradition, but we do not reject it either. We wrestle it: fighting it and making love to it at the same time. We try to touch it with our lives."[1] This experiment in feminist thought was not an objective scientific experiment. My involvement in a particular tradition that stressed obedience to biblical authority seemed to clash directly with a developing feminist consciousness that looked with suspicion on this very same authority. This study took on the character of a wrestling with God, as I sought to clarify the significant connections as well as major distinctions between a hermeneutics of obedience and a hermeneutics of suspicion.

The methodological assumption that allowed this experiment to flourish was the value of relational thinking. The rejection of a subject/object polarity allowed me to describe aspects of the Mennonite hermeneutic community and of the feminist hermeneutic community as I had experienced them and as I had encountered them in their own written literature. It allowed both the tensions and the connections between the modes of authority in these communities to surface. At the same time this description was not done in isolation. I consciously did my study in the context of a larger framework of discipleship, a framework that encouraged theological and biblical scholarship to interact and to challenge each other.

This wrestling with the tradition, with feminist consciousness and with the biblical text seemed at first to move me into conflicting directions. The first direction, which asserted the relationship between the divine and human, was not surprising, for it is assumed in my methodology and was only clarified more clearly through the process of study and reflection. The second, which insisted on the radical difference between divine and human authority, interrupted my assumptions, forcing me to change and qualify some of my earlier convictions. At first glance, these two directions seem to present opposite ways of articulating the power and authority of God in history. However, as I reflected more deeply, I began to suspect that both are needed in order to do justice to both the nature of God and the nature of humanity.

The intermingling of divine and human creativity in text, community and interpretive process suggests that divine and human authority are intimately related in the history of the disciple community. Therefore, notions of biblical authority cannot be articulated in terms of a polarity between God and humans. To use a Marcan metaphor, this intermingling of divine and human creativity suggests that both God and humans are involved in the sowing of the seed, in the working of the soil and even in the composition of the soil itself. To attempt to categorically separate God's work from human

145

work is to miss seeing God at work in the world through human mediation, through human servants or through a human-authored text. Or alternatively, it is to fail to acknowledge the human embodiment of God's revealing presence on earth through Jesus, or through the witness of the Bible or the community of disciples.

The attempt to clearly separate God's authority from human authority tends to work itself out in a subtle domination of the other. A false polarization is created in which one's own interpretive practice is associated with the divine, while that of other communities is associated with the human. Self-critique is stifled, while critique of the other is easily justified. When this happens, God's authority is limited and human involvement in the interpretive process is given too much power and authority.

In a general way, both Mennonite and feminist hermeneutic communities acknowledge an intermingling of the divine and the human in the interpretive process. However, when the methodological approach is reduced to either obedience or suspicion, the tension is dissolved and one of the partners of the creative work on earth becomes invisible. Thus Mennonites have difficulty in acknowledging the human aspects of the church's involvement in the hermeneutic process. They often fail to be self-critical of their own tendency to oppress the marginalized voices in the name of God. Feminists are suspicious of male domination in both the Bible and the interpretive process. They have difficulty acknowledging the presence of the divine outside of their own feminist communities of interpretation. This creates its own form of domination.

The Gospel of Mark suggests that the people of the first century struggled with the inherent ambiguity surrounding the authority of Jesus, the authority of the religious leaders and the authority of the "others" who were challenged to proclaim the message of Jesus. The divinity of Jesus did not overwhelm people in such a way that his human nature was obscured. The political and social power of the religious leaders could not easily be separated from the relationship to the divine that their positions in the religious institutions gave them. The seemingly weak and powerless such as the women at the tomb, could not easily be seen as authoritative proclaimers of the Word of God. However, the gospel testifies to God's divine presence within human history, and challenges the disciples to discern its presence despite the ambiguity created by the human embodiment of that authority.

The difference between divine and human authority is so great that it must be clearly articulated in terms of a duality that explicitly differentiates between the authority of God and the authority of humans. Therefore, notions of biblical authority cannot be articulated solely in terms of a connectedness between the human and the divine. A clear difference is asserted in the Gospel of Mark between divine and human authority. The disciples were given a choice; they had to choose between two opposite kinds of authority. The typological descriptions of the leaders, as well as of the ones who chose to be healed, encourages the readers to think in terms of drastically opposite alternatives. The Gospel of Mark therefore clearly challenges a theology that would stress the identity between God and humanity to the exclusion of a strong statement of difference between them.

The danger of equating human and divine authority became very clear in the analysis of both the Mennonite and feminist hermeneutic communities. When the authority of God became encapsulated by a particular hermeneutic community, choices were taken away from some members of the community. A hermeneutical circle developed that could not easily be interrupted. God's disruptive presence was not easily acknowledged and God's authority to transform the community was limited.

The need to maintain freedom of choice in any community that calls itself church necessitates an articulation of the difference between God's authority and human authority. There must be a way in which freedom is given to persons within the community so that they may critically evaluate and reject interpretation that they see as false. A hermeneutics of suspicion of human authority is therefore a necessary moment in the interpretive process. However, there must also be a way in which the openness of persons to the Holy Spirit in their midst can be expressed. This openness may well be indicated by a hermeneutics of obedience that listens to a text with a view toward responding with wholehearted assent to the voice of God.

A Hermeneutics of Discipleship

These opposite directions pointed me to a hermeneutics of discipleship that could lead me beyond the false polarity implied by obedience and suspicion while affirming a new understanding of both the truth claim of the otherness of God and the reality of human involvement in the interpretive process. Discipleship is a theological concept and a practice dependent on the truth claim asserting God's revealing and saving presence in the world. These truth claims cannot be proved by an appeal to objectivity in methodology, nor supported by a clear division between humans as subject and God as object. Rather, God can best be described as the creator and source of all reality, yet one who became present in history in various ways in order to initiate relationships with humans and to invite a response. This is a faith claim asserted as part of the larger network of beliefs that surrounds the notion of discipleship. The church is that institution that proclaims the story of God's incarnation in Jesus and lives in the awareness of God's initiating grace through God's calling to discipleship through Jesus.

Discipleship can be described in terms of a process of following Jesus, who is clearly confessed as the Lord. This process, empowered by the Spirit, embraces moments of both obedience and suspicion as the way is discerned and the path is followed. This is because God's authority is powerful in its ability to reveal and save but vulnerable in its embodiment in humanity and in human structures. The nailing of Jesus to the cross can be understood as a powerful embodiment in Jesus of this vulnerability and refusal to protect God's authority with violent human power. But it is also a powerful witness to the misuse of the freedom of choice given to all humans, a misuse which leads to abuse and oppression. The church, as a human institution, participates in this misuse of divine authority.

A discipleship hermeneutic connects the church and the Bible in an authoritative process. This process can be energizing and life-giving for the community, as the power of God becomes evident in the healing and liberation that happens. However, it can become violent and oppressive if either the Bible or the church claim exclusive right to God's authority. Disciples are challenged to listen, understand and follow Jesus.

Biblical Authority

What then does all of this mean for biblical authority? What kind of ethos of authority would allow both an assertion of the otherness of God and an equal emphasis on God's initiative to reveal and save through human mediation? What kind of ethos would embrace moments of suspicion and also moments of obedience, but give neither perspective ultimate allegiance?

A hermeneutics of discipleship produces a paradoxical assertion of biblical authority. The Bible remains a vulnerable text, limited by its human authorship, open to abuse and misuse by human interpreters. At the same time, the Bible is affirmed as powerful in its ability to reveal and transform readers. Human involvement in the hermeneutical process implies that this paradox must remain, even in the midst of strong statements that assert God's authority and affirm the Bible as a primary embodiment of God's Word.

This paradox produces tensions within the human community, the *ekklēsia*, that interprets the Bible. This is often articulated as a conflict of authority experienced internally within the individual interpreter, as well as externally between two hermeneutic communities with differing dominant approaches to the Bible. These tensions can lead to polarization and alienation. However, they can also be embraced as necessary tensions that can help us face our human limitations as individuals and as communities.

It is these tensions that can lead to a dynamic conversation concerning biblical texts and their interpretation, a conversation in which all human claims to truth are relativized, yet are listened to seriously as possible sources of God's disruptive truth. This dialectical process between centre and margins of an enlarged hermeneutic community can transform persons and communities. It can produce a dynamic church that does more than proclaim the Bible as God's Word. Instead, in its practice of reading and struggling with the truth claims of particular texts, it can be witness to an openness to hearing God's disruptive Word.[2]

How can this approach to biblical authority be helpful in the interpretation of specific texts? Would the construal and interpretation of the texts change if this view of discipleship authorized the interpretative process?

The household codes could provide a particularly suitable test for this view of authority, since these texts have produced polarization and alienation in many hermeneutic communities. They are texts particularly vulnerable to misuse and abuse because they speak to specific situations and address particular needs. The tensions between interpretations of these texts speaks to the limitations of a human-authored Bible and a human-created community to clearly speak God's word. Moments of suspicion are therefore necessary in order to detect the way these texts can be used to foster unhealthy submission or justify oppressive power, thereby taking away choices and maintaining unjust institutional structures.

But these texts also include truth claims that cannot be ignored. Contemporary readers must wrestle with claims that suggest that returning abuse for abuse is not God's response to injustice (1 Peter 2:23). They must wrestle with the mutuality suggested by a subjection to one another, modelled on Jesus Christ's death for the church (Eph. 5). Neither a suspicion that rejects these texts completely nor an easy obedience that fails to see the freedom of living a new life in Christ does justice to these texts in which the human and divine are so thoroughly intertwined.

Static interpretation is avoided when conversations begin to happen between those committed to both an obedience to God and a suspicion of the use of these texts to legitimate human authority. Different choices become available when the conversation includes a readiness for self-critique as well as an openness to sharing deep convictions. The interpretations of these texts are thereby opened up, allowing new directions to be found through the dialogue. Truth claims of the text will be highlighted in order that a discerning response can be given. Limited visions of particular texts can be pointed out and other texts can be brought into the conversation to enrich the process. Both those on the margins and those in the centre of the community will be invited to assist in discovering possibilities of interpretation that may have been hidden by centuries of misuse of the text. In this approach to the household codes, the text challenges the community to go beyond static interpretation, to discover alternative responses in line with the claim that Jesus embodied God's authority.

This has been an experiment in feminist thought, attempted by someone standing within a Mennonite tradition. I have judged this experiment successful in terms of its ability to invite me to deeper commitment to God, to a renewed openness to dialogue and to more courageous self-critique. The invitation is therefore extended to others to test these findings by exploring the authority relationships in their own hermeneutic communities. Perhaps this ever growing circle of dialogue will lead to a greater sensitivity to God's Word. Perhaps it will lead to biblical authority that will transform churches into hermeneutic communities of commitment and critical discernment. A hermeneutics of discipleship will be successful if the conversation broadens, the discernment deepens and free choices are made as the biblical text is read and studied in community.

Endnotes

1   A.J. Waskow, *Godwrestling* (New York: Schocken Books, 1978), p. 11. This is quoted by T. Drorah Setel, "Feminist Insights and the Question of Method," in *Feminist Perspectives on Biblical Scholarship* (Atlanta:GA: Scholars Press, 1985), p. 42, to stress our experience of the authority of a text.

2   Walter Brueggeman, in his discussion of canonization and contextualization, comes to a similar conclusion. However, I would stress that we also internalize something about the centre and the margins because of our involvement in a variety of hermeneutic communities each of which has its own definitions of the centre and the boundary. *Interpretation and Obedience* (Minneapolis: Fortress Press, 1991), pp. 128-134.

Selected Bibliography

1. Method and Hermeneutical Approach

Bernstein, Richard J. *Beyond Objectivism and Relativism: Science, Hermeneutics, and Praxis.* Philadelphia: University of Pennsylvania Press, 1983.

———. *Praxis and Action: Contemporary Philosophies of Human Action.* Philadelphia: University of Pennsylvania Press, 1971.

Bonino, José Miguez. *Doing Theology in a Revolutionary Situation.* Philadelphia: Fortress Press, 1975.

Brueggeman, Walter. *The Creative Word: Canon as Model for Biblical Education.* Philadelphia: Fortress Press, 1982.

———. *Interpretation and Obedience.* Minneapolis: Fortress Press, 1996.

Cahill, Lisa Sowle. "The New Testament and Ethics: Communities of Social Change." *Interpretation* 44, 4: 383-394.

Detweiler, Robert, ed. *Reader Response Theories to Biblical and Secular Texts.* Thematic issue of *Semeia* 31. Decatur, GA: Scholars Press, 1985.

Fetterley, Judith. *The Resisting Reader: A Feminist Approach to American Fiction.* Bloomington and London: Indiana University Press, 1978.

Fiorenza, Francis Schüssler. *Foundational Theology.* New York: Crossroad, 1984.

Fish, Stanley. *Is There a Text in This Class? The Authority of Interpretive Communities.* Cambridge, MA: Harvard University Press, 1980.

Frei, Hans W. *The Eclipse of Biblical Narrative.* New Haven and London: Yale University Press, 1974.

Gadamer, Hans-Georg. *Reason in the Age of Science.* Cambridge, MA and London, UK: The MIT Press, 1981.

———. *Truth and Method.* New York: Continuum Publishing Co., 1975.

Green, Garrett, ed. *Scriptural Authority and Narrative Interpretation.* Philadelphia: Fortress Press, 1987.

Hanson, Paul. *Dynamic Transcendence: The Correlation of Confessional Heritage and Contemporary Experience in a Biblical Model of Divine Activity.* Philadelphia: Fortress Press, 1978.

Hauerwas, Stanley and Gregory L. Jones. *Why Narrative? Readings in Narrative Theology.* Grand Rapids, MI: Eerdmans, 1989.

Johnston, Robert K. *The Use of the Bible in Theology: Evangelical Options.* Atlanta: John Knox Press, 1983.

Kaufmann, Gordon D. *An Essay on Theological Method.* Missoula, MT: Scholars Press, 1975.

———. *Theology for a Nuclear Age.* Philadelphia: Manchester University Press and Westminster Press, 1985.

Kelsey, David H. *The Uses of Scripture in Recent Theology.* Philadelphia: Fortress Press, 1975.

Lash, Nicholas. *Theology on the Way to Emmaus.* London: SCM Press, 1986.

Lindbeck, George A. "Barth and Textuality." *Theology Today* 43 (1986): 361-376.

———. *The Nature of Doctrine: Religion and Theology in a Postliberal Age.* Philadelphia: Fortress Press, 1984.

Marshall, Bruce D. "Aquinas as a Postliberal Theologian." *The Thomist* (1989): 353-402.
McClendon, James Wm. *Ethics*. Nashville: Abingdon, 1986.
Meeks, Wayne A. "A Hermeneutics of Social Embodiment." *Harvard Theological Review* 79 (1986): 176-186.
Mills, Patricia Jagentowicz. *Woman, Nature and the Psyche*. New Haven and London: Yale University Press, 1987.
Mueller-Vollmer, Kurt, ed. *The Hermeneutics Reader*. New York: Continuum Publishing Co., 1985.
Murphy, Nancy and James Wm. McClendon, "Distinguishing Modern and Post-modern Theologies." *Modern Theology* 5, 3 (April 1989): 191-212.
Pinnock, Clark. *The Scripture Principle*. San Francisco: Harper & Row, 1984.
Placher, William C. *Narratives of a Vulnerable God*. Louisville, KY: Westminister/John Knox Press, 1994.
_____. "Paul Ricoeur and Postliberal Theology: A Conflict of Interpretation." *Modern Theology* 4, 1 (1987): 35-52.
Ricoeur, Paul. *Essays on Biblical Interpretation*. Edited by Lewis S. Mudge. Philadelphia: Fortress Press, 1979.
_____. *Hermeneutics and the Human Sciences*. Edited by John B. Thompson. Cambridge: Cambridge University Press, 1981.
Sanders. James A. *Canon and Community: A Guide to Canonical Criticism*. Philadelphia: Fortress Press, 1984.
Schner, George. "The Appeal to Experience."*Theological Studies* 53,1 (1992): 40-59.
Shapiro, Gary and Alan Sica, eds. *Hermeneutics: Questions and Prospects*. Amherst: The University of Massachusetts Press, 1984.
Thiemann, Ronald F. *Revelation and Theology: The Bible as Narrated Promise*. Notre Dame, IN: University of Notre Dame Press, 1985.
Young, Iris Marion. "The Ideal of Community and the Politics of Difference." Edited by Linda J. Nicholson. *Feminism/Postmodernism*. New York and London: Routledge, 1990, p. 300-323.

2. Mennonite Theology and Interpretation

Anabaptism Today 11 (February 1996).
"The Anabaptist Vision." *The Conrad Grebel Review* 12, 3 (Fall 1994); 12, 4 (Winter 1995).
Bender, Harold S. "The Anabaptist Theology of Discipleship." *Concern* 18 (July 1971): 36-46.
_____. *The Anabaptist Vision*. Scottdale, PA: Herald Press, 1944.
_____. *Biblical Revelation and Inspiration*. Scottdale, PA: Mennonite Publishing House, 1959.
Bender, Ross Thomas. *The People of God*. Scottdale, PA: Herald Press, 1987.
Brandt, Di "The silence of women is a goal of pornography." *Mennonite Reporter* 15, 13 (June 24, 1985): 11.
Concern. A Pamphlet Series for Questions of Christian Renewal. Scottdale, PA, No. 1-18.

Cummings, Mary Lou. *Full Circle: Stories of Mennonite Women*. Newton, KS: Faith and Life Press, 1978.

Confession of Faith in a Mennonite Perspective. Scottdale, PA and Waterloo, ON: Herald Press, 1995.

Dueck, A J., ed. *The Bible and the Church*. Winnipeg, MB: Kindred Press, 1988.

Driedger, Leo and Donald B. Kraybill. *Mennonite Peacemaking*. Scottdale, PA: Herald Press, 1994.

Durnbaugh, Donald F. *The Believer's Church: The History and Character of Radical Protestantism*. London: Collier-MacMillan, 1968.

Dyck, Cornelius J., ed. *A Legacy of Faith: The Heritage of Menno Simons*. Newton, KS: Faith and Life Press, 1962.

Epp, Marlene. "Women in Canadian Mennonite History: Uncovering the 'Underside'." *Journal of Mennonite Studies* 6 (1988): 90-107.

Frantz, Nadine Pence, ed. "Women: Bearing the Cross of Discipleship." *Women's Concerns Report* 89 (March/April 1990): 1-14.

Friedmann, Robert. *The Theology of Anabaptism*. Scottdale, PA, 1973.

Garrett, James Leo, Jr., ed. *The Concept of a Believer's Church: Addresses from the 1967 Louisville Conference*. Scottdale, PA: Herald Press, 1969.

Gingerich, Melvin. "The Mennonite Women's Missionary Society." *Mennonite Quarterly Review* 37 (April, July 1963): 113-125.

Goering, Gladys V. *Women in Search of Mission: A History of the General Conference Women's Organizations*. Newton, KS: Faith and Life Press, 1980.

Good, Martha Smith. *Women in Ministry in the Mennonite Conference of ON and Quebec: Uncovering their Experiences*. D. Min thesis, Toronto School of Theology, 1988.

Hershberger, Guy F. *The Recovery of the Anabaptist Movement*. Scottdale, PA: Herald Press, 1967.

Huebner Harry, ed. *The Church as Theological Community*. Winnipeg, MB: CMBC Publications, 1990.

Hartzler, Tina. "Choosing to Be Honest Rather than Good." *Festival Quarterly* (Summer 1986): 7-18.

"In a Mennonite Voice: Women Doing Theology." The *Conrad Grebel Review* 10, 1 (1992): 1-86.

Jeschke, Marlin. *Discipling in the Church: Recovering a Ministry of the Gospel*. Scottdale, PA: Herald Press, 1988. Originally published 1972,

Kaufman, Gordon D. *Nonresistance and Responsibility and Other Mennonite Essays*. Newton, KS: Faith and Life Press, 1979.

Kauffman, J. Howard and Leland Harder, eds. *Anabaptists Four Centuries Later*. Scottdale, PA: Herald Press, 1975.

_____. *The Mennonite Mosaic: Identity and Modernization*. Scottdale, PA and Waterloo, ON: Herald Press, 1991.

Klaassen, Walter. *Anabaptism in Outline: Selected Primary Sources*. Scottdale, PA and Kitchener, ON: Herald Press, 1981.

_____. *Anabaptism: Neither Catholic Nor Protestant.*. Waterloo ON: Conrad Press, 1973.

_____. "The Nature of the Anabaptist Protest." *Mennonite Quarterly Review* 45 (October 1971): 291-311.

Klassen A.J., ed. *Consultation on Anabaptist Mennonite Theology*. Fresno, CA: Council of Mennonite Seminaries, 1970.

Koontz, Gayle Gerber. "The Liberation of Atonement." *Mennonite Quarterly Review* 63, 2 (April 1989): 171-192.

_____. "The Trajectory of Scripture and Mennonite Conviction." *The Conrad Grebel Review* 5 (Fall 1987): 201-220.

Koontz, Gayle Gerber and Willard Swartley, eds. *Perspectives on Feminist Hermeneutics*, Occasional Papers, 10. Elkhart, IN: Institute of Mennonite Studies, 1987.

Kraus, C. Norman. *Jesus Christ Our Lord: Christology From a Disciple's Perspective*. Scottdale, PA and Kitchener, ON: Herald Press, 1987.

Loewen, Harry, ed. *Why I Am a Mennonite: Essays on Mennonite Identity*. Scottdale, PA and Kitchener, ON: Herald Press, 1988.

Loewen, John Howard. *One Lord, One Church, One Hope, and One God*. Elkhart, IN: Institute of Mennonite Studies, 1985.

Mennonite Encyclopedia I-IV. Scottdale, PA: Mennonite Publishing House, 1956-1959.

Miller, Paul M. *The Prayer Veiling*. Scottdale, PA: Herald Press, 1956.

Nyce, Dorothy Yoder. *Weaving Wisdom: Sermons by Mennonite Women*. South Bend, IN: Womensage, 1983.

_____. *Which Way Women?* Akron, PA: Mennonite Central Committee, Peace Section, 1980.

Packull, Werner. "From Monogenesis to Polygenesis: The Historical Discussion of Anabaptist Origins." *Mennonite Quarterly Review* 49, 2 (1975): 83-121.

Pipken, H. Wayne, ed. *Essays in Anabapist Theology*. Elkhart, IN: Institute of Mennonite Studies, 1994.

Poettcker, Henry and Rudy Regehr, eds. *Call to Faithfulness: Essays in Canadian Mennonite Studies*. Winnipeg, MB: Canadian Mennonite Bible College, 1972.

Redekopp, Calvin Wall and Samuel J. Steiner, eds. *Mennonite Identity*. Waterloo, ON: Institute for Anabaptist and Mennonite Studies, 1988.

Reimer, A. James. "Anabaptist-Mennonite Systematic Theology." *The Ecumenist* 21, 4 (May/June 1983): 68-72.

_____. "The Nature and Possibility of a Mennonite Theology." *The Conrad Grebel Review* 1, 1 (1983): 33-55.

_____. "Further Reflections on a Possible Mennonite Theology." *The Conrad Grebel Review* 1, 3 (Fall 1983): 51-54.

Reimer, Margaret Loewen. *One Quilt, Many Pieces*. 3rd ed. Waterloo, ON: Mennonite Publishing Services, 1990.

Rich, Elaine Sommers. *Mennonite Women: A Story of God's Faithfulness, 1683-1983*. Scottdale, PA: Herald Press, 1983.

Rutschman, LaVerne. "Anabaptism and Liberation Theology." *Mennonite Quarterly Review* 55, 3 (July 1982): 255-270.

_____. "Latin American Liberation Theology and Radical Anabaptism." *Journal of Ecumenical Studies* 19, 1 (Winter 1982): 38-56.

Sawatsky, Rodney. *Authority and Identity: The Dynamics of the General Conference Mennonite Church*. North Newton, KS: Bethel College, 1987.

Schipani, Daniel S., ed. *Freedom and Discipleship: Liberation Theology in an Anabaptist Perspective*. New York: Orbis Books, 1989.

_____. *Religious Education Encounters Liberation Theology*. Birmingham, AL: Religious Education Press, 1988.

Scriven, Charles. *The Transformation of Culture*. Scottdale, PA: Herald Press, 1988.

Simons, Menno. *The Complete Writings of Menno Simons*. Leonard Verduin, trans., John Christian Wenger, ed. Scottdale, PA: Herald Press, 1956.

Snyder, C. Arnold. *Anabaptist History and Theology: An Introduction*. Kitchener, ON: Pandora Press, 1995.

Swartley, Willard. *Slavery, Sabbath, War and Women*. Scottdale, PA and Kitchener, ON: Herald Press, 1983.

_____, ed. *Essays on Biblical Interpretation: Anabaptist-Mennonite Perspectives*, Text-Reader Series 1. Elkhart, IN: Institute of Mennonite Studies, 1984.

_____, ed. *Explorations of Systematic Theology from Mennonite Perspectives*. Elkhart, IN: Institute of Mennonite Studies, 1984.

Toews, John E. and Katie Funk Wiebe, eds. *Your Daughters Shall Prophecy*. Winnipeg, MB: Kindred Press, 1992.

Toews, Paul. "The Concern Movement: Its Origin and Early History." The *Conrad Grebel Review* 8, 2 (Spring 1990): 109-126.

Unrau, Ruth. *Encircled: Stories of Mennonite Women*. Newton, KS: Faith and Life Press, 1986.

Weaver, J. Denny. "A Believers' Church Christology." *Mennonite Quarterly Review* 57, 2 (April 1983): 42-59.

_____. *Becoming Anabaptist*. Scottdale, PA and Kitchener, ON: Herald Press, 1987.

Wiebe, Katie Funk. "The Mennonite Woman in Mennonite Fiction," in *Visions and Realities: Essays, Poems, and Fiction Dealing With Mennonite Issues*. Edited by Harry Loewen and Al Reimer. Winnipeg: Hyperion Press, 1985.

Williams, George H. *The Radical Reformation*. Philadelphia: Westminster Press, 1962.

Williams, George H. and Engel M. Mergal, eds. *Spiritual and Anabaptist Writers*. Philadelphia: Westminster Press, 1957.

Yoder, Elizabeth G., ed. *Peace Theology and Violence Against Women*, Occasional Papers, 16. Elkhart, IN: Institute of Mennonite Studies, 1992.

Yoder, John Howard. *The Fullness of Christ*. Elgin, IL: Brethren Press, 1987.

_____. *The Original Revolution*. Scottdale, PA: Herald Press, 1971.

_____. *The Politics of Jesus*. Grand Rapids, MI: Eerdmans, 1972, rev. ed., 1994

_____. *The Priestly Kingdom: Social Ethics as Gospel*. Notre Dame: University of Notre Dame Press, 1984.

_____. *The Royal Priesthood*. Edited by Michael G. Cartwright. Grand Rapids, MI: Eerdmans, 1994.

_____. "Sacrament as Social Process: Christ the Transformer of Culture." *Theology Today* 48, 1 (April 1991): 33-45.

3. Feminist Theology and Interpretation

Andolsen, Barbara Hilkert. "Agape in Feminist Ethics." *Journal of Religious Ethics* 9 (Spring 1981): 61-83.

Bach, Alice, ed. *The Pleasure of Her Text*. Philadelphia: Trinity Press, 1990.

Bass, Dorothy C. "Women's Studies and Biblical Studies: An Historical Perspective." *Journal of the Society of Old Testament* 22 (1982): 6-12.

Bennett, Anne McGrew. "Overcoming the Biblical and Traditional Subordination of Women." *Radical Religion* 1 (1974): 28-38.

Brock, Rita Nakashima. *Journeys by Heart: A Christology of Erotic Power*. New York: Crossroad, 1988.

Carr, Anne E. *Transforming Grace: Christian Tradition and Women's Experience*. San Francisco: Harper and Row, 1988.

Christ, Carol P. "Embodied Thinking." *Journal of Feminist Studies in Religion* 5, 1 (Spring 1989): 1-15.

Coggins, Richard. "The Contribution of Women's Studies to OT Studies: A Male Reaction." *Theology* 91 (1988): 5-16.

Collins, Adela Yarbro, ed. *Feminist Perspectives on Biblical Scholarship*. Atlanta, GA: Scholars Press, 1985.

Crawford, Janet and Michael Kinnamon. *In God's Image: Reflections on Identity, Human Wholeness and the Authority of Scripture*. Geneva: World Council of Churches, 1983.

Daly, Mary. *Beyond God the Father*. Boston: Beacon Press, 1973.

_____. *Gyn/Ecology*. Boston: Beacon Press, 1984.

D'Angelo, Mary Rose. "Remembering Her: Feminist Readings of the Christian Tradition." *Toronto School of Theology* 2, 1 (Spring 1986):118-126.

Duck, Ruth C. *Gender and the Name of God*. New York: Pilgrim Press, 1991.

Dunfee, Susan Nelson. *Beyond Servanthood: Christianity and the Liberation of Women*. Lanham, ND: University Press of America, 1989.

Fabella, Virginia and Oduyoye, Mercy Amba. *With Passion and Compassion: Third World Women Doing Theology*. New York: Orbis, 1988.

Fiorenza, Elisabeth Schüssler. *In Memory of Her*. New York: Crossroad, 1983.

_____. *Bread Not Stone: The Challenge of Feminist Biblical Interpretation*. Boston: Beacon Press, 1984.

_____. "Commitment and Critical Inquiry." *Harvard Theological Review* 82, 1 (1989): 1-11.

_____. "The Ethics of Biblical Interpretation: Decentering Biblical Scholarship." *Journal of Biblical Literature* 107, 1 (1988): 3-17.

Fulkerson, Mary McClintock. *Changing the Subject: Women's Discourses and Feminist Theology*. Minneapolis: Fortress Press, 1994.

Hampson Daphne. *Theology and Feminism*. Cambridge, MA: Basil Blackwell, 1990.

Hayter, Mary. *The New Eve in Christ:The Use and Abuse of the Bible in the Debate about Women in the Church*. Grand Rapids, MI: Eerdmans, 1987.

Heine, Susan. *Women and Early Christianity: A Reappraisal*. Minneapolis: Augsburg Publishing House, 1988.

Heschel, Susannah. "Anti-Judaism in Christian Feminist Theology." *Tikkun* 5, 3: 25-28, 95-97.

Johnson, Elizabeth Ann. *She Who Is: The Mystery of God in Feminist Theological Discourse*. New York: Crossroad, 1990.

Martin, Frances. *The Feminist Question*. Grand Rapids, MI: Eerdmans, 1994.

McFague, Sallie. *Metaphorical Theology*. Philadelphia: Fortress Press, 1982.

Mollenkott, Virginia Ramey. *The Divine Feminine: The Biblical Imagery of God as Female*. New York: Crossroad, 1983.

_____. *Women, Men & the Bible*. Nashville, TN: Abingdon, 1977.

Moltmann-Wendel, Elizabeth. *The Women Around Jesus*. London: SCM Press, 1982.

Plaskow, Judith. "Christian Feminism and Anti-Judaism." *Crosscurrents* 28 (1978): 306-309.

"Racism in the Women's Movement—Roundtable." *Journal of Feminist Studies in Religion* 4, 1 (Spring 1988): 93-114.

Ringe, Sharon H. *Jesus, Liberation and the Biblical Jubilee*. Philadelphia: Fortress Press, 1985.

Ruether, Rosemary Radforth. *Sexism and God-Talk: Toward a Feminist Theology*. Boston: Beacon Press, 1983.

_____. *Women-Church*. San Francisco: Harper and Row, 1985.

Russell, Letty. *Church in the Round: Feminist Interpretation of the Church*. (Louisville, KY: Westminister/John Knox Press, 1993).

_____. *Household of Freedom: Authority in Feminist Theology*. Philadelphia: Westminster Press, 1987.

_____. *Human Liberation in a Feminist Perspective: A Theology*. Philadelphia: Westminster Press, 1974.

_____, ed. *Feminist Interpretation of the Bible*. Philadelphia: Fortress Press, 1985

_____ and J. Shannon Clarkson, eds. *Dictionary of Feminist Theologies*. Louisville, KY: Westminster/John Knox Press, 1996..

Segovia, Fernando F. and Mary Ann Tolbert, eds. *Reading from This Place*, Volumes 1 and 2. Minneapolis: Fortress Press, 1995.

Stroup, George W. "Between Echo and Narcissus: The Role of the Bible in Feminist Theology." *Interpretation* 42, 1 (1988): 19-32.

Saiving, Valerie. "The Human Situation: A Feminine View," in *Womanspirit Rising*. Edited by Carol Christ and Judith Plaskow. San Francisco: Harper and Row, 1979.

Schneiders, Sandra M. *The Revelatory Text*. New York: HarperSanFrancisco, 1991.

_____. "The Feet-washing: An Experiment in Hermeneutics." *Catholic Biblical Quarterly* 43 (1981): 76-92.

_____. "Women in the Fourth Gospel and the Role of Women in the Contemporary Church." *Biblical Theology Bulletin* 12 (April 1982): 35-45.

Tamez, Elsa, ed. *Through Her Eyes: Women's Theology From Latin America*. New York: Orbis, 1989.

Tetlow, Elisabeth Meier. *Women and Ministry in the New Testament: Called to Serve*. London, New York and Lanham, MD: University Press of America, 1980.

Thistlethwaite, Susan Brooks and Mary Potter, eds. *Lift Every Voice: Constructing Christian Theologies from the Underside*. San Francisco: Harper and Row, 1990.

Tolbert, Mary Ann. "Defining the Problem: The Bible and Feminist Hermeneutics." *Semeia* 28 (1983): 113-126.

Trible, Phyllis. *God and the Rhetoric of Sexuality*. Philadelphia: Fortress Press, 1978.

_____. *Texts of Terror*. Philadelphia: Fortress Press, 1984.

_____. "Feminist Hermeneutics and Biblical Studies." *The Christian Century* (Feb.3-10 1982): 116-118.

Wahlberg, Rachel Conrad. *Jesus According to Woman*. New York: Paulist Press, 1975.

_____. *Jesus and the Freed Woman*. New York: Paulist Press, 1978.

Williams, Delores S. "The Color of Feminism: Speaking the Black Woman's Tongue." *Journal of Religious Thought* 43 (1986):. 42-57.

Winter, Miriam Therese, "The Women-Church Movement." *Christian Century* 106 (March 8): 258-260.

Young, Pamela Dickey. *Christian Method/Christian Theology*. Minneapolis: Fortress Press, 1990.

4. The Gospel of Mark and Discipleship

Beavis, Mary Ann. *Mark's Audience: The Literary and Social Setting of Mark 4:11-12*, Journal for the Study of New Testament Supplement Series 33. Sheffield, UK: JSNT Press, 1989.

_____. "Women as Models of Faith in Mark." *Biblical Theology Bulletin* 18, 1 (January 1988): 3-9.

Belo, Fernando. *A Materialist Reading of the Gospel of Mark*. Maryknoll, New York: Orbis Press, 1981.

Best, Ernest. *Disciples and Discipleship*. Edinburgh: T.& T. Clark, 1986.

_____. *Following Jesus*. Sheffield, UK, JSOT Press, 1981.

Boomershine, Thomas E. "Mark 16:8 and the Apostolic Commission." *Journal of Biblical Literature* 100, 2 (1981): 225-239.

_____. "The Narrative Technique of Mark 16:8." *Journal of Biblical Literature* 100, 2 (1981): 213-223.

Clevenot, Michel. *Materialist Approaches to the Bible*, Trans. William J. Nottingham. Maryknoll, NY: Orbis Books, 1985.

Derret J. Duncan. "Mark's Technique: The Haemorrhaging Woman and Jairus' Daughter." *Biblica* 4 (1982), 474-505.

Dewey, Joanna. "Mark as Interwoven Tapestry: Forecasts and Echoes for a Listening Audience." *Catholic Biblical Quarterly* 53, 2 (April, 1991): 221-235.

Donahue, John R. "Jesus as the Parable of God in the Gospel of Mark." *Interpretation* 32, 4 (October 1978): 369-386.

_____. "A Neglected Factor in the Theology of Mark." *Journal of Biblical Literature*, 101, 4 (1982): 563-594.

_____. *The Theology and Setting of Discipleship in the Gospel of Mark*. Milwaukee, WI: Marquette University Press, 1983.

Dowd, Sharon Echols. *Prayer, Power, and The Problem of Suffering.* Society of Biblical Literature Dissertation Series, 105. Atlanta, GA: Scholars Press, 1988.

Gager, John C. *Kingdom and Community: The Social World of Early Christianity.* Englewood Cliffs, NJ: Prentice-Hall, 1975.

Graham, Susan Lochrie. "Silent Voices: Women in the Gospel of Mark." *Semeia* 54 (1992): 145-158.

Grassi, Joseph A. *The Hidden Heroes of the Gospels: Female Counterparts of Jesus.* Collegeville, MI: The Liturgical Press, 1989.

Harrington, D.J. "A Map of Books on Mark (1975-1984)." *Biblical Theology Bulletin* 15 (1985): 12-16.

Hawkin, David J. "The Incomprehensibility of the Disciples in the Marcan Redaction." *Journal of Biblical Literature* 91 (1972): 491-500.

Hollenbach, Paul W. "Jesus, Demoniacs, and Public Authorities: A Socio-Historical Study." *Journal of the American Academy of Religion,* 49, 4:567-587.

_____. "Liberating Jesus for Social Involvement." *Biblical Theology Bulletin* 15, 4 (October 1985): 151-157.

Hooker, Morna D. *The Gospel of St. Mark.* Black's New Testament Commentaries. London: A & C Black, 1991.

Jeremias, J. *The Parables of Jesus.* S. Hooke., trans. (2d rev. ed.). New York: Charles Scribner's Sons, 1972.

Kealy, Sean P. "Mark: Hope for Our Tragic Times." *Biblical Theology Bulletin* 12, 4 (October 1981): 128-130.

Kee, Howard C. *Community of the New Age: Studies in Mark's Gospel.* Philadelphia: Westminster Press, 1977.

_____. *Medicine, Miracle and Magic in the New Testament Times.* Cambridge: Cambridge University Press, 1986.

Kelber, W. *Mark's Story of Jesus.* Philadelphia: Fortress Press, 1979.

_____. *The Passion in Mark: Studies on Mark 14-16.* Philadelphia: Fortress Press, 1976.

Kingsbury, Jack Dean. *The Christology of Mark's Gospel.* Philadelphia: Fortress Press, 1983.

_____. "The 'Divine Man' as the Key to Mark's Christology—The End of an Era?" *Interpretation* 35, 3 (July, 1981): 243-257.

_____. *Conflict in Mark: Jesus, Authorities, Disciples.* Minneapolis: Fortress Press, 1989.

Lee-Pollard, Dorothy. "Powerlessness as Power: A Key Emphasis in the Gospel of Mark." *Scottish Journal of Theology* 40, 2 (July 1987): 173-188.

Malbon, Elizabeth Struthers. "Disciples/Crowds/Whoever: Marcan Characters and Readers." *Novum Testamentum* 28, 2 (1986): 104-130.

_____. "Fallible Followers: Women and Men in the Gospel of Mark." *Semeia* 28 (1983): 29-48.

_____. "The Jewish Leaders in the Gospel of Mark: A Literary Study of Marcan Characterization." *Journal of Biblical Literature* 108, 2 (1989): 259-281.

_____. "Mark: Myth and Parable." *Biblical Theology Bulletin* 16, 1 (January 1986): 8-17.

_____. "The Poor Widow in Mark and Her Poor Rich Readers." *Catholic Biblical Quarterly* 53, 4 (October 1991): 589-604.

Marcus, Joel. *The Mystery of the Kingdom of God.* Atlanta, GA: Scholars Press, 1986.

Marshall, Christopher D. *Faith as a Theme in Mark's Narrative.* Cambridge: Cambridge University Press, 1989.

Meeks, Wayne A. *The First Urban Christians: The Social World of the Apostle Paul.* New Haven and London: Yale University Press, 1983.

Meye, R.P. *Jesus and the Twelve: Discipleship and Revelation in Mark's Gospel.* Grand Rapids, MI: Eerdmans, 1968.

Milavec, Aaron. "The Identity of 'The Son' and 'The Other': Mark's Parable of the Wicked Husbandman Reconsidered." *Biblical Theology Bulletin* 20, 1 (Spring 1990): 30-37.

Munro, Winsome. "Women Disciples in Mark?" *Catholic Biblical Quarterly* 44 (1982): 225-241.

Myers, Ched. *Binding the Strong Man.* Maryknoll, NY: Orbis, 1990.

Petersen, Norman. "When Is the End not the End? Literary Reflections on the Ending of Mark's Narrative." *Interpretation* 34 (April 1980):151-166.

Pilch, John J. "Healing in Mark: A Social Science Analysis." *Biblical Theology Bulletin* 4 (1985): 142-150.

_____. "Understanding Biblical Healing: Selecting the Appropriate Model." *Biblical Theology Bulletin* 18, 2 (April 1988): 60-66.

Rhoads, David M. and Donald Michie. *Mark as Story.* Philadelphia: Fortress Press, 1982.

Robbins, V. *Jesus the Teacher: A Socio-Rhetorical Interpretation of Mark.* Philadelphia: Fortress Press, 1984.

Schottroff, Luise. "Frauen in der Nachfolge Jesu in Neutestamentlicher Zeit," in *Traditionen der Befreiung.* Edited by Willy Schottroff and Wolfgang Stegemann. München: Kaiser Verlag, 1980, pp. 91-133.

_____. "Maria und die Frauen am Grabe Jesu." *Evangelische Theologie* 42 (January/February, 1982): 3-25.

Scroggs, Robin. "The Earliest Christian Communities as Sectarian Movement," in *Christianity, Judaism and other Greco-Roman Cults.* Edited by Jacob Neusner. Leiden, Netherlands: E.J. Brill, 1975, pp. 1-23.

Selvidge, Marla J. "And Those Who Followed Feared." *Catholic Biblical Quarterly* 45, 3 (July 1983): 396-400.

_____. *Daughters of Jerusalem.* Kitchener, ON and Scottdale, PA: Herald Press, 1987.

_____. *Woman, Cult, and Miracle Recital.* London and Toronto: Associated University Presses, 1990.

Senior, D. "With Swords and Clubs—Mark's Critique of Abusive Power." *Biblical Theological Bulletin* 17 (1987): 10-20.

Swartley, Willard. *Mark: The Way for All Nations.* Scottdale, PA: Herald Press, 1979.

Tannehill, R. "The Disciples in Mark: The Function of a Narrative Role." *Journal of Religion* 57 (1977): 386-405.

_____. "The Gospel of Mark as Narrative Christology." *Semeia* 16 (1980): 57-93.

_____. "Reading It Whole: The Function of Mark 8:34-35 in Mark's Story." *Quarterly Review* 2, 2 (Summer 1982): 67-78.

Telford, William, ed. *The Interpretation of Mark*. Philadelphia: Fortress Press, 1985.

Thiessen, Gerd. *Sociology of Early Palestinian Christianity*. John Bowden, trans. Philadelphia: Fortress Press, 1978.

_____. *The Miracle Stories of the Early Christian Tradition*. Translated by John Riches. Edinburgh: T. & T. Clark, 1983.

Tolbert, Mary Ann. *Sowing the Gospel: Mark's World in Literary-Historical Perspective*. Minneapolis: Fortress Press, 1989.

Trocme, Etienne. *The Formation of the Gospel According to Mark*. Translated by Pamela Gaughan. Philadelphia: Westminster Press, 1975.

Tyson, Joseph B. "The Blindness of the Disciples in Mark." *Journal of Biblical Literature* 80 (1961): 261-268.

Via, Dan O., Jr. *The Ethics of Mark's Gospel—In the Middle of Time*. Philadelphia: Fortress Press, 1985.

Waetjen, Herman C. *A Reordering of Power*. Minneapolis: Fortress Press, 1989.

Weeden, Theodore J. *Mark: Traditions in Conflict*. Philadelphia: Fortress Press, 1971.

Wink, Walter. *Naming the Powers: The Language of Power in the New Testament*. Philadelphia: Fortress Press, 1984.

Wrede, William. *The Messianic Secret*. Translated by J.C.C. Gerig. Greenwood, SC: Attic Press, 1971.

Index of Authors and Subjects

Accountability, 9, 34, 36, 45, 51, 87, 90. *See also* binding and loosing

Anabaptist Vision, 25-28, 47, 49

Anabaptist-Mennonite tradition, xii, 2-3, 8-9, 10-11, 25-28, 29, 31, 33, 35-36, 38, 44, 46, 48, 49-50. *See also* Mennonite

Androcentric, 66, 68, 69

Apocalypticism, 107, 117, 122, 125, 136

Apologetics, xiii, 25-26, 81

Atonement, 73-75

Authority: construal of xi, xiii, 1, 7, 14, 19, 102-104; ethos of, xiii, 1, 6, 21, 28, 39, 44, 54-56, 78, 94-96, 99, 134-141, 148-151; internal sense of, xii, 6, 18, 52, 56, 74, 77, 95-96; in history 37-39, 75-76; mediation of xiii, 15-17, 18-19, 37, 53, 55, 71, 95; practice of, 43-53, 83-92, 120-133; structures of, xiii, 10, 12, 17, 40-42

Authorities, 11, 42, 53, 84, 117-120, 123-127, 132. *See also* leadership

Autonomy, 8, 43, 54, 70, 76, 77, 85, 139. *See also* freedom

Baptism, 3, 34, 51, 84, 89-90, 107, 118

Barrett, Lois, 46

Basileia, 4, 70, 78-79, 82-83, 102. *See also* kingdom of God

Beavis, Mary Ann, 99

Bender, Harold, 8, 25, 27

Bender, Ross, 33

Bernstein, Richard, 5

Best, Ernest, 99

Biblical text: as canon, xiii, 5, 7, 12, 14, 30-31, 38, 39, 55-56, 69, 87, 94; as historical, 30-32, 37-39, 75, 81, 137; as inspired, 2, 26, 35; construal of, 14, 19, 102-104, 137-138; functioning in community, 7, 44-54, 63-66, 78-93, 107, 122-123. *See also* Word of God

Binding and loosing, 11, 35-37, 44-46. *See also* accountability

Bonino, Josè Mìguez, 5

Brandt, Di, 48

Brock, Rita Nakashima, 74

Breaking bread, 45, 49-51, 88-89

Brueggeman, Walter, 94

Cahill, Lisa Sowle, 5, 12

Charisma, 46-47

Choices: freedom of, 34, 52; of authority, 84, 90, 107, 109, 127, 130, 134, 146-150; of identity, 90, 115, 135-140, of hermeneutical approach, xii-xiii, 2, 6, 12, 16, 21, 95, 100; by Jesus, 30, 109-110

Christendom, 3, 33, 86

Church: as community of disciples, 7-10, 25, 31, 32; as hermeneutic community, xii, 3-7, 37; social-political shape of, 33-34, 39, 43, 72-73, 84-88. *See also* women-church, *ekklēsia*

Clevenot, Michel, 126

Commitment, xi, xiii, 2, 4, 10, 12, 15, 17, 19, 21, 30, 33, 34, 37, 38, 40, 42, 44, 50, 63, 70, 71, 90, 100, 101, 107, 119, 149, 150

Consciousness, critical, 4, 16, 63, 66-67, 72, 76, 85, 145. *See also* critique

Convictions, xiii, 6, 18, 20, 100, 145, 149; defined, xi, 13-14; Anabaptist-Mennonite, 1, 3, 8, 10, 28-38, 39, 46, 54, 55; Feminist, 3, 4, 6, 10, 63,

66, 67-77, 81, 85, 87, 93, 94
Creation, 8, 29, 32-35, 36, 47, 48, 51,
    68-71, 72, 76, 79, 90, 94
Critique, xi, xii, xiii, 1, 2, 6, 10-12,
    13-15, 16, 17, 19, 20, 21, 26,
    53-54, 63, 66, 67, 74-75, 76,
    79, 80, 94, 95, 139-140, 146,
    149
Cross, 31, 40-42, 53-54, 74-75, 88-
    89, 91, 99, 109, 114, 123,
    125, 127, 130, 136, 148
Cultural-linguistic, 17-20
Daly, Mary, 66, 74
Dialogue and conversation, xi, xii,
    xiii, 1-5, 6, 8, 10, 12, 13-14,
    16, 18-20, 21, 44, 45, 48, 54,
    55-56, 63, 87, 93, 95, 104,
    139, 148-149, 150
Dirks, Elizabeth, 46
Discernment, 10-12, 35-37, 41, 44,
    47-49, 52-53, 150
Discipleship: as key theological term,
    xii, 2, 7-12, 17, 19; as
    revolutionary subordination,
    39-43, 44, 53-54; as
    subversive memory, 78-83, in
    Anabaptist-Mennonite
    tradition, 8-10, 25-28, 29, 31,
    34, 37 ; in biblical text, 12,
    134-137; in feminist theology,
    4, 7-9, 63, 67, 70, 72, 74, 75,
    76, 78, 93; hermeneutics of,
    147-148
Discourse, xii, xiii, 6, 7, 8, 17-20;
    patterns, xii, 3, 6, 10, 11-12,
    20-21; of feminists, 67, 77-
    93; of Mennonites, 28, 39-54
Domination and oppression, xi, 7, 9,
    17, 41, 56, 63, 65, 66, 70, 74,
    76, 78, 80, 81, 83, 86, 87, 88,
    91, 92, 93, 94, 95, 119, 124,
    129, 132, 133, 134, 135, 140,
    146, 148
Donahue, John, 105
Dualism xi, 21, 68-69, 84, 87, 88, 89,
    99, 105-107, 113, 115, 117-

119, 125, 128, 131-132, 134,
    136, 138-139, 145-147
Dyck, Cornelius J., 31
Ekklēsia, 4, 7, 11, 70, 72, 76, 78, 84-
    86, 94. See also church,
    women-church
Embodiment, xii, 5, 6, 7, 20, 32, 34,
    37, 38, 46, 77; of Jesus'
    authority, 115, 116, 133, 134,
    135, 137, 138, 121; of
    liberation, 73-75; of the
    divine, 37, 38, 55, 56, 115,
    137, 139, 140, 146, 148. See
    also incarnation
Equality, 9, 42, 46, 65-68, 70, 71, 72,
    73, 74, 76, 78, 80, 81, 82, 83,
    87, 91, 92, 93, 94
Ethics, 25, 30, 31, 32, 33, 39-43, 49-
    51, 52, 82-83, 94, 131-140.
    See also justice
Eugene, Toinette M., 91
Experience, xi, 4, 7, 14, 17-19, 20,
    and biblical text, xii, 3, 10,
    13, 14, 16, 17, 92-93; of
    authority, xi, 1, 6, 10-12, 43-
    45, 52-56; of women, 9, 11,
    45, 51, 64, 66, 68, 69, 70, 72-
    76, 80, 81, 83, 85, 92-95
Farley, Margaret A., 69
Fear, 11, 33, 110, 111-115, 129, 132,
    133, 135
Feminism, xi, xiii, 3, 4, 7, 8, 10, 12,
    16, 17, 18, 19, 20, 21, 137-
    140; defined, 9, 21, n. 8; and
    ethos of authority, 63-94
Fish, Stanley, 5
Freedom, 4, 7, 8, 34, 36, 43, 47-49,
    51, 52, 68, 70, 71, 73, 76, 84,
    85, 86, 91, 92, 95, 147, 149;
    of the Spirit, 48-49
Fundamentalism, 26, 28
Gadamer, Hans-Georg, 15-16
Gifford, Carolyn De Swarte, 63-67
God, See Trinity
Graham, Susan Lochrie, 100
Habermas, Jürgen, 16

Healing, 79, 90, 102, 103, 106, 108,
    110, 111, 112, 115, 116, 123-
    124, 125, 128, 129, 130, 131,
    132, 133, 134, 135, 139, 140
Hermeneutical circle 53, 61 n.124, 92
Hermeneutic community: as heuristic
    tool, xii, xiii, 2-7, 13-20;
    feminist, 94-96, 137-141;
    Mennonite, 35-36, 55-56,
    137-141; Marcan, 104, 136-
    137
Hermeneutics of discipleship, 148-
    150
Hermeneutics of obedience, xi, xii,
    10, 15, 17, 21, 63, 67, 68, 69,
    70, 74, 76, 77, 83, 84, 87, 91,
    92, 93, 94, 95, 145, 147
Hermeneutics of suspicion, xi, xii, 10,
    15, 17, 21, 63, 67, 68, 69, 70,
    74, 76, 77, 83, 84, 87, 91, 92,
    93, 94, 95, 145, 147
Hierarchy, 9, 11, 43, 74
Household codes, 41-42, 54, 78-83,
    149
Huebner, Harry, 31
Identity, communal, 3, 4, 9-10, 14,
    20, 25-28, 34, 49, 51-52; as
    disciples, 4, 8, 11, 12, 17, 25,
    27, 32, 36, 37, 110, 114, 115,
    128, 134, 135, 139, 140
Ideological, 12, 17, 63, 75, 81, 116,
    118, 122
Image of God, 32, 68, 69, 74, 76
Incarnation, 29-32 , 35, 37, 43, 75, 83,
    116, 147
Inclusivity, 12, 65, 66, 70, 74, 79, 82,
    83, 84, 85, 87, 91, 92, 93, 123
Inner/outer, 18, 25, 35, 105, 126
Insider/outsider, 42, 105-106, 110-
    113, 115, 116, 134-135
Interpretation: as authoritative
    process, 15, 53-54, 92-93; as
    creative process, 14, 17-20,
    34; as critical process, 16, 20-
    21, 66-67; as performance 39,
    43-44, 53,78 84; as self-
    involving, xiii, 1-2, 13-14, 15-

17, 69, 100; as social/
    political process, 1 4, 5, 7,
    28, 67; as transformative
    process, xi, 14, 20, 31, 81, 83
Intratextual, 19-20
Janzen, Waldemar, 38
Jeshke, Marlin, 36
Jesus movement, 4, 78-79
Johnson, Elizabeth, 69, 72, 73, 74, 75
Justice, 4, 9, 10, 66, 70, 71, 81, 87,
    122, 123, 124, 145, 149
Kant, Immanuel, 5
Kingdom of God, 30, 33-34, 40, 70,
    79, 99, 102, 104, 105, 106,
    129
Koontz, Gayle Gerber, 87
Kraus, C. Norman, 27
Language, xii, 4, 11, 14, 15, 16, 17,
    18, 19, 20, 43, 65, 69, 84, 89,
    120-121, 134, 140; of
    authority and power, 99, 101,
    135
Leadership, 2, 26, 46-47, 52, 55, 112,
    119, 127, 128, 129
Liberation, 9, 66, 69, 70, 73-76, 77,
    78, 81, 82, 83, 84, 85, 91, 92,
    93, 94, 124, 131, 132, 134,
    135, 139, 140; theology, 4 , 5,
    17
Lindbeck, George, 17-19
Lord's Supper, See Breaking bread
Luther, Martin, 25, 30
Malbon, Elizabeth Struthers, 99, 127,
    134, 136
Marginal, 1, 7-9, 12, 17, 49, 54, 65,
    70, 71, 75, 76, 79, 89, 82, 83,
    84, 86, 89, 91, 92, 93, 95,
    131, 135, 139, 146,
Martens, Elmer, 47
May, Melanie A., 45
McClendon, James, 3, 13
McFague, Sallie, 75
Meeks, Wayne A., 5
Mennonite, xi-xiii, 137-140;
    description of, 3, 26-28; ethos
    of authority, 25-55. See also

Anabaptist-Mennonite
tradition
Method, xi, xii, 4, 6, 13-21, 26, 63-
67, 70, 74, 147
Michie, Donald, 109, 112, 117
Munro, Winsome, 100
Myers, Ched, 116, 118, 120, 121, 122,
123, 125, 137
Nonconformity, 33-34, 40, 43, 45, 52,
61
Nyce, Dorothy Yoder, 45
Ollenburger, Ben, 30
Parable as plot synopsis, 103-104
Patriarchy, 4, 9, 11, 16, 43, 46, 63, 64,
65, 66, 68, 69, 70, 72, 75,
76, 77, 79, 80, 81, 82, 84, 87,
91, 92, 95, 119, 136, 150
Peace, 3, 10, 33, 44, 46, 50, 71
Politics, 14, 38, 89, 132, 134; of Jesus
39, 53, 120-125, 128;
subversive 125-133, 142
Power: and discipleship, 39-43, 43-
53, 83-92; creative function
of, 99, 104-116; defined, 1-2,
101-102; of biblical text, 6-7,
37, 55, 67, 82, 148; of Jesus
107-110, 121-125; of the
Spirit, 35- 37, 71-73;
relationships of, 1, 10-12, 15-
17, 38, 41, 43, 89, 93;
subversive function of, 116-
133; unmasking of, 110-115
Redekop, Magdalene, 49, 50
Rhetoric, 17, 101, 103, 106, 113, 121,
122, 140
Reformation, 2, 8, 27, 29, 48
Relativism, 5, 14, 41, 51, 15, 64, 91,
137, 148
Revelation, xii, xiii, 29-30, 31-32, 35,
36, 37, 38, 42, 43, 55-56, 73-
77, 81, 83, 93, 94, 95, 106,
110, 115,-116, 130, 132, 146-
148
Rhoads, David M., 109, 112, 117
Ricoeur, Paul, 5
Ringe, Sharon, 63

Roles, 11-12, 28, 45, 46, 50, 52, 64-
65, 79,, 80, 83, 101, 127, 130,
140
Ruether, Rosemary Radforth, 4, 9, 63,
68, 70, 71, 73, 74
Rule of Christ, 35, 36, 44, 46
Rule of Paul, 35, 48-49
Russell, Letty, 4, 7, 9, 63, 68, 70, 71,
72
Sacrament, 43, 49
Sanders, James, 5
Salvation, xiii, 10, 31, 33, 35, 36, 55-
56, 73, 75, 77, 79, 93, 94, 95,
99, 134, 139, 140
Schertz, Mary, 51, 60 n.89
Schneiders, Sandra, 63, 71, 72
Schottroff, Luise, 4
Schroeder, David, 36
Schüssler Fiorenza, xii, xiii, 4, 7, 8, 9,
63, 67, 70, 72, 119; and
discipleship, 78- 83; and
communal practices, 83-92;
and authority, 92-93
Senior, Donald, 108, 137
Servanthood, 29, 30, 31, 32, 33, 37,
40-41, 46, 47, 52-53, 83,
127-129, 132, 140
Setel, T. Drorah, xi, 150 n. 1
Simons, Menno, 29, 46
Snyder, Arnold, 27
Sophia, 71, 72, 74, 75, 93
Swartley, Willard, 29
Temple, 79-80, 108, 109, 117, 118,
120, 121, 122, 124, 125, 126,
130
Theology: definition of, 13-14; model
of, 20-21
Tolbert, Mary Ann, 16, 103, 106, 107,
110
Torah, 79, 80, 119, 120
Tradition, xii, xiii, 4, 5, 6, 7, 17, 20,
52, 54, 56, 65, 68, 71, 72, 73,
90, 94, 113, 122-123, 145;
authority of, 10-11; feminist
struggle with, 70, 71, 73, 74,
75, 77, 78-83, 85, 88, 89, 90,

91, 92, 93, 94, 95; nature of,
13-15, 25-27
Trinitarian framework: as understood
by feminists, 67-77; as
understood by Mennonites, 28-
37,
Trinity: God, Creator, 32-34, 67-71;
Jesus, 29-32, 73-75; Holy
Spirit, 35-37, 71-73
Truth, xii, 6, 10, 11, 14, 35, 35, 39,
43, 55, 56, 91, 92, 93, 128,
136; claims to, 14, 16, 17, 18,
19, 43, 91, 92-95, 100, 101,
132, 138, 140, 147, 148, 149
Vulnerability: of biblical text 116,
137-138, 140, 141; of
followers, 115-116, 138-140;
of God, 135, 148; of Jesus,
107, 109, 137, 138, 140, 141
Weeden, Theodore, 99
Wenger, J. C., 25, 47
Wiebe, Katie Funk, 86
Wink, Walter, 101-102
Winter, Miriam Therese, 9
Wisdom, 90-92, 111, 114. *See also*
Sophia
Women-church, 4, 7, 9, 70, 71, 72,
76, 78, 79 84, 85, 86, 87, 88,
93; practices of, 86-96. *See*
also ekklēsia
Women's studies, 65-66
Word of God, 8, 35, 37, 73, 107, 128,
146
Yoder, John H, xii, 2, 8, 10, 13, 19, 27,
28, 29, 30, 32-33, 34, 35; and
discipleship, 39-43; and communal
practices, 43-53; and authority,
53-54
Young, Pamela Dickey, 90
Zikmund, Barbara Brown, 63-67

Index of Biblical References

Leviticus
25   40

Psalms
118:22   126

Isaiah
5:1-7   122
5:20-21   123
56: 1-8   123

Jeremiah
7:4   124

Zechariah
9:9   124

Matthew
5-7   31
16   44
18   36, 44, 45

Mark
1:1   106
1:2   127
1:1-2   122
1:1-13   107
1:8   108
1:14-15   108
1:14-8:26   142 n. 29
1:15   122
1:21   108
1:22   119
1:22, 27   102
1:24   123
1:25   128
1:27   102
1:31   131
1:34   109
1:35   108
2   113
2:1-12   109, 124

2:10   102
2:7, 16, 18, 24   113
2:12   109
2:24ff   122
2:25   122
3   106, 113
3:1-28   109
3:5   108
3:12   108, 109, 128
3:13-16   114
3:14   123
3:15   102, 108
3:23   102
3:23-28   125
3:29, 35   106
3:31-35 105, 114, 125
4   104, 105, 106, 122, 133
4:1-9   107, 110
4:1-20   114
4:1-32   103
4:10   105
4:11-12   105
4:12   112
4:15   114
4:20   105
4:21-22   106
4:25   112
4:26   107
4:26-32   110
4:28   107
4:31-32   107
4:33   105
4:33-40   142, n. 20
4:35-5:43   110
5   123
5:1-20   142, n.19
5:9   123
5:19, 43   109
5:20   111, 131
5:33-34   124
5:34   124

6-8   114
6:1-6   109
6:2   102, 108
6:3   108
6:6   108
6:6-13   114
6:7   108
6:8-13   123
6:12   123
6:17   102
6:45   108
7   113
7:1-12   108
7:1-13   119
7:6-8   126
7:6-13   122
7:24   108, 109
7:24-30 108, 111, 131
7:29   124
8:14-15   131
8:14-21   125
8:15   113
8:22-10:52 128
8:26   142 n. 29
8:27-30   109
8:33   108, 114
8:34   127
8:34-35   141 n. 13
8:35   106
9:28-29   128
9:33-37   111
9:33-41   128
9:36-37   106
9:41   106
10   111
10:2ff   122
10:2-12   119
10:11   106
10:13-16   112
10:13-27   128
10:17-31   114
10:18   108, 109

167

10:31	106	14:53-15:39	109	**Ephesians**	
10:35-45	114, 128	14:62	102, 108	2:14-15	32
10:42	102	14:60-62	109	3:3-6	32
10:43-44	106	14:72	129	4	46
10:46-52	124	15:1-39	109	4:13	46
10:52	124, 128	15:2	109		
11	113, 126	15:6-15	109	**Philippians**	
11:1-25	130	15:31-32	109	2:6-11	29
11:7	122	15:34	1-9		
11:15-19	124	15:37-39	29	**Hebrews**	
11:18	113	16:7	106, 114	1:1-2	29
11:23	106				
11:23-24	131	**Luke**		**1 Timothy**	
11:25	131	4:18-19	40	2:8-15	47
11:27-33	109, 117				
11:28, 29, 33	102	**John**		**1 Peter**	
12	133	14:15-24	35	2:9	36
12:1-12	103, 116			4:10	46
12:10	122	**Acts**			
12:11	117	2:14-21	72	**I John**	
12:12	113	15	48	2:3-11	35
12:13-17	118	15:28	36	4:6-21	35
12:18-27	119				
12:24	110	**Romans**			
12:24ff	122	8:19-24	68, 96 n. 14		
12:26	122	8:11	35		
12:28-34	119	12:1	33		
12:29	108				
12:33	116				
12:35	108	**1 Corinthians**			
12:38-40	113	3:11	29		
12:41-44	112	5:17	32		
13	122, 126	10:5	35		
13:5:132		12	46		
13:13	106	13	46		
13:22	108	14:21-29	47		
13:25	102	14: 29, 34	48		
13:26	108	14:26-29	35		
14:6-9	131				
14:12:25	130	**2 Corinthians**			
14:29	129	3:2	33		
14:32-41	108, 129	5:5	35		
14:32-43	109	5:16-17	51		
14:33	108				
14:40-41	129	**Galatians**			
14:48-49	109	3:28	51		
14:50	114	5:5	35		

Series Published by Wilfrid Laurier University Press for the Canadian Corporation for Studies in Religion / Corporation Canadienne des Sciences Religieuses

Editions SR

1. *La langue de Ya'udi : description et classement de l'ancien parler de Zencirli dans le cadre des langues sémitiques du nord-ouest*
   Paul-Eugène Dion, O.P. / 1974 / viii + 511 p. / OUT OF PRINT
2. *The Conception of Punishment in Early Indian Literature*
   Terence P. Day / 1982 / iv + 328 pp.
3. *Traditions in Contact and Change: Selected Proceedings of the XIVth Congress of the International Association for the History of Religions*
   Edited by Peter Slater and Donald Wiebe with Maurice Boutin and Harold Coward
   1983 / x + 758 pp. / OUT OF PRINT
4. *Le messianisme de Louis Riel*
   Gilles Martel / 1984 / xviii + 483 p.
5. *Mythologies and Philosophies of Salvation in the Theistic Traditions of India*
   Klaus K. Klostermaier / 1984 / vi + 549 pp. / OUT OF PRINT
6. *Averroes' Doctrine of Immortality: A Matter of Controversy*
   Ovey N. Mohammed / 1984 / vi + 202 pp. / OUT OF PRINT
7. *L'étude des religions dans les écoles : l'expérience américaine, anglaise et canadienne*
   Fernand Ouellet / 1985 / xvi + 666 p.
8. *Of God and Maxim Guns: Presbyterianism in Nigeria, 1846-1966*
   Geoffrey Johnston / 1988 / iv + 322 pp.
9. *A Victorian Missionary and Canadian Indian Policy: Cultural Synthesis vs Cultural Replacement*
   David A. Nock / 1988 / x + 194 pp. / OUT OF PRINT
10. *Prometheus Rebound: The Irony of Atheism*
    Joseph C. McLelland / 1988 / xvi + 366 pp.
11. *Competition in Religious Life*
    Jay Newman / 1989 / viii + 237 pp.
12. *The Huguenots and French Opinion, 1685-1787: The Enlightenment Debate on Toleration*
    Geoffrey Adams / 1991 / xiv + 335 pp.
13. *Religion in History: The Word, the Idea, the Reality / La religion dans l'histoire : le mot, l'idée, la réalité*
    Edited by/Sous la direction de Michel Despland and/et Gérard Vallée
    1992 / x + 252 pp.
14. *Sharing Without Reckoning: Imperfect Right and the Norms of Reciprocity*
    Millard Schumaker / 1992 / xiv + 112 pp.
15. *Love and the Soul: Psychological Interpretations of the Eros and Psyche Myth*
    James Gollnick / 1992 / viii + 174 pp.
16. *The Promise of Critical Theology: Essays in Honour of Charles Davis*
    Edited by Marc P. Lalonde / 1995 / xii + 146 pp.
17. *The Five Aggregates: Understanding Theravāda Psychology and Soteriology*
    Mathieu Boisvert / 1995 / xii + 166 pp.
18. *Mysticism and Vocation*
    James R. Horne / 1996 / vi + 110 pp.
19. *Memory and Hope: Strands of Canadian Baptist History*
    Edited by David T. Priestley / 1996 / viii + 211 pp.

20. *The Concept of Equity in Calvin's Ethics**
Guenther H. Haas / 1997 / xii + 205 pp.
* **Available in the United Kingdom and Europe from Paternoster Press.**
21. *The Call of Conscience: French Protestant Responses to the Algerian War, 1954-1962*
Geoffrey Adams / 1998 / xxii + 270 pp.
22. *Clinical Pastoral Supervision and the Theology of Charles Gerkin*
Thomas St. James O'Connor / 1998 / x + 152 pp.
23. *Faith and Fiction: A Theological Critique of the Narrative Strategies of Hugh MacLennan and Morley Callaghan*
Barbara Pell / 1998 / v + 141 pp.

Comparative Ethics Series / Collection d'Éthique Comparée

1. *Muslim Ethics and Modernity: A Comparative Study of the Ethical Thought of Sayyid Ahmad Khan and Mawlana Mawdudi*
Sheila McDonough / 1984 / x + 130 pp. / OUT OF PRINT
2. *Methodist Education in Peru: Social Gospel, Politics, and American Ideological and Economic Penetration, 1888-1930*
Rosa del Carmen Bruno-Jofré / 1988 / xiv + 223 pp.
3. *Prophets, Pastors and Public Choices: Canadian Churches and the Mackenzie Valley Pipeline Debate*
Roger Hutchinson / 1992 / xiv + 142 pp. / OUT OF PRINT
4. *In Good Faith: Canadian Churches Against Apartheid*
Renate Pratt / 1997 / xii + 366 pp.

Dissertations SR

1. *The Social Setting of the Ministry as Reflected in the Writings of Hermas, Clement and Ignatius*
Harry O. Maier / 1991 / viii + 230 pp. / OUT OF PRINT
2. *Literature as Pulpit: The Christian Social Activism of Nellie L. McClung*
Randi R. Warne / 1993 / viii + 236 pp.

Studies in Christianity and Judaism / Études sur le christianisme et le judaïsme

1. *A Study in Anti-Gnostic Polemics: Irenaeus, Hippolytus, and Epiphanius*
Gérard Vallée / 1981 / xii + 114 pp. / OUT OF PRINT
2. *Anti-Judaism in Early Christianity*
Vol. 1, *Paul and the Gospels*
Edited by Peter Richardson with David Granskou / 1986 / x + 232 pp.
Vol. 2, *Separation and Polemic*
Edited by Stephen G. Wilson / 1986 / xii + 185 pp.
3. *Society, the Sacred, and Scripture in Ancient Judaism: A Sociology of Knowledge*
Jack N. Lightstone / 1988 / xiv + 126 pp.
4. *Law in Religious Communities in the Roman Period: The Debate Over* Torah *and* Nomos *in Post-Biblical Judaism and Early Christianity*
Peter Richardson and Stephen Westerholm with A. I. Baumgarten, Michael Pettem and Cecilia Wassén / 1991 / x + 164 pp.
5. *Dangerous Food: 1 Corinthians 8-10 in Its Context*
Peter D. Gooch / 1993 / xviii + 178 pp.
6. *The Rhetoric of the Babylonian Talmud, Its Social Meaning and Context*
Jack N. Lightstone / 1994 / xiv + 317 pp.
7. *Whose Historical Jesus?*
Edited by William E. Arnal and Michel Desjardins / 1997 / vi + 337 pp.

The Study of Religion in Canada /
Sciences Religieuses au Canada

1. *Religious Studies in Alberta: A State-of-the-Art Review*
   Ronald W. Neufeldt / 1983 / xiv + 145 pp.
2. *Les sciences religieuses au Québec depuis 1972*
   Louis Rousseau et Michel Despland / 1988 / 158 p.
3. *Religious Studies in Ontario: A State-of-the-Art Review*
   Harold Remus, William Closson James and Daniel Fraikin / 1992 / xviii + 422 pp.
4. *Religious Studies in Manitoba and Saskatchewan: A State-of-the-Art Review*
   John M. Badertscher, Gordon Harland and Roland E. Miller / 1993 / vi + 166 pp.
5. *The Study of Religion in British Columbia: A State-of-the-Art Review*
   Brian J. Fraser / 1995 / x + 127 pp.

Studies in Women and Religion /
Études sur les femmes et la religion

1. *Femmes et religions**
   Sous la direction de Denise Veillette / 1995 / xviii + 466 p.
   *Only available from Les Presses de l'Université Laval
2. *The Work of Their Hands: Mennonite Women's Societies in Canada*
   Gloria Neufeld Redekop / 1996 / xvi + 172 pp.
3. *Profiles of Anabaptist Women: Sixteenth-Century Reforming Pioneers*
   Edited by C. Arnold Snyder and Linda A. Huebert Hecht / 1996 / xxii + 438 pp.
4. *Voices and Echoes: Canadian Women's Spirituality*
   Edited by Jo-Anne Elder and Colin O'Connell / 1997 / xxviii + 237 pp.
5. *Obedience, Suspicion and the Gospel of Mark: A Mennonite-Feminist*
   Exploration of Biblical Authority
   Lydia Neufeld Harder / 1998 / xiv + 168 pp.

SR Supplements

1. *Footnotes to a Theology: The Karl Barth Colloquium of 1972*
   Edited and Introduced by Martin Rumscheidt / 1974 / viii + 151 pp. / OUT OF PRINT
2. *Martin Heidegger's Philosophy of Religion*
   John R. Williams / 1977 / x + 190 pp. / OUT OF PRINT
3. *Mystics and Scholars: The Calgary Conference on Mysticism 1976*
   Edited by Harold Coward and Terence Penelhum / 1977 / viii + 121 pp. / OUT OF PRINT
4. *God's Intention for Man: Essays in Christian Anthropology*
   William O. Fennell / 1977 / xii + 56 pp. / OUT OF PRINT
5. *"Language" in Indian Philosophy and Religion*
   Edited and Introduced by Harold G. Coward / 1978 / x + 98 pp. / OUT OF PRINT
6. *Beyond Mysticism*
   James R. Horne / 1978 / vi + 158 pp. / OUT OF PRINT
7. *The Religious Dimension of Socrates' Thought*
   James Beckman / 1979 / xii + 276 pp. / OUT OF PRINT
8. *Native Religious Traditions*
   Edited by Earle H. Waugh and K. Dad Prithipaul / 1979 / xii + 244 pp. / OUT OF PRINT
9. *Developments in Buddhist Thought: Canadian Contributions to Buddhist Studies*
   Edited by Roy C. Amore / 1979 / iv + 196 pp.
10. *The Bodhisattva Doctrine in Buddhism*
    Edited and Introduced by Leslie S. Kawamura / 1981 / xxii + 274 pp. / OUT OF PRINT
11. *Political Theology in the Canadian Context*
    Edited by Benjamin G. Smillie / 1982 / xii + 260 pp.
12. *Truth and Compassion: Essays on Judaism and Religion*
    in Memory of Rabbi Dr. Solomon Frank
    Edited by Howard Joseph, Jack N. Lightstone and Michael D. Oppenheim
    1983 / vi + 217 pp.

13. *Craving and Salvation: A Study in Buddhist Soteriology*
    Bruce Matthews / 1983 / xiv + 138 pp. / OUT OF PRINT
14. *The Moral Mystic*
    James R. Horne / 1983 / x + 134 pp.
15. *Ignatian Spirituality in a Secular Age*
    Edited by George P. Schner / 1984 / viii + 128 pp. / OUT OF PRINT
16. *Studies in the Book of Job*
    Edited by Walter E. Aufrecht / 1985 / xii + 76 pp.
17. *Christ and Modernity: Christian Self-Understanding in a Technological Age*
    David J. Hawkin / 1985 / x + 181 pp.
18. *Young Man Shinran: A Reappraisal of Shinran's Life*
    Takamichi Takahatake / 1987 / xvi + 228 pp. / OUT OF PRINT
19. *Modernity and Religion*
    Edited by William Nicholls / 1987 / vi + 191 pp.
20. *The Social Uplifters: Presbyterian Progressives and the Social Gospel in Canada, 1875-1915*
    Brian J. Fraser / 1988 / xvi + 212 pp. / OUT OF PRINT

Available from:

WILFRID LAURIER UNIVERSITY PRESS

Waterloo, Ontario, Canada   N2L 3C5
Telephone: (519) 884-0710, ext. 6124
Fax: (519) 725-1399
E-mail: press@mach1.wlu.ca
World Wide Web: http://info.wlu.ca/~wwwpress